SAM & MANDY STELLMAN'S
CRUSADE FOR SOCIAL JUSTICE

WHAT TWO CAN DO

CHRIS ROERDEN

Badger Books Inc.
Oregon, Wis.

© 2000 by Chris Roerden
Published by Badger Books Inc.
Printed by McNaughton & Gunn of Saline, Mich.
Cover photo from *Milwaukee Sentinel,* June 9, 1982, page 6, part I, Dale Guldan, photographer © 2000, Journal Sentinel, Inc. Reproduced with permission..

First edition
ISBN 1-878569-68-6
Library of Congress Card Number: 00-102346

Publisher's Cataloging-in-Publication
(provided by Quality Books Inc.)

Roerden, Chris.
 What two can do : Sam & Mandy Stellman's
crusade for social justice / Chris Roerden. -- 1st
ed.
 p. cm.
 Includes bibliographical references and index.
 LCCN: 00-102346
 ISBN: 1-878569-68-6

 1. Stellman, Sam. 2. Stellman, Mandy.
3. Human rights activists--Milwaukee--Wisconsin--
Biography. 4. Social action--Milwaukee--Wisconsin
--History. 5. Social advocacy--Milwaukee--
Wisconsin--Biography. 6. Abused women--Legal
status, laws, etc.--Milwaukee--Wisconsin--History.
7. Women--United States--Social conditions--
History.   I. Title.

HV1444.R64 2000   361.25'0922
                       QB100-484

Information and opinions contained in this book that are not annotated or attributed to another source were provided to the author by L. Mandy Stellman and Sam Stellman in the form of extensive interviews and numerous letters, articles and other materials from their personal collections.

Badger Books Inc., P.O. Box 192, Oregon, WI 53575
Toll-free phone: (800) 928-2372
Web site: http://www.badgerbooks.com
E-Mail: books@badgerbooks.com

Dedication

To the volunteers and staff of organizations that work for the rights of women and children, all royalties earned by this book are being donated to help support your efforts.

III

Acknowledgements

Pat Meller, Kim Wilson, and Julie Kleppin have been extremely helpful in the writing of this book. Pat organized the Stellmans' half-century of archival material, conducted many interviews of Mandy, edited the manuscript, and provided wise counsel and tireless support since the project began. Kim interviewed more than 30 individuals, researched hundreds of questions, and cheerfully expedited the handling of all photographs and other editorial tasks. Julie conducted a number of interviews with Sam and served as a welcome reminder of the good times we'd had working for women's rights in the seventies and eighties.

Mary Schieffer and Barb Schieffer gave invaluable insight into the life of a police officer. Dorothy Austin, Elizabeth N. Hoffmann, and Morris Gandelman helped edit the text; Gayle Schindler, Donna Utke, Barbara Lightner, Carolyn Keith, and Carolyn Washburne reviewed it. Kathy Manglos, Leah R. Carson, and Jamakaya conducted the earliest interviews.

Kim Baugrud, Cherie Maris, Bill Winter, Dawn Drellos, and Barbara Ulichny graciously consented to review key sections of the manuscript in addition to furnishing important background. Among others who offered much-needed information are John Steen, Melanie Moore, Deb Billings-Nelson, Stu Driessen, Lois Hoiem, Barbara Labrie, Duane Dudek, Bob Reitman, Doris Schermer, Pat Gowens, Doris LaBrasca, Andrew Kane, and Larry Kipperman.

Abigail Van Buren and Jeanne Phillips generously gave permission to reprint the "Dear Abby" columns and letters.

Above all, Mandy Stellman and Sam Stellman have been role models for us all by their vision, activism, generosity, and chutzpah. Their wish is that you read their story and feel inspired to continue the work of *tikkun olam*.

Contents

MANDY AND SAM STELLMAN, a remarkable duo. Mandy possesses the prudential judgment that is key to knowing when to litigate a legal issue and when to settle it. She is a fearless woman who aggressively seeks justice no matter what the effort requires or the personal cost to be paid by her.

Sam brought an utterly unflagging energy to assisting those caught in the snares of the law but who would be better served by alternative dispositions. The community has and will continue to benefit from the insightful programs Sam created to reduce recidivism and help offenders turn their lives around.

Mandy and Sam as a team had those rare human qualities to agitate but not antagonize, to be outspoken but not offensive, to be quite persistent but still remain pleasantly persuasive.

Their patent passion for justice so felicitously graced their work that those who might otherwise bridle at their efforts for reform instead came not only to deeply respect them but indeed, beyond that, to have a genuine affection for them.

E. Michael McCann
District Attorney
Milwaukee County
Wisconsin

PART ONE: OUTRAGE

Never doubt that a small group of thoughtful committed citizens can change the world. Indeed it's the only thing that ever has.

Margaret Mead

1. A Crime Next to Homicide

"How old did you say?"

"Eighteen." She sat in the interrogation room, defensive under the barrage of questions. "I got lost. I've been in Milwaukee only a couple of—"

"How much money did you get?"

"M-money? I needed directions. He...his car...." Her tears began.

"How did you pick him up?"

"I didn't.... He said he'd drive me.... He said...."

"What kind of way is this to be dressed?"

"But he...I don't know what you mean. C-can I talk to a woman?

"What are you wearing under that?"

"Please...he...I...I'm.... He raped me."

###

It was a late Friday afternoon in 1973. The phone on the hall table was ringing as Mandy Stellman walked in the door. Tired at the end of a long work week, coat still on, she heard a breathless voice ask her to come down to the police station right away. It was a volunteer from the Women's Crisis Line.

"A woman's been raped, and all the detectives questioning her are male," said the volunteer. "She wants to talk to a woman, but the police won't *let* her!"

"That's outrageous! I'll be right there."

Mandy bolted out the door, anger sweeping away her fatigue. In twelve minutes she was at police headquarters—one block from the law office she had just left.

"I want to be present during the interrogation," she announced to the detective in charge.

"No."

"I *insist* on being present." She looked the detective in the eye, though he towered over her five-foot height.

"No," he replied. "You aren't admitted during the interrogation."

"You mean to tell me," she retorted, her eyes flashing behind large black frames, "that an alleged criminal can't be questioned without an attorney present, but my client, who is a victim, has fewer rights than a rapist? Or a bank robber?"

When Mandy realized that arguing was getting nowhere, she shifted tactics. "I insist that a female officer be present during the interrogation."

This was also denied.

"All right," she said. "I'm calling the newspapers."

Attorney Stellman soon had the ear of the *Milwaukee Journal* and the *Milwaukee Sentinel,* as well as that of the district attorney, E. Michael McCann. She simply let it be known she was planning to sue the police department for depriving her client of the right to have an attorney present during the initial interrogation.

Her threat worked. Eventually, she was allowed to see the frightened eighteen-year-old. Mandy learned that the woman, a newcomer to Milwaukee, had been offered a ride by a young man who seemed friendly at the time.

Mandy learned that when the young rape victim arrived at the police station with the volunteer from the Women's Crisis Line, Sharon Senese, they'd heard an officer say, "If women want to prevent rape, they should keep their legs crossed....How many rapes do you really think are rapes?"[1]

This remark—and the power wielded by the Milwaukee police in cases of rape—so incensed Mandy and other Crisis Line volunteers that they vowed to make changes. They did not anticipate at the time how successful they would be or how widely their changes would be felt.

If the police were insensitive to women, the court system was insulting—unabashedly so—as many women discovered.

Helen was a long time coming home from the store. Her children, waiting in their northside Milwaukee duplex, were starting to worry. They had reason to.

As their mother was loading grocery bags into her car in the parking lot of the neighborhood Kohl's supermarket, a man came up behind her. She resisted, but he forced her into her car and made her drive to a dark, secluded spot. There, he raped her.

Later, paging through high school yearbooks, Helen (not her real name) was able to identify her assailant, and shortly thereafter he was captured. Wanting to learn what her role would be in the trial, Helen called the district attorney's office.

"You may be the victim," she was told by the D.A.'s office, "but you are only a witness—a witness for the prosecution. It's not your trial, it's the State's trial."

Helen's hand on the receiver started to tremble. She could find no words to express her shock.

"My job is to protect society's rights," the D.A.'s office

explained. "We'll want your testimony in order to put this guy in jail, but you are a witness. This isn't your case."

Already traumatized by the rape, Helen felt further assaulted by the criminal justice system. A woman in her forties, she was being treated as a child, a nonperson. She decided she wanted no part of it.

But Helen's friends referred her to Mandy Stellman. Mandy, barely containing her own outrage, helped the woman to eventually realize she could make a difference by bringing her assailant to justice. Finally, Helen agreed to play the role of witness, the only role the system allowed. But she had never been in a courtroom before, and she was terrified of having to tell her story before an all-male court. So Judge Max Raskin—whom Mandy often described as "a brilliant, brilliant man"—suggested that Attorney Stellman sit with the victim during the trial.

When the case came to trial, Mandy sat beside Helen in court, holding her hand when things got rough. When the time came for Helen to testify, she was able to speak effectively because Mandy had explained what would take place and reviewed the types of questions the defense might ask to rattle her. In less than two hours her assailant was found guilty and sentenced.

"I didn't interfere with the case, and I didn't ask questions. As a lawyer I knew I wouldn't be allowed to," Mandy explained afterward to one of the many classes of college students she addressed each year. "The defense attorney would have screamed about that, and he would have had every right to. But the mere fact that I walked in and out of the courtroom with the woman made a difference. In those days, *nobody* would accompany the victim in a rape trial and she'd go bananas. It was frightening."

###

To the best of Mandy's knowledge, she was the first attorney in the American judicial system permitted to represent the *victim* in a first-degree rape trial. Even though she had no official role in the trial, she was allowed to accompany the other attorneys when the judge called them into his chambers for discussions out of earshot of the jurors.

"I know for a fact that a lot of sexist jokes go on in chambers among the male prosecutors, the male lawyers, and the male judges," Mandy confided to the college students. "The jokes are all at the expense of the victim. She'd never know about it, of course. But with me there it *didn't happen.*"

As Mandy told the students about these "firsts," she realized that many of her listeners had not even been born at the time. Knowing her listeners took for granted the presence of women in many professions, she said, "Today it's a whole different ball game, because today there are female prosecutors and female judges. Even so, the old game isn't over yet. We're still working on it," she emphasized. "It takes a long time to change things. I'm continually outraged by the system's treatment of women."

###

It was this outrage that led the volunteers at the Milwaukee Women's Crisis Line to secure the support of a broad coalition of women's organizations—including the YWCA, the League of Women Voters, and the National Organization for Women (NOW). They formed Milwaukee's first Anti-Rape Coalition in 1974. Under the leadership of Sharon Senese, the Coalition lobbied the district attorney for Milwaukee County, E. Michael McCann, to reform the criminal justice system's treatment of women who'd been raped. In only one year the women succeeded in establishing a unit within the D.A.'s office to provide the kind of support Mandy had pioneered in Judge Raskin's courtroom. "McCann is very fair, and one of the best prosecutors in the country," Mandy explained to the students. "Today, this Anti-Rape/Witness Support Unit is a whole department that tracks a case."

But in 1974 such a unit represented a major change in the system, all the more impressive because the Crisis Line and its sponsoring organization, the Women's Coalition of Milwaukee, had been in existence only since 1972. Mandy had been active in helping to found both groups. In 1973 she drew up the Coalition's articles of incorporation, and not long after served as its president.[2]

Also rooted in the collective action of these upstart groups, an even greater change began to take shape. It involved no less than a complete rewriting of the state's laws concerning crimes of sexual assault. Those laws, originally written in the era of the flapper and based on centuries-old beliefs about women as property, had legitimized the insensitive treatment of rape victims by the police as well as the dehumanizing status assigned by the courts.

These changes began with Jane Mace, who was used to dealing with trouble—she was a teacher at North Division, one of Milwaukee's inner city high schools. One night as she was heading home, she was attacked, but she managed to fight off her assailant by jabbing her car keys into her attacker's face and slamming her foot onto his instep.

After the man fled, Mace rushed to the local police station to report the crime.

"Why are you dressed that way?" demanded the officer, ignoring the fact that the person before him wore a denim pantsuit and was a schoolteacher in her mid-fifties.

"What were you doing out at this time of night?"

"What bar did you just come from?"

The police officer's line of questioning so infuriated her that she took immediate action. For Mace not only was used to dealing with trouble, but as a teacher in the public school system she also was a city employee. And she believed in keeping city government accountable to its citizenry.

She started by telephoning Milwaukee Mayor Henry Maier in the middle of the night to complain. The next day she phoned Mandy's office from the teachers' lounge. That's when she learned about the state's rape law and how it contributed to the problem.

"Exactly what's *wrong* with the law?" she asked.

"Plenty," Mandy replied, settling back in her leather swivel chair in anticipation of a long phone conversation. "If a woman has cuts and bruises, the chances of winning a case are excellent. Injuries are proof that a struggle occurred. But if she is not visibly injured, it's difficult to convince a judge and jury that a struggle occurred, because under the law you have to show that you *fought for your life.*"

Mace found it hard to believe what Mandy explained next: that the legal system considered a victim to be merely a witness to her own rape.

"Not only that," added Mandy, "if she closed her eyes during the rape, the case could be thrown out of court. Technically, she would no longer qualify as an eyewitness because she didn't *see* the rape!"

Mace was incredulous.

Mandy shifted the receiver and continued, punctuating the air with her free hand. "The attitude of the law is, 'Look, woman, we'll believe you if you bring us a witness.' But rape doesn't occur in the front window of Gimbels Department Store at high noon! The only witness is usually the victim herself. So her word is treated as circumstantial evidence. Then when the case comes to trial, her past is exposed. I warn her that her sexual life, even though it has no bearing on the trial, will be brought out into the open."

Mandy's biting perspective on the law turned Mace's disbelief to outrage. Galvanized, she began by joining the National Organization for Women (NOW) and forming the organization's first state task force on rape. Mace initiated self-defense clinics, which Juana Sabatino and other women helped conduct, and she earned an appointment by the mayor to chair his Community Committee on Crime.

By the mid-seventies, Mandy's already-demanding schedule of speaking engagements began to reflect the public's growing interest in the issue of sexual assault. Soon, increased media awareness began to capture her pithy remarks.

"The rape statute reads like a dirty law," the quick-witted attorney was often quoted as saying, "because the people who passed it were, for one thing, all men, and for another, very old and possibly hung up on sex." Mandy never lost an opportunity to point out that "rape doesn't have anything to do with sex. I'm sure they thought sex was something dirty and possibly a bit funny." And as she was aware, similar attitudes within her own profession at the time hadn't matured much since the laws had been written half a century before. "To most lawyers and judges and D.A.s," she said, "taking rape *seriously* is a big joke."

The source of Mandy's greatest outrage had always been a system of justice that heaped *in*justice on those who turned to it for help. This was nowhere better illustrated than in the contrasts between the legal rights of the accused and those of the accuser, which Attorney Stellman articulated to more than one group of engrossed listeners.

"Unless the past of the accused rapist has some immediate bearing on the trial, *he* cannot be questioned about *his* past sexual activities. But it's open season on women."

To those who still didn't "get it," Mandy offered a fitting

analogy: "When my home was burglarized, all the police found was circumstantial evidence, but they believed me. No one asked me about my sex life, or whether I was getting along with my husband. If it had been sexual assault, I would have been asked all kinds of other questions."

###

Soon after being appointed to chair the mayor's Committee on Crime, Jane Mace stopped by Mandy's office. With her came a young social studies teacher from Nicolet High School named Barbara Ulichny.

"We don't have a lot of time," Ulichny apologized. She took one of the two visitor's chairs facing the large desk.

"Okay," said Mandy. "What can I do for you?"

"Tell me all you know about rape," Ulichny asked.

Mandy started to laugh. "You're in a hurry? You want me to tell you all I know about rape? Tell you what, let's look up the statute."

Swiveling around in her chair to the bookshelves behind her, she picked out one volume of statutes and began leafing through its pages. "Life and bodily security..." she read aloud, the title under which the crime of rape might be expected to fall. It wasn't there. Nor was it listed under crimes against public health and safety. That category, Mandy told her visitors, dealt with crimes such as "the unsafe burning of a building, disarming a peace officer, and endangering safety by use of a dangerous weapon." As she kept turning pages, the large number of serious criminal activities that did not address issues of sexual assault became increasingly evident.

"...Crimes against property...crimes against reputation, civil liberty.... Ah, here it is: crimes against sexual morality."

As Mandy spoke the words "sexual morality," she observed the reaction of her visitors: "They nearly fell out of their chairs in shock, and I knew we were on to a good thing."

Mace and Ulichny had instantly recognized the peculiar rationale behind the law. By classifying a violent, vicious act of bodily assault as a crime against *morality*, the men who had written the laws were implying that the real victim of such an act was society—in other words, husbands, fathers, and brothers—themselves!

"The laws were created by men who considered their own rights of ownership violated if *their* wives or *their* daughters were violated," Mandy explained to her visitors. "In the eyes of the law, rape had nothing whatsoever to do with the rights of the *woman* who was attacked."

Any doubts that Mace and Ulichny might have had about the accuracy of this interpretation were dispelled as Mandy read aloud the other behaviors the original lawmakers had placed in the same category as physical violence against women: "bigamy, incest, fornication, adultery, sexual gratification, lewd and lascivious behavior, obscene material or performance, prostitution, patronizing prostitutes, soliciting, keeping a place of prostitution...and," she added with sarcasm, "all the rest of that good stuff."

What section 1 of Statute 944.01 actually said was:

> *Any male who has sexual intercourse with a female he knows is not his wife, by force, against her will, may not be imprisoned more than thirty years.*

"How does the law define 'intercourse'?" Mace asked. "Only by penetration? Must it involve only a penis and a vagina?"

Jane Mace had immediately recognized one more weakness in the law—its silence about objects of vaginal penetration other than a penis. And the law remained equally silent on whether the definition of intercourse applied if a man forced his penis into some other bodily orifice.

"It's a double injustice for the victim," Mandy said. "She may be viciously penetrated with a broomstick, but because of the narrow definition of rape under the law, she could see her case reclassified as assault, not rape."

Although section 2 of the law sought to clarify section 1, it only added confusion:

> In this section the phrase "by force and against her will" means either that her utmost resistance is overcome or prevented by physical violence, or that her will to resist is overcome by threats of imminent physical violence likely to cause great bodily harm.

"What does the law define as 'utmost resistance'?" asked Mace. "A cry for help? A physical struggle? Wouldn't her resistance depend on whether her attacker was holding a knife at her throat?"

Although Mace and Ulichny had claimed to have little time, they stayed in Mandy's office more than two hours taking copious notes and getting an education in the omissions of the law. Its classification of rape as a crime against morality gave them added incentive to work for legislative change, which Mandy was fully prepared to support.

Over the next two years, she crisscrossed the state, her knowledge of the law invaluable in helping NOW and Milwaukee's Anti-Rape Coalition build grassroots support for important legislative changes.

Wisconsin's state mascot is the tenacious badger, an apt symbol for the state's history of progressivism. True to this tradition, the new sexual assault law proposed in 1974 would—if passed—be the most progressive in the nation.

A large number of women in leadership positions throughout the state, Mandy among them, came together for a summit meeting initiated by Kathryn Morrison and Barbara Ulichny. Morrison, a Democrat from Platteville, was elected to the State Senate soon after. (Ulichny won election to the

State Assembly in 1978 at age thirty-one, then to the State Senate, and later became an attorney in private practice.)

The mission of the women's summit was to draft the basis for a new sexual assault law, a complex and lengthy process involving a host of meetings and numerous individuals. Key players included attorneys Sandra Edhlund, Sara Bates, Julilly Kohler, and Linda Roberson.

The proposed law was designed to close the loopholes in the existing rape statute and bring it into the twentieth century. It established four categories of sexual assault, ranging from touching without permission—which no law prohibited at that time—to forced intercourse. Each category would carry a different penalty, a strategy designed by the women to head off the attitude of many male judges that sexual offense was rarely "serious enough" to warrant putting an offender away for as much as thirty years. It was this boys-will-be-boys attitude that produced the state's shameful record of suspended sentences, freedom for rapists, and the inevitable repeat offenses.

Few judges—indeed, few men—had the ability to see the issue from the perspective of Mandy's husband, a long-time advocate in his own right for women's equality. Sam Stellman, a professor of criminal justice, always maintained that rapists should be given the most severe penalties possible.

"They are among the most dangerous people, because there is no cure for sex offenders. Rape is not a sex act," he repeatedly insisted, "it is an act of violence. Next to homicide, rape is the worst crime."

The proposed law was designed to change even the name of the crime from "rape" to "sexual assault" to encompass the range of offenses actually committed and to get beyond the stereotypes that inhibited criminal prosecution.

Whenever Mandy offered her audiences examples of such stereotypes, she added her own style of dramatization to ridicule the myths she was about to debunk. "For centuries, rape meant a stranger coming out of the dark," she would pantomime, "and having his way with some young, innocent, virginal type." She understood that after so many centuries of custom, it was hard for people to expand their image of rape. "But the actuality is that fathers rape daughters, husbands rape wives, boyfriends rape girlfriends, uncles rape nieces. These aren't strangers at all," Mandy emphasized. "So the words 'sexual assault' mean it could have been your best friend's husband, your best friend's boyfriend, someone you know."

The proposed sexual assault law sought progress on two additional fronts: one, to end the presumption that unless a woman could prove how much force she had used in fighting back, she had consented to being attacked; the other, to shield her prior sex life from the court's scrutiny.

"It used to be if a woman was not a virgin, the guy would get off," Mandy continued. "It used to be believed that rape was something that could happen only to a virgin—meaning that all other women asked for it!" She would often add, "You have to give credit to the women, the feminists, who brought this to the attention of the legislators."

At the time, Milwaukee newspapers were reporting a 102 percent rise in the number of rapes in the city between 1972 and 1973. As the numbers continued to climb in cities and towns throughout the nation, skeptics were quick to question whether the increase wasn't due simply to better reporting methods, or even to a greater willingness on the part of victims to come forward. Either explanation, observed the Stellmans, paid tribute to the women's movement for its exposure of one of the nation's nastiest secrets.

On September 23, 1974, the proposed legislation was launched at a public forum held on the Milwaukee campus of the University of Wisconsin. The speakers included Jane

Mace, Sandra Edhlund, and Mandy Stellman.

That year, the legislature took no action on the new bill. Introduced early the following year by Senator Bill Bablitch, it passed the State Senate thirty to one. In the State Assembly it was launched by Representative Mary Lou Munts, and it passed ninety-six to one.[3]

Wisconsin's Sexual Assault Act of 1976 was soon recognized as the best statute in the nation for dealing with rape, and it became the model for reforms in other states.

But with all the advances since the early seventies, was Mandy satisfied with where things stood?

"NO!" she thundered.

Do we need to move faster?

"We need to move *mountains*."

A few miles from Wisconsin's State Capitol, where the new law on sexual assault had recently gone into effect, a sixteen-year-old girl was cornered in a stairwell at Madison's West High School. Three boys surrounded their fellow student after class on the afternoon of November 8, 1976, and took turns holding her down while she was raped. The response of the judge who gave the boys a slap on the wrist made it all too clear that among the mountains still to be moved were the attitudes of those entrusted with implementing the new sexual assault law.

The leniency of the sentence for the admitted rapists—home detention—might not have attracted quite as much public notice if the judge, Archie E. Simonson, had not also decided to deliver a courtroom lecture during sentencing. His subject: women's provocative styles of dress. Even though the teenaged girl who'd been gang-raped had been wearing jeans and a loose sweatshirt—hardly a seductive ensemble—Judge Simonson did not let these facts color his opinion. From the bench during the juvenile court hearing, he held forth on Madison's climate of sexual permissiveness, the prevalence of commercialized sex, and women's clothing.

His treatment of the case provoked a public furor, and NOW asked him to apologize or resign. He refused. The Committee to Recall formed within twenty-four hours.[4] As if his diatribe from the bench were not enough to prove his bias, he attempted to defend his sentencing by asking, "Are we supposed to take an impressionable person fifteen or sixteen years of age who can respond to something like that and punish that person severely because they react to it normally?"[5]

An uproar followed, during which Simonson, surprised by the public reaction, managed to make his humiliation even worse. He defended his view of what constituted "normal" male behavior by proclaiming, "I'm trying to say to women to stop teasing."

The Stellmans were livid. Mandy wrote a well-argued opinion piece pointing out the fallacies in the judge's thinking.

During the Victorian age when women wore clothing from neck to ankle and massage parlors were unknown, when television did not exist and X-rated movies were not in vogue, rape still occurred.

Citing the thousands of documented rape cases of women in their seventies and eighties, as well as girls under the age of five, Mandy drove home her point: "Five-year-old girls do not 'tease'; eighty-year-old women do not wear see-through blouses and provocative clothing." Declaring there is nothing normal or healthy about a teenager or a man of any age who attacks a woman, Mandy added: "Rape has never been a normal sexual activity."

Her strong but eloquent article was published as an "In My Opinion" piece by the *Milwaukee Journal*, June 20, 1977.

"Rape has been and is a violent crime," she insisted. "Violent acts have been condemned by all cultures and all societies in all times. Then along comes a Dane County judge, Archie Simonson, who ignores the past and proclaims rape a 'normal activity.'"

Citing changes in the sexual assault law, Mandy pointed out that the judge's decision "is not based on Wisconsin law. In fact, it is not based on any law. The judge has rendered a decision based on the thesis that 'a normal man—including a teenager—cannot be responsible for his sexual drives'—particularly if he is 'provoked.' Well, we have a message for the judge," Mandy concluded, alluding to a recall petition that was swiftly acquiring the requisite number of signatures. "You have provoked the entire community. We demand your apology and resignation."

Simonson continued to proffer a lame self-defense. Claiming that his right of free speech was being attacked, he went on to assert that he himself was being "gang-raped" by the press—a metaphor that further insulted women. The issue, of course, wasn't the judge's freedom to express himself; it was his suitability to sit in judgment of others. And that was the issue galvanizing thousands of men and women.[6] Eagerly they signed their names to the recall petitions—as did hundreds more whose considerable distance from Dane County made them ineligible to be counted. Nevertheless, the recall succeeded, and in the special election that followed, Simonson was removed from the bench. He'd been defeated by a woman, Madison attorney Moria Krueger, age thirty-three.[7]

"Revenge," proclaimed Sam, "was sweet."

###

2. Who's Bringing Up the Boys?

The first ring woke Sam, and he groped for the phone in the dark.

"I don't know what to do," came the desperate voice. "I'm at a pay phone. My husband...he beat me and...and he threw me outta the house."

Over the woman's convulsive sobs, Sam could hear the crying of a child.

"I'm out of my m-mind. I don't have no place to go, no clothes for the k-kids for school tomorrow. The operator gave me the, uh, Crisis Line, and a woman there told me, call the Stellmans."

"Stay where you are," came Sam's gentle voice. He was now fully awake. "I'm going to call a cab for you. Tell the driver to take you to the Continental Motel. They'll give you a room and something to eat. Tomorrow," a glance at the clock told him it was already tomorrow, "someone from the Task Force on Battered Women will be in touch with you and arrange for help. Now," he added, picking up the note pad and pencil that were always ready on the night stand, "tell me where you are so I can send the cab."

"Another one who threw his wife and kids out?" asked Mandy, also fully awake by that time.

Sam nodded and dialed the cab company. Next he called the motel and made a reservation. All costs were to be charged to the Stellmans. Finally, Sam called the woman waiting at the pay phone to reassure her that the cab was on its way.

That was early in 1977, a year before the first shelter for battered women would open, and before hospitals began establishing their own special units for victims of domestic abuse. Prior to 1975 when the Task Force on Battered Women officially got underway—and before 1973 when the Crisis Line began operating—Sam Stellman was the one who telephoned the local welfare office the morning after a late-night call for help and tried to get emergency assistance for these women and their children. Sometimes it took two hours of calling around before he could get any action. Sam was the one who picked up the family at the motel the next morning and drove them to the welfare office, waited for them another hour or two, and drove them to whatever temporary housing he'd been able to arrange.

No one ever kept count of the many midnight calls or cries of terror and physical pain to which the Stellmans responded. And no chronicle of their quiet generosity exists—except that which their canceled checks might reveal.

When the Sojourner Truth House was established in 1978, it became the first shelter for battered women in Wisconsin.[8] Mandy served as its legal advisor and arranged for its incorporation. The Stellmans were among its founders, and although they continued to give it their full support, they understood that creating the necessary safe harbor for abused families would do nothing to alter the dynamics of abuse. To activists such as the Stellmans, a shelter represented the imbalance of power between men and women, one in which the batterer remains in control of what he continues to see as his property—"his" woman, "his" children, and "his" domicile.

Many nights after being roused by a crisis phone call, the Stellmans sat in their small kitchen with cups of hot coffee. They found it helped them unwind enough so they might catch some remaining hours of sleep. At two or three A.M., Sam's hair would be especially unruly, gray wisps flying outward from his temples almost whimsically, in contrast to his craggy features and the deep seriousness of his voice.

"*He's* the one who should be out in the cold! *She* should be in the house!"

Such passion surprised people who saw only the gentle professor. But Mandy knew Sam's outrage because she shared it, and the two made a powerful team.

Men who batter women are potential murderers! They should be seen as men who are dangerous to the safety and security of our society!

These words leapt from the pages of the scores of proposals and articles Sam authored over a twenty-year period. They startled audiences who attended his talks and workshops; they generated annoyance among the counseling community and, at times, among local prosecutors, judges, and other law enforcement officials.

That's because Sam told it like it was, reserving his sharpest rebukes for the professionals—even though he, too, was a professional, a member of the social service community he so often skewered. Yet his contributions went beyond merely voicing negative observations. A lengthy list of accomplishments attested to his lifelong record of taking action to make lasting change.

For Sam, a plan of action was always developing, whether

he sat in the kitchen cooling off after a midnight call for help or stood before an audience moving others to action.

"Men who beat women often beat their children," Sam would tell his skeptical audiences. "And we're learning that these same men often rape the women they say they love."

The setting was typical: a dimly lit, poorly heated high school auditorium in northern Wisconsin in the late seventies. An assortment of helping professionals, community leaders, and anyone else who wandered in sat uncomfortably in molded gray plastic seats. Sam was on a statewide tour to build community sponsorship for a program he initiated called Deprogramming Men Who Batter.

"Men who strike their wives or girlfriends are nasty, dangerous men who use hitting as a way of controlling 'their' women," Sam said matter-of-factly from the bare stage. His voice was soft, but everyone heard his powerful words. "These men function as if they own the women. Yet the professionals, who are supposed to be helping those who've been battered, too often say these men are just angry people who are otherwise 'nice guys.' I absolutely disagree!"

Sam's listeners huddled in their coats, chilled as much by the topic as by the custodian's having forgotten to turn up the thermostat in time for the scheduled meeting.

"These men don't hit because they're angry—they hit to assert control. The most accessible object of control is a woman or a child," continued Sam. "A significant factor in their accessibility is the belief that it's *appropriate* for women and children to be under the control of men."

Sam felt this belief was so ingrained in our culture that even professionals who should know better allowed it to influence their judgment. Hence, while violence against women made him angry, it was the attitude of many people in the so-called helping professions that filled him with the energizing emotion of outrage.

"I encounter no shortage of counselors, clergy, and prosecutors who tell couples to go home and work it out," he told his audience, loosening the mike so he could move closer to them. "I encounter no shortage of police and other law enforcement officials who are called to the scene of the violence and tell the man to cool off and take a walk around the block. Or doctors and nurses who ignore the cause of the bruises they see and the broken bones they set. And there's no shortage of trained professionals in *all* of these categories who consistently ignore the woman's story of her beatings."

Sam stepped to the front of the stage without the microphone. "These are the very people a woman is told to get help from. *That* is what's so *outrageous.*"

A heavyset man in the back row pulled his coat closer.

"All these people are equally culpable if women who cry out for help continue to be battered, especially if they are ultimately killed."

Tragically, many are killed. In the United States, between 5,000 and 7,000 women are murdered each year by their husbands and boyfriends, while those seeking medical or hospital care as a result of battering number in the millions.

"Yet the professionals," continued Sam, "too often treat the beating of a woman as a 'family matter' or a 'lover's quarrel,' not as the violation of the laws of assault and battery that it is."

A man's voice called out, "It's not only men. Plenty of women beat up on their husbands, too."

"Nonsense!" Sam replied, stepping down from the stage. "That just doesn't hold up with the research. Men are the prime instigators, harassers, and brutalizers of women."

Looking into the eyes of his listeners, he identified the reason: "Too many men are brought up to see women as inferior to men and therefore as less valuable members of society." Several women in the audience silently nodded.

Sam Stellman was a rare member of the male population. A former college athlete, he defined himself as "anti-men-who-batter," and he used whatever power and authority he had to stop abuse. From 1973 until he retired in 1988, Sam directed the University of Wisconsin's Criminal Justice Institute. His corner office on the eleventh floor of Enderis Hall offered him a striking view of Milwaukee and of Lake Michigan, which formed the city's eastern boundary—a broad panorama matching the scope of his view of community issues. More an activist than an academic, he spent considerable time outside this coveted top-floor office, taking the issues to the people who could act on them.

Throughout his long career, Sam pioneered numerous programs to address specific community needs, from getting kids off drugs to reducing recidivism by pairing probationers with volunteer mentors. He tackled issues of shoplifting, illiteracy, mental retardation, and poverty.

Sam never developed a program just to fill a university's need for programming. His work was part of a larger mission reflecting his personal philosophy. Adept at recognizing how people's individual experiences are part of broader social issues, Sam had a knack for putting his finger on a problem before others discovered it was an issue. The hard part was getting others to join him in taking the kind of action needed to make a difference.

"If an agency or a school or a task force somewhere—or a government group or university—wants to run with an idea," he often said, "I'm eager to help."

Social progress, Sam believed, requires many people taking up each challenge. Too often he saw how progress stalled each time someone with a good idea became entrenched in the role of controlling how that idea was carried out. Wisely, Sam limited his own involvement in a program to designing it, getting it off the ground, and training others to carry it forward. He was then able to do the same for the next problem.

"New tactics are needed all the time," he said. Believing that creative thinking does not come from a committee, he found that a group approach in the initial stages had the result of impeding progress.

"I'm not a team player," he often admitted, chuckling but not smiling. "I cook up and develop a program, and *then* I hand it over to a team."

In this manner he set up many problem-solving programs in Wisconsin and helped other states develop variations of those programs. Over the years, his methods for dealing with batterers influenced several thousand professionals. Some of these he reached as they gathered in modern hospital training facilities; some, in drafty high school auditoriums throughout Wisconsin.

As the high school's cranky furnace began making its existence felt, members of Sam's audience started to shed their coats.

Sam was describing the eight-hour program he developed for deprogramming men who batter. "It's based on an important belief," he emphasized. *"Men who batter are potential murderers.* Everything comes back to that fact."

A red-gloved hand in the front row shot up. "How did you get the deprogramming under way?"

Sam sensed that the questioner was hoping for a similar

program to be established in her community. Standing at the same level as the molded seats, he began. "Well, they all start about the same way. Somebody calls with an idea that makes sense, one that can be implemented. The only mystery to me," he added with a characteristic chuckle, "is how they get my name, except that I make things happen, and they hear about it somehow or other."

Sam would admit to being a good "managing problems" person: give him the problem and he'd come up with a workable plan of attack.

"It might start with a judge identifying a particular problem. Then I take it on, develop a program, and get the judge to bring other judges in to review it. I haven't seen a judge who changed a program yet. They may raise a question like, 'What are you going to do with that part of it?' But never a real challenge or change. Then we set a starting date and establish ground rules—such as if there will be a fee—and so on."

Referring to Deprogramming Men Who Batter, Sam explained that the men themselves paid the fifty-dollar fee. "Few plead poverty, because the alternative is incarceration. The program costs the taxpayers nothing."

Modestly, he often credited Mandy, and the victims who came to her for legal help, with making him aware of the severity of the problems facing women. And he often acknowledged that political support and funding for some of his efforts had come about for reasons other than their benefit to women.

The red-gloved woman asked what that meant. So Sam told how he had been invited by the Division of Probation and Parole, part of Wisconsin's Department of Corrections, to develop a treatment program for men who batter. The division had a real concern—but not for the women who were being beaten. If the men on parole or probation for other offenses were found to be beating their wives or girl-friends, their probationary status could be revoked. The number of men who might have to return to prison would add to the state's existing problems with seriously over-crowded jails. That was the system's real concern.

As Sam continued to describe the program he was justifi-ably proud of, he skipped over the part that still caused a twinge of bitterness. When he'd developed the deprogram-ming concept in 1975, he'd requested $6,000 to pay the program's major instructor, Dr. Carlton Beck, a professor of education counseling at UW-Milwaukee. But the probation and parole department refused to allocate the money. Two years passed before the funds began to flow and the pro-gram could be implemented.

In its first year of operation, 1977, the eight-hour treat-ment program served about one hundred men.

"The next year I got a call from the Kenosha County fam-ily court commissioner,"[9] Sam continued. "He told me, 'We have an awful lot of guys who batter women here.' So I went to Kenosha, and out of that came what's got to be the long-est-running treatment program in the state, maybe the coun-try. Now it's run by the university at Parkside. They've expanded it and gotten other programs going."

But the Milwaukee program was short-lived, operating from 1977 to 1980 and then dying for lack of funding.

"Milwaukee always has a money problem," Sam observed wryly.

However, in other Wisconsin communities—Janesville, Fond du Lac, Racine—his programs remained alive. Similar deprogramming efforts, with some modifications, kept op-erating in Texas, Montana, and Alaska,[10] where Sam and Mandy had been invited to present their unique workshops.

"It doesn't take much to support a program," Sam said. "What it needs is one person to take action."

From the third row, a man with a neatly trimmed brown beard identified himself as a therapist and asked, "How do you structure your eight hours?"

"We divide the session into four parts," replied Sam, guessing that the therapist favored long-term programs. "First we get the D.A. or assistant D.A. to come in to talk about the law and use a scare tactic, like telling these S.O.B.s, 'If I ever see you again in my office, I'll do everything I can to lock you up.' I always tell the D.A. to hit hard on this theme."

As Sam talked, he slowly moved up the center aisle, looking into the eyes of each listener. "Then we get them in a group with a highly trained counselor. The men sit in small groups and talk about why they think they batter. We've heard every damn thing under the sun. 'She doesn't bring me my beer'...'She doesn't keep the kids quiet when I'm watching TV.' We've heard everything."

Sam shook his head. "I can give you the whole list. There are all kinds of excuses. And lies." Approaching the back of the auditorium, he noticed that the heavyset man hunched down in the last row would not make eye contact.

"Men who batter are the greatest liars you've ever heard. No matter what their social class, they are the biggest con artists you've ever seen." Sam turned and moved back down the aisle. "They've convinced themselves that their reasons are good reasons. But we refute all their excuses—*all* of them—and tell them that battering is not acceptable for *any* reason. There's a lot of discussion, and eventually they have to admit that the problem is in themselves, not the women. *That's* the point where they begin to change their beliefs."

Next, Sam described the part of the deprogramming that involved a woman—often Mandy. "She's a professional, and she talks about a woman not as someone who just cooks you your meals and gets you your beer. She talks about the value of a woman in the family, the value of a woman in the community, in society. When they see this professional person, well-dressed, articulate—most of the guys on probation don't have much sophistication, besides not having much value for women—it just shakes them up." Sam indulged in his familiar chuckle.

"And then the instructor goes from there to what I call alternatives to battering. Like having a friend to talk to, day or night. That's the most successful alternative. First, get away from the immediate situation, then call the friend. Or go to the gym, jog, or get some new interest. We don't necessarily tell them to go to counselors," added Sam, catching the eye of the man with the brown beard. "At the end of the day, we reinforce the message we started with: 'If you still want to continue what you're doing, we'll do everything we can to see that you are locked up.' We don't want these guys to go home and forget."

Sam shared with his audience how some of the men at the end of a deprogramming session often asked him to call their wives or girlfriends to certify that they'd changed.

"'Absolutely not!' I tell them. 'Show by your *actions* that you've changed!'"

Brown Beard interrupted. "I can tell you that eight hours simply isn't enough time to really turn these men around."

With Sam's reading of the therapist's viewpoint confirmed, he replied, "If they don't get the message in eight hours, I doubt they will ever get it."

"Where's your research?"

"Lack of research is one of the problems," Sam admitted. "Even when a man enters therapy, the likelihood he will continue to be violent either during or after therapy is high. However, from what we've been able to determine, there are very few repeaters among the batterers who experience deprogramming."

Sam added that since no one can predict future violence with any accuracy, counselors who run such programs need to make clear to everyone concerned that "successful completion of the program" meant no more than that. It meant an individual's performance in counseling was sufficient to meet the program requirements, but it implied no guarantee of future behavior or safety for potential victims.[11]

"From my experience as a therapist," continued Brown Beard, "such men as you describe belong in long-term treatment and need a peer support group."

Sam knew this was coming. "Hogwash!" he responded. "Before we started, as I looked around the country at what was available, the few programs going were running fifteen weeks, twenty weeks, thirty weeks, with once-a-week sessions. I would call and ask, 'How do you pick the number of sessions?' They had no idea. I'd ask, 'What do you do the thirteenth week?' They had no idea.

Sam observed the jaw tightening behind the beard.

He continued. "Here's what they do in those sessions. The leader says, 'Hey, John, tell us about how you got here,' or whatever, and when he finishes, the leader says, 'Hey, Jim, whaddya think about what John says?' The leader plays no role except to facilitate. It's crazy. These batterers learn the language. They're not stupid. It's part of the con: 'Well, ya know, we were battered.' Or 'My father beat my mother.' When they leave those sessions, they tell other people, 'I know why I batter, blah blah blah....'"

Sam's audiences always listened carefully to his unequivocal opinions. "Peer support groups are good for *victims* but very questionable for perpetrators of violent crimes," he explained. "A support group lets victims learn from each other's experiences that they aren't the only ones with the problem, and that they aren't the cause of their own victimization. But in support groups for sex offenders, drunk drivers, and others who commit serious crimes, the perpetrators show very little remorse—a necessary component of any effort to bring about a change in behavior. Men who beat women don't believe they've done anything wrong."

That's why Sam favored having such men adjudicated before they are sent to treatment. "They need to be told by a judge that they are guilty of a crime, and that there are penalties for not participating in a treatment program." As for support groups, Sam found that "the men usually end up reinforcing each other in rationalizing why they hit."

The auditorium had finally warmed up, but Sam noticed that the man in the back row remained hunched inside his coat.

"With many of those other programs, I don't think the goal is clear. Instead, they give you all the language—like, 'We're gonna make 'em a better person.' Psychobabble! My goal is very clear: Stop the battering!"

A young woman in the sixth row raised her hand. "But these men are sick, aren't they? If eight hours have some effect, wouldn't long-term treatment be even more effective?"

"It's a myth that men who batter women are 'sick' and their sickness should be 'understood.' Battering is a form of male power. It must be stopped." He pulled a well-worn sheet of paper from his back pocket. "Here's a list of the characteristics of the batterer. He thinks he has done nothing wrong," read Sam. "He plays down the extent of the damage. He plays down his own involvement in creating the damage. Following a beating, he expresses remorse. 'I will never do it again.' But he does it again—and again."

Sam carefully refolded the paper and looked up, noticing that the back row was empty.

"There's no such thing as a single battering," Sam pointed out. "Which relates to another myth—that the batterers hate their violence. Not true! They get their biggest kicks when they're hitting someone. Men who batter are bullies and they're dangerous. They're very dangerous. Thirty percent of all homicides of women are by the men who beat them."

Circling back to the matter of long-term programs, Sam explained that they tended to become so institutionalized their goal got lost. "Too many people forget that the goal of any program for batterers of women is to *stop the battery.*"

Though Sam never raised his voice, his words echoed from the walls. "Most counselors working with batterers are simply not outraged enough. To stick to the goal you have to be *continually outraged.*"

###

3. "Dog Bites Man" Is News

No one will ever know exactly when the woman loaded the shotgun or precisely what her husband was about to do at the time she blasted the hole in his head.

She never denied shooting him, hiding his body in a shed, or attempting to set their debt-ridden farmhouse on fire. But the thirty-two-year-old mother of two daughters would not talk about the beatings, the incest, the rapes. For who would define it as rape when a man took what the law allowed from his own wife? Not in 1977. Certainly not in the Wisconsin farming communities around Waupaca.

The prosecutor wanted this farm wife found guilty of premeditated murder. But her brother, as well as the brother of her dead husband, wanted her acquitted on grounds of self-defense. To achieve this, they felt they needed a "big city lawyer." Impatient with their local attorney, the family called Milwaukee's Alan Eisenberg. Alan called Mandy Stellman.

"I need some help, Mandy," said the familiar voice on the phone. "I've got a woman who's being charged with first-degree murder. She wants to commit suicide, believes she's a terrible person. Her first lawyer wanted her to plead guilty!"

As Mandy heard "plead guilty," her eyes widened in disbelief.

"I'm trying to get her out on bail," continued Alan. "She isn't opening up, and I need to have someone talk to her so I can help her."

When bail was raised and the prisoner released pending trial, the woman drove to "the city" to see Mandy. The July heat and the age of her Ford pickup made the journey from Waupaca to Milwaukee seem longer than 128 miles, and it was nearly 4:30 in the afternoon when Jennifer Patri entered the office building at 536 West Wisconsin Avenue. It was well after dark when she left. A slight breeze from nearby Lake Michigan hinted at the relief to come.

In her small office that summer afternoon, Mandy became the first person to hear the Waupaca woman's story— a painful one of sexual and physical abuse. Mandy advised Jennifer to talk to the women at the Milwaukee Task Force on Battered Women—another vital service among the many that Mandy and Sam had helped establish. Its goal was to help women with the court system.

"The women at the task force are trained to talk with you about this," Mandy told the farm woman. "I'm trained in my role as an attorney, and right now I don't want to confuse the two." Getting too close to Jennifer wouldn't be wise, Mandy knew, because she wasn't the attorney handling the defense. Eisenberg was. Stifling her desire to befriend the depressed woman, Mandy thought, "It wouldn't be good for her to have different things coming at her. Not knowing what Alan is planning, advice from me could confuse her."

An expert trial lawyer, Alan Eisenberg was well known for his unpredictable and often unorthodox tactics in and out of the courtroom.

Less well known—especially to those who crowded into

the Waupaca County Courthouse that December hoping to be titillated by the testimony—was the identity of the diminutive woman seated alongside the accused. It was Mandy, also a respected legal professional, whose record of fighting for the rights of the powerless predated her law degree by many years. To those who held traditional expectations of older women, her fighting spirit always came as a surprise.

"An extremely warmhearted, generous woman of motherly demeanor," wrote Steven Englund in *Man Slaughter,* his book about the Patri case.[12] "Mandy was also an *engagée,* a lawyer-feminist of seniority and visibility in the Madison-Milwaukee axis, who believed passionately in the 'social significance' of *Wisconsin v. Patri....* [S]he kept life even more interesting at the defense table than it would have been without her...."[13]

When interviewed for Englund's book, Mandy confided to friends that its author "thought I would just tell him what he wanted to hear. I didn't. I kept challenging him. I told him he was sexist."

As a result, he described Mandy as "a tough interview, for she had a tendency to reverse the roles and interview the inquirer, aggressively."[14]

Only twenty minutes into her interview by Englund she had told him, "I'm just glad you're not on the jury."

The outcome of this courtroom drama lay in the hands of nine men and three women—Jennifer's peers. They had to weigh the argument that this woman had shot her husband because he'd come at her with a butcher knife, and they had to determine the extent to which her self-defense was premeditated.

Though the purveyors of sick humor may have categorized the shooting as a form of husband beating—a rare phenomenon, in actuality—the violent member of the Patri family was not Jennifer. Shooting her husband was a reaction against thirteen years of abuse and the fear of what her abuser had been threatening to do next.

Robert Patri had been known in the community as a bully. He was a problem drinker and a philanderer. He ran an unsuccessful auto repair shop in town, but it was Jennifer who supported the family by raising hogs and toiling long hours on the farm. At the time of the shooting, Robert was living with a woman he intended to marry after divorcing his wife. His plan to seek custody of their two little girls terrified Jennifer, who was convinced he'd already attempted to fondle their eleven-year-old.

He was a father who played pornographic tapes on the car's audio system when his wife and young daughters were present. He was a husband who repeatedly threw food into his wife's face, made her submit to oral and anal intercourse, and further assaulted her by forcing his hand up her vagina. Several times he had threatened to kill her. Family and neighbors testified that they saw bruises on Jennifer's face and noticed her wearing sunglasses to church to hide the marks. A third pregnancy ended after one of many beatings.[15]

Jennifer lived with this abuse because she felt their daughters deserved both a mother and father, and she firmly believed marriage was for life, no matter what. And because her self-esteem was so totally crushed by thirteen years of her husband's unremitting abuse—verbal, physical, sexual, and psychological—she had come to believe she was responsible for all that befell her.

This type of self-blame is now characterized by psychiatrists as typical of the classic battered woman syndrome. But in December of 1977 when the Patri trial began, few citizens of Waupaca, or anyplace else, for that matter, had heard of this phenomenon. Mandy had heard of it, however, and she knew who would have accurate information about it. She got Dr. Katherine Bemmann of Waukesha to give Jennifer a thorough psychiatric examination. Then she secured the psychiatrist's testimony on Jennifer's behalf. As a result, the jury believed a measure of self-defense existed, and they returned a verdict of manslaughter instead of first-degree murder. All things considered, the defense felt victorious.

As soon as Jennifer began serving her ten-year sentence for manslaughter at Taycheedah Correctional Institution, the defense team began preparing to answer the separate charge of arson. One year after the first trial, a second trial was held, this time at the opposite end of the state in LaCrosse.

"Any further west and the Mis'sippi would be wettin' them lawyers' briefs," proclaimed a local wit.

The new location proved to be less contaminated by the media coverage of the first trial than Waupaca County to the east.

The composition of the second jury was just the reverse of the first—three men and nine women. They proceeded to accept the theory presented by the defense: that once Jennifer saw her dead husband and realized what she'd done, she experienced a psychotic episode in which she had no control over her actions in starting the fire.

"Here's a churchgoing woman who'd taught Sunday school," explained Mandy after the trial. "She'd raised two children and been president of the parent-teacher association. She couldn't handle it and went into this psychotic episode. Katherine Bemmann was able to get the jury to understand this. Her testimony was absolutely crucial. It was quite a case."

Jennifer, who'd already served one year of her sentence

by the time the final verdict was handed down, was declared not guilty by reason of insanity and moved from Taycheedah to a state mental hospital. Granted a parole in 1981,
she returned home and quietly resumed her life on the farm.

At the time of the arson trial, Mandy was interviewed by
a Madison reporter for an article on the subject of women
holding strong religious beliefs who are battered.[16]

Although the syndrome is similar for all battered women,
with many of the women blaming themselves for having
done or not done something or other, "the woman who is
religious convinces herself that it's not happening or it's
not that bad," explained Mandy, "because if it were, she'd
have to deal with the question of 'How could God do this to
me?' or 'This is not the God I believe in.'"

Mandy reached this conclusion based on her conversations with men and women who had been in concentration
camps many years earlier. "They told me that when things
are so terrible, if you *believe* what is happening to you, you
are not able to tolerate it. I suspect that the more religious
the woman who's being battered, the more likely she needs
to convince herself that this most gruesome experience could
not be true."

The Patri case was one of the most controversial cases to
inflame the emotions and opinions of citizens all across the
country, and Mandy Stellman had been asked to play a role
in it. Fifty-five at the time, she had been out of law school
only six years. She performed her duties *pro bono*, and although Alan Eisenberg paid her expenses, she had to pay
other lawyers to handle her cases while she was out of town.
"It cost me thousands and thousands of dollars," she admit-

ted. "I literally closed my office. But I don't regret it."

Amid the national attention focused on the Patri case, *Newsweek* expressed its greatest concern for the husbands and boyfriends who were becoming the new "victims" of the "trend toward violence" on the part of abused women.[17]

The *Newsweek* article cited a case in which a pregnant woman's provocation for stabbing her husband had been that the man had come at her with a broomstick. The jury had acquitted her of stabbing her husband, although, as the article's writers declared, "she was in little danger of being killed by a broom-handle blow." Apparently *Newsweek's* editors seemed unable to understand how a broomstick could be enough of a threat to a woman seven months pregnant that she should be acquitted for defending herself with a knife.

Outraged, Mandy got several other women to join her in mailing broomsticks to *Newsweek's* publisher, Katherine Graham, suggesting she test the object for its lethal potential.

Mandy's letter added:

The entire article smacks of the old double standard where men are protected by the laws of self-defense and women are criticized for availing themselves of these same laws. According to Newsweek, *wife-beaters are encouraged to use broom-handle justice against their pregnant wives, and women who defend themselves are accused of using frontier justice. Let the whole world be put on notice...that women shall continue to defend themselves against brutal and brutalizing attacks by men.[18]*

This clash of views took a grisly twist sixteen years after the Patri case. The same magazine ran an article about a group of high school athletes who cheered as several of their friends used a broomstick *and* a baseball bat to sexually assault a mentally retarded seventeen-year-old girl.[19]

###

Of all the publicity generated by the Patri case, perhaps the most meaningful media event occurred when Mandy got a small item printed in the *Weyauwega Chronicle*. Its very simplicity makes this accomplishment noteworthy, and anyone wondering how to get started as an activist could apply the same strategy to other situations.

"It began the evening the jury was out, and we had nothing to do but wait," Mandy recalled. The defense team was staying at a little hotel in Weyauwega, not far from the courthouse. "So we went to have coffee with the locals. It was about five o'clock. The editor of the paper was always there wanting to get more information. I got into quite an argument with him over whether there was a high percentage of women in that rural county who were battered.

"'No way,' he said. 'I know everybody here.' So I challenged him to run a survey in his paper to find out. He said okay because he was so sure it would be a big joke. But it wasn't."

On December 15, 1977, Dick Prideaux, the newspaper's editor, ran the questionnaire Mandy created. It was captioned: "Battered Women in Waupaca? Let's Find Out." Nine questions followed, ranging from "Has your husband ever struck or beaten you?" to "Do you think a man has a right to hit his wife?"

Women were asked to respond anonymously.

What happened next was described by Steven Englund in *Man Slaughter:*

> *The survey was the brainchild of Mandy Stellman, who had endeared herself to locals by offering to conduct free therapy sessions for "disturbed men" who beat women. [The survey] produced results sufficiently shocking for the editor to decide neither to announce nor detail them. Instead, a few issues later, buried in a column of sundry editorials, Prideaux quietly averred that yes, "more such people are living in their own little hells [here]."*[20]

"So he finally admitted it in the newspaper," said Mandy. Of the fifteen responses received, four were from men who jokingly referred to themselves as battered husbands. The newspaper editor found the topic equally funny, adding his own little warning to men to "never date a girl you can't lick, let alone marry one."

Englund continued:

Prideaux the humorist was followed by Prideaux the psychologist. A woman wrote to say that she had never been beaten or verbally abused by her husband, but if she had been, "I certainly wouldn't have killed him." This reply, wrote the editor smugly, "is, of course, the healthy emotional response," which, he felt certain, "a large majority of women would probably make."

But what of the other ten responses? The editor of the *Weyauwega Chronicle* played down the replies that did not exhibit what he considered to be the healthy emotional response, even though they represented fully two-thirds of the surveys returned to him. Instead, wrote Englund, the editor noted:

"...from comments scribbled on the borders of the form, one or two correspondents appear to be almost desperate, seeking some avenue of escape from their domestic situation," and he concluded that "definitely, there are battered women in Waupaca County." And that was that. He said no more, published no quotations from this large unhappy majority of respondents, and never again adverted to the subject. Thus, with silence about a profound social issue [revealed] in its own midst, did the Weyauwega Chronicle *perceive and fulfill its obligation to its readers.[21]*

"Of course there's a higher proportion of battered women in rural communities," said Mandy when interviewed later at her office, "because you can hide it. Nobody sees you every day. You're not on the street, going to an office. You're doing your farm work. The cows, pigs, and horses see you. Jennifer was a pig breeder. The pigs aren't going to make a phone call to the sheriff. But at least if someone—like my secretary—came to my office battered," Mandy leaned forward and pounded her desk, "I'd *do* something about it!"

###

4. Blowing the Whistle

Sam slipped into an old blue denim jacket and backed the Oldsmobile down the driveway, heading south along Green Bay Avenue toward Wisconsin Avenue. It was 4:05 P.M. in a city that begins its weekday exodus to the suburbs at three, and Sam had just gotten the call from Mandy he'd been expecting, marking the end of another of her demanding days of seeing clients and appearing in court. Though Sam retired at age seventy, Mandy's workload was showing little sign of winding down.

Sam had driven his partner to and from work each day since 1971, when Mandy broke her right leg in a fall. In fact, the husband and wife team seemed to go everywhere together. Sam even began all his speeches with the line, "I never go anywhere without my attorney, Mandy." After work they sometimes drove directly to a fundraising event, or stopped for supper on the way to a meeting. They served on the boards of a number of organizations—usually individually, occasionally together—and meetings occupied one or more nights a week.

However, Sam did not show up at meetings of all the groups he supported with his membership. "All they talk about is

how great they are. Meanwhile, the problem they're supposed to be solving gets worse." He recognized the pattern:
another instance of the means becoming the end. It infuriated him.

Occasionally Sam admitted to one overriding character
flaw: an unwillingness to listen and to compromise. "I don't
listen as well as I probably should, but I don't hear a lot of
good ideas."

During the day Sam and Mandy each read the same articles in the newspaper, and when they got together in the
evening they found they were angry about the same thing.

This evening, a policewoman was expected to stop by after supper for some career advice. So after meeting Mandy
at her office, Sam turned the Oldsmobile toward home, a
comfortable, unpretentious house in Glendale, a suburb north
of Milwaukee. Mandy made dinner, as she did most nights.
She enjoyed cooking, and Sam boasted that her potato lat-
kes were the best in the world.

At seven the doorbell rang, and Sam ushered the off-duty
officer into the wood-paneled family room at the rear of the
ranch-style house.

Rebecca had met Sam during one of his training sessions
for police officers. Impressed by the professor's quiet charisma, she had also been inspired by his get-tough attitude
toward wife beaters.

She told Sam how, as a rookie on the police force and a
woman, she had gotten used to the overt sexism and petty
harassment directed at her from her male colleagues. But
she was finding it harder to witness the cynical attitudes of
some of the veteran police officers because she did not want
to similarly lose hope in her own ability to make a difference in people's lives—especially the lives of abused wom-
en. So she had been trying to decide whether she would be
more effective in reaching her goal if she changed careers.

"Remember, the police weren't trained to handle domestic violence," the soft-spoken professor began, gesturing to the couch. "Well, in Wisconsin they're trained *now*, because state law says they have to be."

Rebecca ignored the couch and instead picked a wooden chair facing Sam's deep easy chair.

"Mandy has to sit in one like that too. Her back...."

Mandy could be heard moving about in the kitchen, and Rebecca voiced the hope that the busy attorney would be able to join them.

Sam continued to focus on the subject he knew so much about. "Domestic violence cases are probably the most difficult for the police. In that I'll support them. Still, the law says they should be arresting batterers, and they're not doing it."

Rebecca looked troubled. "It's not so easy, Sam. Sometimes when we answer a call, one or both people turn on us ...even the ones who called for help. And I don't always get support from my partner to stay and investigate. There's such a macho 'cowboy' mentality on the force, and many cops seem to believe the woman who is being beaten deserved it."

"I know that male cops often side with the batterer," he acknowledged. "The woman is considered inferior. I suspect that many of the officers—most of them are male, of course, but it is getting better, as you know—still, I'm inclined to suspect that many are themselves wife batterers." He shook his head of wispy hair, thinning except for unruly white tufts at his temples.

"Some can be really rough with the woman who's been beaten," said Rebecca. "I've seen officers arrest the wife or girlfriend just because the guy says *she* was hitting *him*. Even if she's the one who is bleeding and bruised."

"When I go to meetings and raise sticky questions about

enforcement," said Sam, "they think I'm a—I don't know what—!" He chuckled briefly but remained serious. "I get all kinds of excuses. If the guy's drunk, the attitude is, 'Well, we all get drunk sooner or later.' Or, 'She drove him to it.' I can't accept the rationalizations." His voice became angrier but not louder. "The law says there has to be an arrest. Women are being injured and even killed. Most of it can be *stopped.*"

Rebecca added that in responding to a call for help, some of the sergeants reinforced the anti-woman attitudes of their male officers.

Sam told of being asked to train the Kenosha police in how they should handle such calls. "I'd say to the officers, 'When you come up to the door, what should you do?' Let's say there's been a call from the woman or a neighbor. Usually the man comes to the door and answers, 'Nothing's wrong. Go away and leave us alone!'

"What you do, I tell the police, is you put your nightstick in the door before he can close it. You say, 'We had a call and we're here to investigate.' And if the man becomes abusive or looks dangerous, let him close the door, then call your back-up quickly—very quickly."

Sam believed that when the police enforce the law, the law can be effective. "But it hasn't been that effective, because I know the police aren't following it carefully enough. We're losing the effort to turn this thing around, mainly because the people involved in the issue are not outraged enough. That's different from being angry. You have to be *outraged!*"

"It's not just the police who need to change their outlook," said Rebecca. "There's so much leniency at every stage of the criminal justice system. Even if we do arrest a batterer and he's charged and prosecuted, the courts sentence him to probation or allow him to bail out until the next

court date. Then he goes right back to beating his partner."
Rebecca quoted the estimate she'd heard: "At least four
women are killed every day by their husbands, boyfriends,
or ex-partners. Every fifteen seconds in the U.S. a woman is
beaten!"[22]

Sam remained quiet. Then he said, sardonically, "It takes
no hard investigative work by police departments to find
these men." On the fingers of his right hand he enumerated
the ways of finding the batterers. "They're reported to the
police; their victims keep seeking relief from the courts;
district attorneys have volumes of records on great numbers of these men; and judges see them in court over and
over again."

The dark-haired young woman leaned forward to hear her
mentor's voice. Her brown eyes were intense as she said,
"The problem is that the system is bogged down at every
level. And the jails are full! So plea bargaining is a common
way out. Everyone from the police to the district attorneys
to the judges make their own discretionary decisions."

Sam sat forward in his easy chair. "The question is, what
can be done to stop the battering in the first place? One of
the ways *not* to stop it is to send the couple back to 'work it
out.' That just means more hitting. Another way that isn't
stopping anything is to send the man to 'treatment' without bringing him into court."

Sam also opposed joint counseling. "In any joint session,
he controls the session even if he says nothing. The woman
has learned to read his body language. She knows she'll get
another beating as soon as they get home."

Sam's voice remained soft despite his strong feelings.
"Same with mediation. You can mediate child custody. I've
set up a program to mediate disputes between neighbors.
But you can't mediate violence, because there are no com-
promises. Men run the show. The best way, if there is one, is

for the police to arrest the man on the first call for help, then for the district attorney to prosecute him vigorously. Finally, the judge has to impose a penalty that sends a message to this guy that his behavior is *not* acceptable and that the beating of women is a serious crime."

The policewoman nodded, adding, "If you did the crime, you do the time."

"At least," said Mandy, entering the room, "any restraining order a woman has been able to get from the court should be fully enforced to keep the man away."

"And it should be issued immediately," added Rebecca, turning to acknowledge Mandy's arrival. "Before the man is released."

"Mandy had a case—more than one," Sam was saying, "where the woman was beat up by her husband, went to her doctor, and the minute he found that she'd gone to the district attorney the doctor said he wouldn't treat her. He didn't want to get 'involved.'"

"Absolute, actual truth," said Mandy, settling into the remaining straight-backed chair. "So I called my own doctor and he said 'Sure, send her over.' And my doctor saw her. I knew he would, because I wouldn't pick a doctor who wasn't socially conscious."

"Mandy and I did some in-service training at St. Luke's Hospital for their medical personnel. The training was approved for a couple of hours of credit from the AMA...."

"...It was June 1978," Mandy interjected, tucking a small pillow behind her. "I remember because it was after the Jennifer Patri case had made headlines, and Alan Eisenberg asked Sam and me to appear with him."

"The program was called 'Another Social Disease—Battered Women,'" added Sam. "Mandy brought some pictures taken of a client after she was brutally beaten by her husband. We taped over her face in the photos, but you could see the bruises on her arms, breasts, back. And we passed out the photographs to the audience."

Mandy picked up the story. "I asked them to raise their hands if they'd ever seen a patient like that. Most of the hands went up—these were doctors, nurses, support staff. Then I asked them to raise their hands if they ever wrote in their notes, into the record, that this was a beating of a woman by a husband or somebody. Not one hand went up. They didn't want to get involved! You know how flat this part of the country is?"

Rebecca looked confused by the seemingly unrelated question. Mandy began telling about the time a woman had been brought to an emergency room bruised and bleeding, saying she "fell off a cliff."[23]

"Not one medical professional asked her any questions!" Mandy was indignant. "That she fell off a cliff was actually in the *records*. Do you see any cliffs around here?"

Mandy continued. "Since the medical records actually said she fell off a cliff, how was I going to prove it was her husband who'd caused those awful injuries? She wasn't going to tell the truth with him standing right there. But once he left the hospital room, the wife whispered to the nurse, 'My husband beat me up. He broke my glasses and broke my nose.' The wife then confided in me, and I eventually convinced the nurse to testify. What woman would feel comfortable telling such personal violations to a man? Women have felt male lawyers sold them out. They're right—it's happened too often."

Rebecca wondered aloud if maybe she could do more good as an attorney than as a police officer. Though she wasn't getting any direct advice about making a career change— the purpose for her visit to the Stellmans—she was listening intently to what they were saying.

Mandy began to tell about appearing on a local cable TV

show with the author of the book about the Patri case. "He kept saying there was no medical evidence produced by any of Jennifer's doctors that she'd been a bruised, beaten, battered woman. So I confronted him—on television."

Mandy jabbed the pillow behind her to adjust it. "I said that I had done a lot of questioning of battered women and gotten them to get their hospital and medical reports from their doctors. I said that in all these cases, not one doctor had ever written down that the husband or boyfriend had beaten her. Even when the doctor suspected it and with a few questions could have established it. That's because the police were involved. So if there were something in the records, the doctor could be subpoenaed to testify. The doctors did not want to get involved."

"I've seen that happen with many violent crimes," Rebecca added. "Whether it's the criminal or the victim talking to the doctor or nurse about the violence, the medical staff hesitates to tell the police. They don't want to have to take the time to go to court."

Sam said, "It took until 1992 for the AMA to come out with a statement that doctors had better start putting down in their notes that women are being beaten and that this is a social disease, a real national disease. They actually used the word 'disease,' and Mandy and I thought, we've been waiting twenty years for the doctors to say this."

Rebecca glanced at the elegant chime clock behind Sam. Though it was growing late, she was held by the stories, and neither Mandy nor Sam seemed reluctant to continue talking. Sam's quiet voice did not necessarily mean he was tired—it was his way of talking, even when he was very, very angry.

"Speak up, Stell," prodded Mandy. "We can't hear you."

"People are either ignoring the problem or joking about it," Sam went on a little more loudly. He told about the time that Mandy, in all seriousness, sent the editor of the *Weyauwega Chronicle* a rape whistle for his wife to carry.

"He made it into a joke," said Mandy. "He told me, 'Maybe I need it because of women attacking me,' and all that crap."

The rape whistles were something the Stellmans bought by the thousands, paying for them as a contribution to the Women's Crisis Line. "The whistles had the phone number of the Crisis Line on them," explained Mandy. "Years ago we gave them out wherever we went."

###

Rebecca drove home to her tiny apartment on the East Side, and she carried into her bedroom a manila folder Sam had given her. It contained copies of letters and newspaper clippings going back at least fifteen years. Though Rebecca had an early morning appearance in court, once she opened the folder, she sat up until midnight reading each piece.

She began with a letter to the editor from Mandy, published by the *Milwaukee Journal* as its "In My Opinion" column for September 26, 1976.

The police had been there many times before. They knew Patricia and her husband very well. While Patricia, now five months pregnant, was feeding her two-year-old son, her husband demanded his dinner, and when it didn't come immediately, he grabbed Patricia by the throat, kicked her in the stomach, and beat her unmercifully with fists and elbows.

This scenario was well known to Rebecca in her police work.

[Patricia] went to the hospital with a ruptured spleen that had to be removed. She lost the baby. The husband was ordered to appear in the office of the district attorney. He was never prosecuted for a crime and Patricia lives in fear of another attack.

Not until twelve years after Mandy wrote this piece did the Wisconsin legislature consider a bill making arrest mandatory when police were called to a domestic violence scene. Sam had lobbied hard for that change in the law, and the bill passed with a minimum of opposition. That was in 1988—the same year Sam retired and Rebecca graduated from the police academy.

Even with the law's passage, "mandatory arrest"—as Rebecca had seen in her short time on the force—represented a fine concept but was seldom taken seriously. Getting the authorities to enforce the law took repeated effort—the manila folder bore testimony to that ongoing effort.

Among the techniques employed by the Stellmans, the writing of newspaper articles and letters sought to publicly humiliate those who failed in their responsibilities to serve the people. The D.A.'s office earned its share of such humiliation.

Rebecca continued reading Mandy's "In My Opinion" piece from 1976:

And then there is Elizabeth. When the police responded to a neighbor's telephone call, they found Elizabeth with red welts on her face, neck, and arms. Her nine-year-old daughter was crying. "Daddy wouldn't stop hitting Mommy."

Rebecca stirred uncomfortably and skipped the next few paragraphs.

Few cases ever result in prosecution of the man who beats a woman. What we have in Milwaukee is selective prosecution of the battery law; a man attacking a man is battery; a man attacking a woman is often considered a "domestic quarrel."

Mandy's *Journal* piece not only called for an end to this double standard but also blew the whistle on another practice the public was unaware of:

*Until very recently, almost all cases involving wife bat-
tering were handled by the district attorney's office, even
though few ended with prosecution in the courts. Recently, the district attorney and city attorney, ignoring Wisconsin law, have decided together that women being
beaten by men should be given an even lower priority.
Now [the women] have been turned over to students as
part of the law school training.*

*Now these students can "play judge" with the lives of
powerless women, most of whom are of low income....*

*Almost all police departments and law enforcement agen-
cies have treated, and continue to treat, the battered
woman problem as a domestic issue and not as a serious
problem involving violent criminal activity....*

*According to the police and the district attorney's of-
fice, most battered women who come to their attention
are a problem because they don't follow up on the charges against the men.*

Though many people found such reluctance hard to understand, it was a familiar theme. Mandy's article went on
to explain why.

*It starts with the woman being economically dependent
upon the man who is the breadwinner and totally in control of the family money. If the husband or boyfriend is a
heavy drinker, and/or beats her, unless the woman has
job skills and a place to provide for her children, she is
literally trapped in an economic bind that forces her to
remain with the husband or boyfriend, or—almost as a
last resort...become a welfare recipient.*

As Rebecca read on, a siren sounded a few blocks away on
Downer Avenue heading for St. Mary's emergency room.

*Battered women are emotionally beaten down, too. Their
self-esteem is low, as they feel ashamed of their "family
problems." They avoid neighbors who may hear the*

screaming and the crying. The battered woman lives in isolation, reluctant to involve others with her problems. She somehow feels she has brought this upon herself, that she deserves what is happening. She not only lives in fear—she lives with no hope for the future.

When children are involved, the mother must deal with their fears and must often protect them from the rage of the man. Life is a constant state of terror for her and her children.

What does this all add up to? It adds up to an abomination! A woman gets little help from the prosecutor's office, and certainly no protection from further attacks by her assailant—who has no worry, since he faces little chance of the battery laws being enforced.

The one exception to non-enforcement that Mandy's editorial noted was when it came to murder—when a batterer eventually killed the woman he'd been tormenting. Such crimes were all the more tragic because most were preventable—*if* the police and district attorney's office had been willing to define earlier calls for intervention as incidents of battery and to enforce the laws that applied.

The final case referred to in Mandy's letter to the editor concerned Teresa, a woman who had come to Mandy's office one day saying, "He's gonna kill me."

The attorney had called the police and hidden the woman in her back office all day. But that evening Teresa had gone home. A couple of days later, the tragic consequences of Teresa's decision to return home were reported in the newspaper.

Mandy's editorial identified the role of the police and the district attorney in those consequences:

The police...had been called many, many times to Teresa's residence, at least 10 times in the past two years for "domestic quarrels" and beatings. Twice her husband was ordered to the district attorney's office; never was he charged with a crime. The last time the police were called was to pick him up for first degree murder. He had put a pillow over Teresa's head; she died in a few minutes.[24]

Rebecca turned slowly to the next set of photocopies, two pages of fine print, which indicated that two of Mandy's articles on the subject of battering had been read in their entirety into the *Congressional Record* of October 12, 1977.

She had written the second article a year after her condemnation of the double standard in prosecuting violent men. It had originally been published in the *Milwaukee Sentinel* under the banner "Battered Women Encouraged to Expose Brutish Men."

With more women starting to "come out of the closet" about their brutalization, Mandy's article proposed a way around the lack of enforcement:

Since the police, the district attorney and the city attorney are obviously of no help to a battered woman, now what the woman can do is to publicly announce to all she comes in contact with—the butcher, the baker, the milkman, and particularly his employer—my husband is a wife beater!

That should do it! Let's start shouting![25]

The failure of the professional community to address wife-beating—which the Stellmans had been calling attention to for some time—began drawing notice from the media in the seventies, as well as from politicians seeking support for pet projects. The *Sentinel* ran a series on battered women in the summer of 1977, and Mandy seized the opportunity to write to the editor, praising the series and reinforcing its message by adding her opinions and some inside information.

The women who have been beaten saw doctors, lawyers,
clergy, social workers, psychiatrists, psychologists, mar-
riage counselors, and a whole host of other "experts."

Where have these concerned experts been over all these
years of seeing women so conspicuously covered with the
evidence of physical abuse—black eyes, bruises, broken
bones?

In fact, there seems to be some evidence that many of
these experts told the women that the women had brought
this upon themselves. Others told these women to go back
to their violent spouses and "make up"—knowing or sus-
pecting that the husbands would beat them again....

Unflinchingly naming names, Mandy's article castigated
David Felger, Milwaukee's Assistant City Attorney, for "sending the battered women to talk with Marquette University
law students who also handle neighbor arguments about
garbage and music playing too loud."

Rebecca recalled Sam and Mandy's conversation earlier
that evening about how they had visited Marquette and
seen for themselves how pointless the program was. And
how they became so outraged that they fought to eliminate
the student involvement, even though their stance meant
confronting some of the community's most powerful officials—the district attorney and the city attorney—who had
established the program with federal money.

Mandy's article also named District Attorney E. Michael
McCann as the one who had sent the cases to the City Attorney's Office, "knowing full well that they will end up
with students who haven't even been oriented as to the
problems of battered women...."

The article concluded by analyzing the failures of the police. Rebecca read these paragraphs intently; it was because
she wanted to make a difference that she became a police
officer. The Stellmans were an example for her of what one

person could do to make a difference, even if that effort didn't change the world all at once. She picked up the clipping again.

If a man beats another man...without the police being present, that man will be arrested. The police don't have to be present, they don't have any concern about being charged with false arrest, or about being reprimanded by their superiors.

With respect to a man beating...a wife or a girlfriend, then the police have a different set of rules of their own not based on the law. Now, for reasons which only the police have decided, when a woman is battered, the police have to be present when the assault takes place for them to do anything; they claim they might be accused of false arrest—even though the woman is standing in front of the officer with all the evidence of the battering showing....

So, if a cop wishes to "cop out" of responding to a call by a beaten woman, he rationalizes [his] brushing off wife battering as unimportant by saying that women love to be beaten. Or [he uses] every tactic possible to discourage the woman from filing a complaint against her husband or boyfriend and then joyfully announces, "But she won't prosecute, so why do anything?"

Mandy's article suggested that these attitudes toward women reflected the private lives of police officers in the United States, borne out in the professional literature's statistics about the high rates of divorce, alcoholism, and family problems among the police officers themselves.

The issue interested Rebecca because, as she'd admitted to Sam, she didn't know whether the male cops she worked with developed such attitudes in the job, or if the macho guys attracted to this kind of work already held those attitudes.

The last letters she read before turning out the light were contained in three clippings that Sam had placed at the back of the folder.

###

"How dare L. Mandy Stellman put down the police just because women are beaten up by their spouses?" asked one Milwaukee letter writer, who identified herself as "Cop's Wife."

Her words openly displayed the very attitude Mandy had said was operating within the police community.

"Cop's Wife" continued:

> *If a woman is beaten up repeatedly by a man and choos-*
> *es to stay with him, she deserves to get beaten up. I'm*
> *sick and tired of hearing how these women expect the*
> *police to stop their husbands from beating them up but*
> *refuse to stay away from such men. I don't feel a bit*
> *sorry for them! It's their own fault. Don't they have any*
> *pride or dignity?*[26]

Another letter writer took issue with Mandy's views from the anonymity afforded by the initials B.K.

> *As a police officer, I found the L. Mandy Stellman letter*
> *on the battered women articles to be both amusing and*
> *disgusting. Amusing because of all the misconceptions*
> *regarding police work and disgusting because people read*
> *and actually believe these misconceptions.... In order to*
> *arrest a person, male or female, for a misdemeanor, that*
> *misdemeanor must occur in the presence of a law en-*
> *forcement officer. If it does not, AN ARREST CANNOT BE*
> *MADE. That's the law.*[27]

B.K.'s understanding of "the law," which he or she expounded with all the power that capitalization could add to modern typography, was contradicted a week later in a letter from Janesville, Wisconsin, signed "Another Cop."

Sorry, B.K., that is not the law. Wisconsin law provides for the arrest of any person for a felony or misdemeanor based on the officer's reasonable grounds to believe the person is committing or has committed a crime.

Thus, an arrest of one person for intentionally injuring another may be based on reasonable grounds and probable cause without the actual act of striking occurring in the officer's presence. State Statute 968.07(1)(D) gives the officer the authority to make an arrest in that manner. [28]

Mandy did not need this vindication, but coming from "another cop" it must have carried some weight with readers. More important, it proved the strategic value of the Stellmans' letter-writing techniques. By exposing abuses and furnishing convincing details, Sam and Mandy often instigated a debate that kept an issue alive until something was done about it. The strategy was similar to Sam's starting a community program and bringing in the people who could carry it on.

Rebecca clipped a piece of paper to the manila folder, which she would return to Sam the next day. On it she wrote: "None of us has to save the world. We just need more people like you to get things rolling and create opportunities for others to pick up a share of the battle against injustice."

A battle it is, and Mandy and Sam fought it all their professional lives on behalf of women, children, and the "little guy." They took on every layer of the law enforcement system as well as doctors, therapists, social service agencies, the clergy, the media, and major corporations. Neither big nor small officials who perpetuated abominations of justice escaped being skewered by the sharp pen of the Stellmans.

Though the couple bestowed their charity anonymously, when it came to demanding social change, the full names of Samuel D. Stellman and L. Mandy Stellman appeared as bylines in many hundreds of articles and letters written over more than fifty years. Their incisive words—written, spoken, broadcast in interviews, and delivered from lecterns—have educated, informed, criticized, lambasted, and provoked hundreds of thousands of people. Their words together with their deeds have furnished fuel to legislators and lobbyists, empowered victims to act in their own best interests, and given acid indigestion to bureaucrats and bumblers.

How did these two become so committed?

###

PART TWO: SOURCE

True modesty, like underclothes
Does its job, but seldom shows.
                                    Sol Mandlsohn

5. Acorns Don't Fall Far from the Tree

On Monday evenings, Abraham and Rose Mandlsohn walked the four blocks to the neighborhood movie house, leaving their oldest boy, Sol, in charge of the family grocery store. Although Mondays were quiet at the A&M grocery, the store stayed open until eleven o'clock because second-shift workers stopped on their way home to pick up a bottle of milk, a loaf of bread, and a couple of slices of bologna for the next day's lunch. If they spent eighty cents, they'd spent a great deal. It was 1935 and the middle of the Great Depression in Canada, just as in the United States.

One Monday night around eight o'clock, the bell hanging above the door jingled as Marta P___ walked in, a baby in her arms, a toddler clutching her hand, and three tow-headed kids straggling behind.

"Five pounds of macaroni, please, five pounds of potatoes, and two pounds of hamburger."

Behind the wood-block counter, seventeen-year-old Sol Mandlsohn ground the beef, weighed it, and wrapped it in white butcher's paper just as he had learned to do from his father. The boy's thirteen-year-old sister, Mandy, who was helping in the store, saw the needle on the scale touch the big number three, but she said nothing as Sol rang up the price for two pounds. Her brother was doing exactly what all the Mandlsohn children had seen their father do. This was normal; they never talked about it.

Earlier that day, Mandy had accompanied her mother to the courthouse in another familiar ritual. Franz W___, a factory worker who lived in the neighborhood, had been arrested early Sunday morning, having gotten drunk on Saturday after being paid on Friday. Because he could not make bail on Monday, Rose Mandlsohn—in broken English—pleaded his case, just as she had done many times for many others. All the judges had gotten to know her.

"Well, Rosie," the judge said, "will you vouch for this man?"

As usual, Mandy's mother agreed to see that the now-sober Franz would not get in trouble again, and the shame-faced offender was released on her recognizance.

And what was Rose's relationship to Franz—or to Stepan, or Hans, or any of a dozen other factory workers for whom she vouched? Simply that these men and their families lived in the neighborhood and shopped at the A&M grocery at 783 Queen Street West, Toronto. True, those families also shopped at the A&P across the street, but *there* they couldn't buy on credit as they could at the A&M.

It made no difference to Abie and Rose that the beneficiaries of their intervention were not Jewish.

Along with thousands of other Jews from eastern Europe, the Mandlsohns had emigrated to Toronto in 1912 from a region near Minsk, Russia. They settled in a neighborhood made up mostly of Church of England immigrants and white Protestants from central and western Europe.

In the thirties and forties when the Mandlsohn children were growing up, families experienced the same social problems as today—they just weren't called "social problems" then: domestic violence, alcohol addiction, child abuse, sexual harassment, homelessness, and dysfunctional families. Nor were such problems handled by trained social workers or counselors. Those professionals were scarce. Instead, a family's problems were handled, often with great skill and wisdom, by the local grocer, butcher, bartender, and barber—those unassuming men and women who lived and worked in the same neighborhood as their "clientele." Their neighborhood businesses served as community centers, and the proprietors functioned as community workers for the neighborhood.

Rose Mandlsohn was one of the best of these. She and her husband served as role models for the entire community as well as for their three daughters and three sons, who learned that caring about others is a way of life. Rose's values were reflected first within her own family, where the chores were shared by six youngsters whose ages spanned no more than twelve years altogether—and then in the family store, where husband and wife shared equally in the work. After the birth of every baby, Rose put on her apron and went back to work alongside Abie.

The family lived above the store on the second and third floors of a tall, narrow brick building. "We had live chickens in the back," recalled Mandy some sixty-five years later. "Today it wouldn't pass the health inspector. We had a shed behind the store—today it would be a garage—with chicken coops in it.

"My mother would be cooking something on the second floor where the kitchen was and she'd say, 'I need six eggs.' We'd go downstairs, shoo the chickens away, and bring up six fresh, warm eggs."

Early in the week, well before payday, customers would come into the grocery store without money. "So my father would give them a little notebook and he would write in it that they bought milk, ten cents, and bread, ten cents, macaroni, five cents. He'd add it up by hand, put the date next to the total, and hand the book to the customer. He kept no records. Or he'd write on the outside of the grocery bag, add it up, and put the amount in the notebook. People would bring in the notebook each time and my father would add more." On payday, he or Rose would total what the customer owed. Rose performed all the calculations in her head.

"I can picture very vividly particular women coming into the store with their five, six, or seven children," Mandy said. "They would buy five pounds of potatoes, maybe a pound of sugar—we sold it loose—a pound of rolled oats, a bottle of milk—there were no cartons then, just bottles— and a couple of loaves of bread. I recall very vividly my father saying, 'Would you like any meat?'"

Recounting a story, Mandy played all the parts, taking different voices and getting into character for each.

"The woman would say, 'Ah, the kids don't like to eat meat, and my husband is tired of it.' But my father knew she didn't have the money, so he'd say, 'Well, I've got three pounds of this ground meat left over and I have to throw it out because I'm cleaning out the ice box'—it was a walk-in cooler where you put blocks of ice in the top section—'so why don't you take it. And here's some beef bones we're gonna throw out.'"

It was the Mandlsohn version of what we now call a food pantry. The Mandlsohns were not affluent, and they never owned an automobile, but they always had enough to eat because they had the grocery store. Whatever assistance they provided, the Mandlsohns always preserved the dignity of those they helped—even the occasional shoplifter.

Watching for pilfering was one of the children's responsibilities, in addition to bagging groceries, making home deliveries, and cleaning the store. But no one was to be accused. When it came time to total the groceries on the counter, the practice was to add to the bill—with the purchaser looking on—those items that had disappeared into his or her pocket. No words were exchanged about the pilfered goods. Respecting the dignity of the individual was sacred. It was a powerful lesson in humanity.

When Mandy was no more than a toddler, she began receiving gentle lessons in values. "We weren't allowed to eat candy or oranges in the yard or playground. My mother would make us finish our food in the house." To the children's predictable "why?" Rose would explain that some of their playmates had hardly any food.

Often, people the children did not know moved in with the family. Or a stranger appeared at the dinner table and was introduced as a distant "cousin." No one asked where they came from or how long they were going to stay. These visitors, treated like members of the family, were the homeless of the thirties.

"My parents were doing social work," Mandy explained. "They never lectured about what they were doing. We learned by watching what they did and by participating."

If someone needed legal advocacy or got a ticket for a misdemeanor, intervention was there in the person of Rose, the quasi-lawyer, whose formal education—in Yiddish—had stopped before high school. If someone in the multilingual community needed a letter translated or a bill from the gas company explained, clarification was there in the person of Abraham, the business manager, who had taken English lessons in night school after arriving in Canada with a high school education. Despite the limits of their schooling, Rose and Abie knew more languages than most people. They spoke Yiddish and Russian fluently, as well as some Polish and Ukrainian.

Because Mandy grew up in a neighborhood where six or more different languages were spoken, she did not learn to speak English well until she entered kindergarten.

This fourth child—a second daughter—was born at home, as was the custom. Dr. Levine charged two dollars for his trouble. He never got around to registering the event, so Mandy never had a birth certificate, and her date of birth was always a little uncertain. Rose remembered the event's taking place around the time of Children's Day at the Canadian National Exhibition. In 1922 that occurred on August 22, so that is the date the family celebrated each year.

The little girl was named Leah, Hebrew for Lillian. But everyone called her Mandy, a shortened version of the family name, Mandlsohn.

A bright student and fast learner, Mandy loved school. All six Mandlsohn offspring earned good grades. "My mother and father valued education," she recalled. "We just automatically knew you had to get good grades. There was no question." After completing Niagara Street Elementary School she went on to high school at the Parkdale Collegiate Institute, a short ride by streetcar. But Mandy nearly always walked the two miles each way.

As a teenager, pretty, dark-haired Mandy was unable to have dates on Saturday nights because the store was busy. Although the Mandlsohns kept a kosher home and bought their own meat at a kosher butcher shop, they carried non-kosher food in the store and stayed open to meet the needs of their customers on Saturday, the Jewish Sabbath. So Mandy's dates usually took place in the middle of the week.

In the thirties, discussing sex was taboo, and daughters didn't get much advice from their parents. Nevertheless, when Mandy went to a party, she knew that if the lights were turned off it was time to leave. A typical date for her meant playing a couple of games of Ping-Pong at the YMHA, the Young Men's Hebrew Association.

Instead of giving her three daughters advice, Rose simply gave each a hatpin and said, "Take it with you when you go places like the movies." Whenever the girls asked the hatpin's purpose, their mother would simply nod and say, "You'll see." And they did. One time at the movies, a man sat down next to one of Mandy's sisters, and the usefulness of the hatpin suddenly occurred to the young woman. A single quick jab into the hand that had come to rest on her knee sent the man quickly to the nearest exit.

As for the women who came into the store brandishing a black eye and bruises, the type of advice Rose dispensed was more direct: "Go home and tell your husband that if he hits you again, you'll wait until he goes to sleep and you'll hit him with a Coca-Cola bottle."

Mandy's mother was a quiet but effective woman.

Rose and Abraham reared their sons and daughters with no sex-role distinctions. As a result, Mandy was a feminist long before she ever heard the word.

"I would visit friends at their homes and see their fathers yelling and their mothers cooking and cleaning. My parents discussed business and politics. I didn't see that anywhere else I went."

In fact, Mandy used to wonder whether the mothers of some of her friends were still living, because she never heard an inquiry of any kind about mothers. The parents of her friends always asked their children's friends, "And what does your father do?" but never "What does your mother do?"

During an era when young men were brought up to be breadwinners and young women were expected to find husbands who would support them and their children, the Mandlsohns were equal partners. Although Rose and Abraham assumed their children would marry—and all but one did—they gave particularly shrewd advice to their daughters: "Don't marry a doctor, be a doctor," and "Don't play house, buy a house."

They were as supportive of the first-born, Ettie, who chose to become a homemaker, as they were of the last-born, Sandy, who chose a career as a nurse. As for their sons, brilliant Sol became a successful businessman, actor, and poet. Archie, who died young, worked in the family store, and Willie became an accountant.

This large and loving family was part of a network of relatives who had established a beneficent society in Toronto around the time that Rose emigrated from Russia. As in Jewish communities all over North America, immigrants pooled their resources to fund funerals and take care of other emergencies, to provide loans for family members who wanted to start a small business, and to help the more recent immigrants. The Mandlsohns always contributed in their quiet way, and people would pay back the loans when they were able to. This social service club was called *Mishpocha*, the Yiddish word for family. Membership grew to several hundred, and the group eventually bought a building for its social events and its administration. For many years at Hanukah and Purim, two Jewish holidays, Rose and Abraham hosted parties for this extended family, furnishing the coffee and cake and the treats for the children.

"No one ever got up and thanked Rosie and Abie," Mandy observed about the charitable behaviors and expressions of *tzedakah* that defined her environment. "I didn't know the meaning of all these things until I analyzed them years later. It was the Judaic sense of values. You shared what you had, and you didn't brag."

In English, the Hebrew word *tzedakah* is often incorrectly translated as *charity*. A more accurate translation is *justice* or *what is just*. Thus, helping others is considered a responsibility, an obligation—not an option.

Of course, not everyone in the Jewish community met that obligation in the quiet and loving way the Mandlsohns did. Their sense of values not only shaped Mandy's beliefs but also nourished her conviction and courage to act on them. And even though her siblings shared the same values, it was this fourth child of six who became the most outspoken on behalf of those values, and the most active.

The first of many times that Mandy made headlines occurred on March 11, 1941. She was eighteen. It was the week of exams, and after school she went to study at a friend's house. Intending to spend the night, she changed her mind after dinner and walked home. What moved her to return home and sleep in her own bed that night she never knew. It must have been *b'sheart*—destiny—because in the middle of the night she awoke coughing and choking from the smoke that had already filled the three-story building.

A soldier going by saw the smoke and turned in the alarm. Her sister Sandy, who shared a room with her on the third floor, fled down the stairs, as did the other children, whose rooms were on the second floor. Her mother must have managed to get down the stairs with Sandy, but by the time her father reached the stairs the smoke was so thick he had to turn back. From the master bedroom at the front of the building, he climbed out on the third-floor ledge and waited for the fire department.

And Mandy? She realized that the tenants renting the back bedroom next to hers were trapped. Instead of taking an immediate escape route, she led the family along the smoke-filled hallway, through her parents' bedroom, and to the ledge. By then the fire department had arrived.

The next day's headlines read:

> *"Six Perch On Third-floor Ledge Until Rescued by Firemen; Girl Insists On Being Last As Four Adults And Child Are Helped Down Ladder."*[29]

For her heroic action, the high school senior received the Certificate of Valour from the Canadian National Exhibition. In addition, for "safety, bravery and valour," she was presented with the Lowney Young Canada Club Honour Award Medal, the highest award given by the organization.

She also received love letters from a soldier, who saw a picture of the pretty hero in the newspaper. He was eager to meet her, and offered to present her with one of his own medals. Mandy politely declined.

Another event took place the night of the fire that the newspaper did not report. At one point the woman Mandy rescued had thought her five-year-old boy would be trapped inside. She became hysterical.

"So I hit her," said Mandy, always a person of action.

###

When Mandy graduated from high school a few months after the fire, her choice of profession was motivated by an unspoken heritage of commitment to helping others. Thus, she sought the most humanitarian of the professions known to her—nursing. But no anti-discrimination laws existed at the time to level the playing field and allow a capable and dedicated nineteen-year-old to prove her worth. In a personal interview at St. Elizabeth Hospital in Toronto, where she tried to enroll in nursing school, she was told that a facility in New Jersey was where the Jewish girls went for their nursing education and training.

Mandy reacted to this bitter disappointment with an "I'll show them" attitude, enrolling instead in the Toronto Normal School to become a teacher. A year later, in June 1942, she graduated with an elementary teaching certificate. Immediately she began job hunting, armed with her certificate and previous experience as a camp counselor. Toronto's City Parks Department hired her for the summer as a recreation specialist. But when she applied for a permanent teaching post in the city's public school system, she was promptly turned down.

"We have our quota this year," she was told. "We already have a Jewish teacher."

Profoundly hurt by this second rejection, she could scarcely comprehend what she was hearing. After nearly two decades of believing in the principle of equality and the rewards of merit and hard work, she was entering an unjust adult world that attempted to thwart her life's objective. Though wounded, she felt another, stronger emotion, like anger but more focused. Recognizing that the hurt produced by an unfair, unjust system was not to be tolerated, she experienced the rising of outrage.

This outrage became the catalyst for her first battle against the status quo. Having grown up with her self-esteem intact, Mandy was determined to fight back. But she had not yet learned the strategies of radical action—in the literal sense of "radical" meaning "root"—which strives to make changes at the root of a problem. She did not yet know that such change had to be made to a *system* so it would neither discriminate against her nor perpetuate discrimination against others who would come after her.

But she did have the intelligence and determination to seek change for herself. And she used the most accessible strategy available to her at the time: personal connections.

One of the members of the board of education happened

to be Jew. He also happened to be Mandy's cousin, and he agreed to use his influence. That fall his well-qualified niece was hired as part of what was referred to at the time as "occasional staff." She became a substitute teacher, grades one through eight.

Mandy was a natural teacher, and she loved her work. But it didn't take long for her to see the limitations of teaching as a means of making an impact on the lives of young students. After a few years in front of a classroom, she took the next deliberate career step—one in a series, each reflecting an increasing awareness of her role in *tikkun olam*, the Jewish sense of duty to repair the world. When she left teaching, she believed she could effect more meaningful change as a social worker interacting one-on-one with the people who needed her help.

The limitations of social work, her third career choice after nursing and then teaching, took her less time to recognize. Years later, as soon as she received her bachelor's degree in social work, she took the next step closer to the root of effecting change and enrolled in law school.

Building on the traditions of her heritage and the influence of her parents as role models, Mandy was determined to pursue a life's work that would make the greatest difference in the lives of the greatest number of people.

Two miles from Queen Street West where the Mandlsohn children were growing up, the neighborhood changed. Also a community of immigrants, most of the pushcart vendors along that part of Dundas Street could be heard hawking their wares in Yiddish, rather than in any of the diverse languages heard in the A&M grocery. Storefronts bore only Hebrew letters, and the boys playing stickball against the curb wore the traditional yarmulkes.

Shortly after the turn of the century, it was this impover-
ished Jewish ghetto in Toronto that became home to Fanke
Weisblum, an intelligent, well-educated, and politically
aware young woman who, in her twenties, had left Warsaw
and her prosperous family to find a new life away from the
increasingly oppressive anti-Semitism in eastern Europe.

When Fanke arrived, she was already able to read and
write English fluently—only one of several languages she
knew. She also adopted an English nickname, "Fannie.

The young man she met and married, Schiach Stellman,
worked as a milkman. His family originated in Belgium.
When the couple's first two children were three and one,
the young family left Canada hoping to find greater economic opportunity in the United States. But only five years
later—1922—Fannie returned to the same poor Toronto
ghetto, an indigent widow with four children, Pauline, two;
Shalom, four; Minnie, six; and Lillian, eight.

The Stellmans had left Canada in 1917 filled with opti-
mism. They had headed west, planning to continue to California. But they got no farther than Detroit, the first city
beyond the Canadian border; it was the same year the United States was drawn into the war in Europe. One year later,
on November 11, 1918, the armistice was signed, and the
Stellmans' third child was born—the first Stellman to be an
American citizen by birth. In celebration of the new age of
world peace, they named this baby, their only boy, Shalom,
the Hebrew word for peace. Not until he entered school was
he called Samuel, or Sammy. His adoring sisters gave him
their own nickname: Sambo.

Sammy was four when his father was killed in an accident. In those days, there were no pensions, no unemployment insurance, no worker's compensation, and no social

security. The need for benefits for widows and children was just beginning to be recognized, but only in certain industries. "Welfare" was an even more despised word in the twenties than it became in the early nineties, and the only social welfare system in existence for the indigent at the time offered but three choices: the almshouse, the community, and the family.

The young Stellman children had no grandparents on this side of the Atlantic. The Stellmans were living in Radom, the Weisblums in the Apetow region—areas of Poland that were part of Russia at the time. Fannie's closest relatives lived in Toronto.

The Widow Stellman was a survivor, however. With no means of support, financial or emotional, Sam's mother packed up and returned with her four young children to the immigrant neighborhood in Toronto where her two sisters were rearing their own families. For a time the Stellman family of five moved in with Fannie's sister Tinka and her husband, Anshel Wise. The Wises had three children of their own. Fortunately, their house at 183 Beverly Street was large.

It was during this time that Sam's awareness and understanding were shaped by the courage and philosophy of his mother, a woman who was raising four children as a single parent, a status better known in the thirties as the "Poor Widow." It was during this time, too, that Sam's values and commitment were molded by the social activism and humanitarianism of his Uncle Anshel.

Anshel Wise owned a candy and cigar store on Dundas Street at the corner of Bay. He also acted as an agent for various steamship lines, selling tickets and making travel arrangements. Because everybody who emigrated from the old country came by boat, Anshel was widely believed to be the conduit for bringing over more Jewish immigrants from Europe than anybody else in all of Canada. He not only cared about helping people, he also knew what strings to pull to get them out of Europe. When the immigrants arrived, he went further, getting them settled, running interference with the Canadian government, and obtaining and translating the proper documents. He was a one-man resettlement agency, making sure that everyone and everything had been taken care of. To many people he was a savior.

Although Sam was too young to understand the importance of his uncle's activities, he realized it later. To the fatherless boy, Anshel Wise was a great role model, a caring, compassionate man who used whatever power he had to help those in need. He regularly sent money to his family in Poland, attended night school, and in later years became a commissioner of licensing. Eventually he took a position with the Canadian immigration department and continued his work of helping resettle immigrants.

A handsome man with a fair complexion and very blue eyes, Anshel appeared taller than his five feet eight inches because he carried himself well, despite a limp that in later years caused him to use a cane.

With the help offered by the Wises, Fannie and her children eventually were able to move to an eight-room house on Ross Street where she could take in boarders. The house was situated just around the corner from the Wise home. At least once a week, Sam continued to drop in at the candy store to visit the uncle he loved and admired, and whose commitment to helping others profoundly influenced his own values.

Like the Mandlsohns, Fannie was a social activist in her own way, stretching the limits of her resources to share with others. An avid reader, she kept well-informed about current world and national issues and was vocal about social injustice. The common theme defining her interests and outlook was justice for the working person and ways of making life fair for all.

The Stellman household became the center of activity for numerous young adults, from union organizers to volunteers on their way to join in the fight against fascism in Spain. Many others were homeless and unemployed, but driven by their fervent belief in the possibility of a better world.

Every night around the heavy oak dining table, heated discussions raged on every subject of concern to these socially conscious idealists: Hitler and the frightening growth of the Nazi movement...the Depression...communism and the Soviet Union...the war in Spain under General Franco... strikes by workers for better wages...the deliberate gunning down of union organizers.

Through the double doors that remained open between the dining and living rooms, the children would hear:

"It's the extremes of capitalism. The 'haves' do everything they can to keep the workers down."

"It's the Henry Fords and John D. Rockefellers. They don't give a goddamn about the rest of the people."

In the middle of every discussion could be heard the voice of Fannie Stellman, champion of the poor and the oppressed—not to mention a great cook. Whether her guests agreed or disagreed with her opinions on world events, she fed them and, when necessary, let them sleep on the living room couch—or wherever else an empty bed could be found in the eight rooms.

Taking all this in were the four Stellman children. Too young to understand the discussions, they absorbed the message of caring and the search for justice in a hostile world of business, industry, and government. Such messages etched themselves in the Stellman psyches as the three girls and one boy grew into adolescence and adulthood. They learned from example as well as from words.

Such daily discussions provided the philosophical underpinnings for the real situations that the children were witnessing for themselves in their own household and among their relatives. They witnessed the impact of miserly wages, the hiring and firing of employees at will, and the need to organize for health and safety on the job.

That people ought to help one another, no matter how little they themselves had, became clear to the Stellman children as they developed sensitivity toward both the unemployed and the working poor. And they took for granted that a well-informed woman, feisty and vigorously vocal, could hold her own with a predominantly male population of varying shades of political opinion.

These were people fighting for a cause. To Sam, the Depression era in which he grew up, and the burning issues of social justice all around him, formed an integral part of the Jewish values he absorbed.

A quiet boy, Sam was both intelligent and athletic, participating in every team sport available to him: baseball, rugby, and basketball. In addition, he served as the scribe for his athletic clubs because he was the only one of the jocks who could read and write well enough—his inscrutable penmanship notwithstanding.

Pauline, Sam's little sister, enjoyed Sam's popularity in other ways. She often pestered him until he let her come with him to his ballgames. But instead of introducing her to his friends, as she'd hoped, Sam would sit her down with a yearbook to read. Pauline would get back at her brother by waiting on the porch, intercepting his friends when they came to call for him, and not letting him know.

Sometimes Sam would let his little sister retrieve the balls that went out of bounds. He collected five cents a ball and she collected scraped knees—willingly. Pauline was so proud of Sam that she made sure everyone knew she was his sister. Because he was popular, she was popular.

Fannie often worried that her athletic son would get hurt. "Don't go ice skating, you'll break a leg," she would warn. "Don't play rugby where they all land on you." So whenever Sam came home bruised he made sure to wear a long-sleeved shirt to hide his bandages. One day his little sister touched him on the arm and asked how he was feeling. It was one of the few times the young man showed anger. "Shut up," Sam growled.

The other times he got mad were when Pauline would take his roller skates, and would turn down a date solely because another girl liked the same boy. Sam would scold, "If there's a boy you like, go after him."

Every day after public school, Sam and his sisters went to Peretz Schule. This was one of many secular schools operated throughout Canada and the United States by the Workmen's Circle, an organization that represented the secular side of the Jewish community. It was dedicated to improving the practical rather than the spiritual aspect of people's lives.

The high school Sam attended, Harbord Collegiate, was 95 percent Jewish. He became captain of the championship Harbord Collegiate football team and also played with the Lizzies, a Toronto Parks Department team. The year Sam was captain of the Lizzies, 1937, the team won the city, province, and dominion championships for rugby and basketball.

Over the years, pictures of Sam with his teammates appeared often in the local newspapers, as did sports page items such as these:

"The big hitting noise of the evening was big Sammy Stellman, who had a perfect performance in the batter's box, collecting three singles in three times at bat."

"Stellman led his team up front, setting up numerous plays and scoring 10 points himself, canning 6 free throws out of a possible 6, and in the back court picking up scores of rebounds off his own backboard...."

"Sammy Stellman, hero of the series, again played a standout back-court game for the winner, and also accounted for seven useful points."

"Sammy Stellman...the only player to consistently make gains."

"[The] plunging sensation, Sammy Stellman, romped through the Red and Black centre for 20 yards...."

And, to his mother's dismay:

"Sammy Stellman, who had pieces of flesh torn out of his elbows in the game early in the week, was their most effective ball-carrier."

When Sam's sisters graduated from high school, they went right to work as all young women did in those days, becoming secretaries and earning very little. When Sam graduated from Harbord in 1936 he too worked—as a gym instructor at the Toronto YMHA.

After three years, the Y gave him an athletic scholarship to attend the University of Minnesota. Few of his contemporaries went to college directly from high school, if ever, because few could afford it. Sam couldn't afford it either, and despite his scholarship he needed two hundred dollars for living expenses, a lot of money in 1939. Anshel Wise co-signed his nephew's bank loan, proud of the first one in the family able to attend college.

Sam viewed his education and his uncle's continuing support of it as "kind of an ethnic thing with us, a Jewish belief in education generally."

After his freshman year in Minneapolis, Sam returned home for the summer. He was of draft age. It was 1940, and Canada was already embroiled in World War II. National security measures on both sides of the border were heightened, so when he attempted to return to Minnesota for his sophomore year, the United States would not allow the American-born Canadian resident to re-enter the country. As a result he lost his scholarship. Although he enrolled at the University of Toronto instead, his family felt the financial sacrifice.

In college Sam quickly established himself as a leader. He became the first president of the new Physical and Health Education Association and captain of the rugby team. He played basketball and volleyball for University College while continuing to work full-time as a gym instructor. When the YMHA basketball team won its 1941–42 championship, Sam was its coach.

The following year he became one of sixty-three athletes honored by the University of Toronto as "University College Colour Holders."

The most memorable aspect of Sam's college experience had to do with gender. The year he enrolled marked the first time the University of Toronto extended its previously all-woman physical education program to men.

Five males in addition to Sam enrolled, but five dropped out because they found the course work too difficult. Sam became the first male to complete the program. When he graduated in 1943 with a B.S. in physical and health education, Sam was the lone male among sixteen women in his graduating class.

On the occasion of its fiftieth class reunion, this "Pioneer Class" was featured in the alumni news. Dr. Stellman, having by then achieved many advances on behalf of women, was quoted as attributing "much of my feminism to the groundwork I received as the lone male among women who understood the importance of promoting the status of women at a time when women were not held in the highest esteem in the working world, including the Physical and Health Education field."[30]

In fact, Sam had come to understand the importance of promoting the status of women at an early age, having grown up with three intelligent sisters and a courageous, socially conscious mother.

Sam's egalitarian attitude remained at odds with the view of women prevailing in the thirties through the mid-forties. He was well aware at the time of the goal of mothers for their daughters—to see them married, even if they did go to college. Because it was almost unheard of for women to enter other fields, physical education was considered "a big thing" for women during that period of history.

It was in his senior year, while Sam was teaching a women's gym class at the YMHA, that the middle Mandlsohn daughter enrolled in his class.

###

6. How Low Can Higher Education Get?

Mandy closed her eyes and began to explain what had attracted her to Sam. "He was...."

"Intelligent," Sam interrupted.

Opening her eyes she looked at him coquettishly. As vivacious and sharp-witted at seventy as she was at nineteen, Mandy asked, "Why did I like you?"

Sam smiled. "And visey versey?"

They shared a private laugh, almost a giggle. These married partners never fought, never belittled or demeaned one another, never exchanged a harsh word.

For two people who spent their lives together as a well-coordinated team, it seems fitting that they met on a gym court. Fifty years later, Mandy referred to that athletic young woman in the gymnasium as "the dumpy one in the school rompers." In reality, that athletic young woman possessed a nice figure that carried just a few extra pounds. Though she would never be called skinny, she was not heavy. And she always dressed attractively, despite owning only two blouses in those early years—which she washed by hand and ironed every other day.

Nineteen-year-old Mandy rushed home from her first evening of volleyball class. Almost out of breath, she ran to find her big sister. "Ettie, let me tell you...I met someone! He's an instructor at the Y. He's tall, and good looking. And he's so nice! His name is Sam Stellman."

Ettie replied matter-of-factly. "I know him. I'm in one of his daytime exercise classes. I've known him for years."

"Why didn't you ever tell me about him?"

"You never asked."

It wasn't long before Sam began walking the pretty young woman home from the Y. Because four miles separated the Mandlsohn house from the YMHA, the pair had a lot of time to become acquainted. Mandy talked about teaching and Sam talked about athletics—which each of them loved.

Soon the young couple began meeting Friday evenings at the University of Toronto, where Sam was enrolled. Mandy signed up for a night class toward her B.A. in education. Sam, wearing the uniform of the Canadian Officer Training Corps (the equivalent of ROTC in the United States), walked her home after class. Sometimes the couple stopped to share a nickel Coke, and although money was scarce, they sometimes splurged a dime and split a Kosher corned beef sandwich.

Although Sam talked easily with his new companion and a few close friends, he spoke very little around most people. The only boy in a family of females, he'd grown up in a world of listening and analyzing issues. This demeanor provoked Mandy's mother to ask at one point, "Doesn't he talk?"

When Mandy announced she wanted to marry the quiet young athletic instructor, her family was supportive. But when Sam's family contemplated sharing the only male among them with another woman, their reaction was lukewarm. It didn't take too long, however, before they became proud of their Sammy's wife.

The wedding was planned for August following Sam's June 1943 graduation from Toronto University. With his new bachelor's degree in Physical and Health Education, Sam got a summer job as director of Camp Frailoch, an all-boys' camp fifty miles west of Toronto in Muskoka. Thirty miles from Muskoka, Mandy found a summer job as a counselor at Camp Winnebago, a private camp.

It was a hot day at the beginning of July when Sam, twenty-four, received his long-anticipated notice from the Canadian draft board. Quicker than most shotgun weddings, the ceremony was moved up to July 11. Mandy called her sister Ettie from camp on a Thursday to see if their parents could make the wedding that very Sunday.

"We almost didn't make it ourselves," chuckled Sam fifty years later.

"We nearly missed the train back to Toronto from Muskoka. Stelly, I'll never forget you running down the platform to catch the train."

He grinned. "I'm still tired."

Because Sam didn't own a suit, he'd had to borrow a jacket and trousers. Two hundred guests showed up despite the short notice. Right after the wedding, the couple took the train back to Camp Frailoch, where Mandy had been hired by Sam to run the arts and crafts program. She was the only woman at the camp except for one kitchen worker.

They began a rainy honeymoon in a leaky tent, but their spirits never dampened.

###

Sam received his basic training in Brantford, Ontario, a location that allowed the newlyweds to see each other on weekends. That fall, Mandy accepted a position at Dewson Street school, teaching a class of fifty gifted fourth graders. Gifted herself, she couldn't have been happier. But seeking that post introduced her to yet another form of discrimination. The school system had a regulation against hiring married women. Without hesitation, Mandy put her wedding ring on her other hand and turned it around so the diamond wouldn't show. It was her first act of civil disobedience.

In November Sam was transferred to Medicine Hat, Alberta, and Mandy chose to leave her job. Their new housing was located in a cellar, and their bed occupied a place by the furnace. It was a difficult move for Mandy because she was pregnant. Whenever her mother sent a package with items from the grocery store, she cheered up a little. One day she awoke to find a two-dollar bill—everyday currency in Canada—with a note from Sam that read, "Go get your hair done." Mandy was so touched by her young husband's gesture that she always kept the note and the two-dollar bill.

While stationed in Medicine Hat, Sam served as a translator for German soldiers being held in a POW camp, and in his spare time he played basketball and baseball. A natural as coach of almost any team on which he played, Sam continued getting rave reviews from the local press.

"Sammy Stellman, playing coach of the army Meds, went on a scoring rampage to run up a total of 24 points...."

"Stellman had the fans and the opposition bordering on hysterics while he was nonchalantly popping up foul balls...."

"Not generally considered to be a good hitting team,
the W.E.T.P., inspired by slugging Sammy Stellman, went
on a rampage of their own...."

In February, Slugging Sammy was ordered overseas. But
he had a request. If only his departure could be delayed by
three months—after all, he was about to become a father.
His commanding officer thought otherwise, saying, "It may
have been necessary for you to be present at the laying of
the keel, but it's not necessary for you to be present at the
launching of the ship."

Sam said good-bye to his wife on Valentine's Day 1945.
Mandy saved all his letters. "When we retire," she told him,
"I'll let you translate them for me. I can't read your hand-
writing."

Sam was stationed twenty miles outside London in Alder-
shot, and he served briefly in Belgium and Germany. Mandy
went to live with her parents and worked in the store until
the baby was born. Then she accepted the invitation of her
sister Ettie and brother-in-law Joe Milne to move in with
them and their eleven-year-old daughter in their two-bed-
room apartment.

Steven Dale Stellman arrived on May 7, 1945, missing by
one day the long-awaited V-E Day. But halfway around the
world where Sam eagerly waited to learn the news from
home, it was already May 8. Thus, the child did enter the
world on a historic day of world peace—a significant event
similar to the occasion of his father's birth twenty-seven
years earlier on Armistice Day.

Steven was given the Hebrew name Simcha, which means
celebration or joyful event. And indeed the world responded joyfully to the news of peace. Only a newborn could have
slept through the celebrations. The maternity ward rever-
berated with noise as if it were New Year's Eve, while the
staff and all the patients who were capable of celebrating

toasted the end of World War II with jubilation and champagne.

Transportation home from Europe after the war was limited. Sam passed the time by coaching a men's volleyball team of Canadians stationed in England. But some men were less patient, and they rioted when they could not get space aboard a returning ship. First to be sent home were servicemen with the skills Canada needed to recover from the war. Because of Sam's work with the YMHA, he was granted early leave and sent home in November 1945.

Among the civilian activities this sports-minded new father undertook was the writing of articles for *Baby News,* which claimed to be Canada's only newspaper on baby health. For five cents a copy, Toronto parents could read "From Crib to Kindergarten" and "Baby Exercises: Laughter and Fun To Teach Coordination"—authored by S.D. Stellman, a man ahead of his time in recommending exercise for babies.[31]

The YMHA in Toronto gladly rehired Sam after the war. But when he asked for a raise because he was married and had a child, he was turned down. So the offer of a position in Youngstown, Ohio, delighted the young couple. Sam became the physical education director of the Jewish Community Center at $3,400 a year. For an additional $1,000 he was to direct the JCC's Tri-City Summer Camp, which drew the children of Jewish families in Akron, Canton, and Youngstown. Adequate housing was part of the arrangement.

Together with eleven-month-old Steven, the Stellmans left Canada in April 1946. Because they lived in camp that first summer, where Mandy also worked as a volunteer, the JCC did not have to provide them with the promised housing immediately. And at summer's end, the director of the Jewish Center took the Stellmans into his own home until the young family could find a place.

"They were very nice to us," Mandy observed. "They had a

little boy themselves. But we wanted our own place, and we didn't like imposing on the director's good will."

Yet thousands of other recently reunited families were also looking for housing, and apartments were scarce.

"We were shown little holes in the wall," recalled Mandy. "All kinds of absolutely unacceptable little dives—real crap. Landlords were getting three hundred to five hundred dollars under the table just for the key to an apartment."

When the promise of housing could not be kept, the Stellmans felt betrayed. They knew that a number of board members owned real estate and could have found them a nice apartment. "But they didn't," Mandy said. "In good conscience they couldn't ask a Jewish Center worker to give them 'key money.' We wouldn't have anyway. So we said, 'Sorry, this is not what we want to raise our child in.'"

Sam decided to resign and find another position. As things turned out, the job found him—a phenomenon that repeated itself, to his never-ending surprise, for each career move thereafter. Others always recognized his quiet charisma.

Shortly after the close of camp that first summer in Youngstown, Sam was attending a national conference of Jewish Center leaders when the director of the Syracuse JCC met him and hired him on the spot to head up the center's physical education program. When Sam returned home he informed the Youngstown JCC that the Stellmans were moving to Syracuse, New York.

"They just didn't believe we would leave," recalled Mandy. "They underestimated the Stellmans—as many others have over the years."

In Syracuse, the Stellmans finally had a place of their own after three years of marriage—half of which they had spent apart, the other half in schlepping from one army

base to the other or bunking with relatives and other bene-
factors.

Places were as hard to find in Syracuse as in the rest of
the country after the war, but the Stellmans were able to
rent an apartment on the second floor of a house owned by
the Jewish Appeal Fund, whose offices occupied the ground
floor. Located on Genesee Street, the house was magnifi-
cent—indeed, a mansion—and Mandy was ecstatic.

When the Hebrew school needed to take over the entire
second floor, the Stellmans moved upstairs to the attic. It
offered two bedrooms and a small bathroom, but no kitch-
en, so they set up a two-element electric hot plate and a
pressure cooker in the entry hall to the bedrooms. Dishes
were washed in the bathroom sink; the baby's diapers, in
the bathtub. But at no time did they feel deprived. Living
in their own place in a beautiful setting, they felt fortu-
nate to be together as a family.

Mandy defined herself as "basically a housewife" during
these early years of marriage. For her, this definition encompassed community activity. Saturdays, when the members of an orthodox congregation attended *schule* in the
building across the street, she ran its children's program.
Because the organization, called the Young Israel, was orthodox, the children were not allowed to draw, write, use
crayons, or do crafts on the Sabbath. So Mandy had to be
exceptionally creative. "We sang a little bit, danced, played
games, and learned about the bible and history." She enjoyed the experience as much as the children did, and admitted to being very good at dancing.

The Stellmans got to know other young couples also strug-
gling to make a living. Often, they got together at the apartment of the Stellmans, the first couple in the group to own
a television set. It boasted a seven-inch screen.

In 1948 the Stellmans had to vacate their attic because

the entire building was being converted into a Hebrew school.
Housing was still scarce. The Jewish community newspaper
highlighted their plight:

> *Stellmans are Desperate*
> *They Need an Apartment Quick...Please Help!*
> *Sam Stellman and his charming wife and son...are forced*
> *to find a 4–5-room apartment.... Sammy and Mandy, a*
> *young, devoted couple with a wonderful son (he's very*
> *good and behaves fine), are directing the day camp for*
> *the local Center....*

The Stellmans found another place to live, although the
"attic apartment"—their first real home—always held a
special place in their memories.

Shortly after this move, Canadian-born Leah Mandlsohn
Stellman became a U.S. citizen.

###

For three and a half years, Syracuse remained home for
the young family. Sam was promoted to program director,
and his initial salary of $4,000 increased to $4,300. His role
was to create and teach programs to meet the needs of the
community. Some challenging situations arose, but he solved
them, often in unique ways. For his men's and boys' basketball programs, for example, Sam rented space from several
area high schools because the Jewish Center occupied an
old building without a gym of its own. Getting the necessary equipment to and from one of these schools posed an
additional obstacle, so on Tuesday and Thursday evenings
Sam would take the bus, toting a large canvas duffel bag
filled with half a dozen basketballs, towels, and other equipment. His students called him Santa Claus.

Sam also booked space at a high school for the Jewish
Center's women's programs. One day a scheduling conflict
led him to ask Mandy to fill in. The women liked her so

much that she continued teaching the classes. On her bus rides she carried the badminton net and racquets.

About five miles east of Syracuse lie the clear waters of Green Lake. The Jewish Center had its summer day camp at the lake. As camp director, Sam organized four two-week sessions each summer, each session serving about one hundred children at a time. Mandy worked as program director and helped Sam interview and train camp counselors. Young Steven went along, too.

Sam engaged a restaurant in Syracuse to make sandwiches for the day campers, and every morning, after the crates of milk, sandwiches, and dessert had been loaded on the buses, the drivers picked up the kids waiting at designated street corners in the city and delivered the entire cargo to the camp at Green Lake.

The second year Sam added a ten-day camp for seniors.

In 1950 Sam and Mandy traveled to Atlantic City for the national conference of Jewish Community Centers. There, Sam met the executive director of the Columbus, Ohio, JCC, Mayer Rosenfeld, who happened to be looking for staff for a new center opening that fall. The two men hit it off immediately, and Sam jumped at the job offer because the director who had originally hired him for the Syracuse position had just left, and the assistant director who moved into that vacancy did not agree with Sam's vision for the future role of the Jewish Center. That vision formed an essential part of Sam's strong sense of purpose.

His efforts at the Syracuse Jewish Community Center did not go unrecognized, however. A respected community leader and member of the local board, Aaron Beckwith, wrote to the National Jewish Welfare Board highlighting some of Sam's qualities and skills:

> *I have had the pleasure of working with Samuel D. Stellman for a few years and have yet to find a weakness in his character or ability. I have seen him take a run-down Day Camp and build it into the most flourishing organization in Syracuse, so that even the well-established Christian Day Camps of our city have turned to him for advice. Working without the help of a Center Building, he has managed to keep a tremendous gymnastic project going on a year around basis.*
>
> *However, I have always felt that Sam is much more than a Gymnastic or Youth Director. His overall planning policies are most intelligent and thoughtful. He has a knack of making his committees work, so that his plans are capably and smoothly carried out. I have learned to appreciate the ability of Samuel Stellman who, in my opinion, encompasses all the attributes needed in the field of professional workers.*[32]

###

The Stellmans were on the move again. Sam's contract as physical education director of the Columbus JCC stipulated a salary of $4,800 and a one-month paid vacation after one year of service. Intangible benefits included the pleasure of developing his own physical education program in a beautiful new building with an attached outdoor swimming pool— not to mention the boost to his ego as he succeeded in reaching his objectives for the community center.

This new challenge proved a massive undertaking, but Sam was a natural activist and organizer. His early successes included demolishing an old dump that sat behind the JCC. Within a year he turned the dump into three lighted baseball diamonds and got the county to do the grading. He also managed to get all the materials donated and a couple of tennis courts thrown in.

Another of his projects involved starting one-day camps, which he then expanded to three days. One camp was held on the site of the former dump, since the new baseball diamonds were used only at night. He also convinced key people in the community to donate money to purchase a site for a day camp on a lakefront.

Every coach who was hired received training in Sam's "no-bench-warmer" policy. "Every kid has to play," he told them. As for the national Little League programs that let only the best kids play, Sam said "that's their business." He explained, "We have our own philosophy about equality. On our teams everybody plays for half the game, good or bad, no matter if they have three feet."

His principles of equality included de-emphasizing competition, putting the best players on the poorer teams, and forbidding any father from managing a team with his own child on it. Sam also opposed embarrassing anyone who lacked skill—a sensitivity that extended to adults, as well. He'd found that many of the men playing in the volleyball leagues he'd organized lacked athletic coordination, so in his gentle way he took each inept player aside and said, "If you want to come at another time, we'll try to help you." Unfortunately, few came back.

Under Sam's direction, the JCC offered everything from weight lifting, handball, and baseball to swimming, sailing, and amateur wrestling. There was no boxing. "A JCC would never have boxing. It's totally against much of what we believe in," he once explained to a visitor to the new center. "It's dangerous and it's not a healthy activity—we don't believe in violence. There were some Jewish boxers in the thirties in the Depression," he added, "but there haven't been any since—well, maybe one."

Sam enticed local sports celebrities, such as Woody Hayes, coach of the Ohio Buckeyes at Ohio State University, to speak at athletic banquets. These events often drew as many as five hundred people and usually generated extensive press coverage.

To help keep boys out of trouble, teach them a worthwhile trade, and give them a lifelong hobby, Sam devised the Youth Car Mechanics Program and developed it together with Sister Miriam, head of the Social Science Department of nearby Bishop Hartley High School. Three high schools participated in addition to the JCC. The local newspaper called it "one of the best community relations programs ever developed for the benefit of teenage boys in eastern Columbus."[33]

Sam's career direction can best be understood—and its true significance appreciated—by recognizing the role that the Jewish Community Centers played in the life and culture of their communities. Such institutions were intended primarily to promote Jewish values, and the JCCs succeeded in becoming pivotal in the survival and strength of Jewish culture. A central principle of the JCCs is that decisions should be made by lay people along with the professionals.

It's true that Sam's athletic abilities underlay the various programs he developed—from baseball diamonds carved out of a dump to impromptu basketball games that helped divert the riot-prone energies of soldiers waiting to ship home after the war. But his activities were always fueled by a drive deeper than the mere hormonal stirrings of a superjock. Sam recognized that community sports, along with health and education in general, were part of the broader sense of social outreach that Jewish immigrants brought with them to North America. Wherever they settled, their need to establish Jewish community and to nurture Jewish values surfaced.

These were the same values and cultural imperatives that had moved Anshel Wise, Sam's uncle, to run interference with the Canadian government on behalf of newly arriving immigrants. It was the same motivation that had led Rose Mandlsohn, Mandy's mother, to plead the case of a neighbor arrested for disorderly conduct.

As deliberately as Mandy sought the arenas of nursing, teaching, and social work to realize her mission, Sam was drawn to creating group activities at the Jewish Community Centers to realize his. The same mission spoke to each.

In this nurturing environment of the Columbus Jewish community, the Stellman family thrived. A second son, Leslie Robert, was born on July 19, 1951. That same year, Mandy became the JCC's director of women's physical education, a role she held for the next thirteen years.

She found that few people in the fifties cared whether girls had equal opportunity in sports. But she cared. She and a well-known Columbus golf pro, Anne Richardson, developed the Girls Sports Clubs—a first in the area. Girls in grades four through eight participated in badminton, floor hockey, basketball, trampoline, calisthenics, volleyball, and other team sports. The Stellmans saw to it that girls got equal time in the gym. These activities were of such high caliber that Mandy was convinced two of the girls could have become Olympic contenders.

Ten years later the *Ohio Jewish Chronicle* reported:

This program has become one of the most popular physical education activities at the center. The expert leadership of Mrs. Sam Stellman has attracted hundreds of women to the center gym.[34]

Mandy was no armchair director. In July 1961 she became the champion of the women's golfing league, undefeated in six games. She had the second lowest handicap in the league.

Nor was her commitment to providing opportunities limited to young people. Recognizing the unique needs of the elderly, Mandy volunteered for more than seventeen years in a program known as the Golden Age Club. She taught folk dancing and helped write skits. The group put on plays, sang, danced, wrote poetry, went on trips, and attended summer camp.

In addition, Mandy worked to interest members in the passage of Medicare. Instead of busying senior citizens with card-playing and shopping trips, this activist took the Golden Agers in busloads for an outing to the office of Governor Michael V. diSalle.

Every year at the end of their eight-week commitment to the summer camp for kids, Mandy and Sam volunteered an additional two weeks each summer for ten years at a camp for people sixty to eighty-seven. The Emma Kaufman Farm Camp, located near Pittsburgh, was one of the first camps for the elderly in the country.[35]

Somehow Mandy also found time to train Head Start and Vista workers, to serve as an appointee to the board of the Hebrew school, and to teach the Sabbath school at their conservative synagogue, Tifereth Israel Congregation. Her tenure on the board of the Hebrew school was short-lived, however.

"I got kicked off because I was too aggressive about making changes," Mandy said. She demanded equality for girls and insisted they update the curriculum. "They were using books from year one."

Eventually, of course, all the innovations she recommended came to pass.

###

Four years after the Stellmans arrived in Columbus, Sam added to his workload by enrolling at Ohio State University to earn his Master's degree, then his Ph.D. He attended classes part-time and did his homework late at night. In 1958 he received his M.S.W.—a Master's in Social Work. Shortly thereafter, the National Jewish Welfare Board asked him to serve as a consultant to the National Association of Jewish Centers. This meant catching a flight on Fridays after a regular work week at the Columbus JCC and assisting another JCC somewhere during its "interim period"—that is, after its director had been fired and not yet replaced.

His first assignment took him to St. Paul, Minnesota. As Sam walked into the JCC building, he noticed that the windows had not been washed for some time and the whole place exuded a musty odor. Knowing who would be the best source of information about any JCC, he sought out the bookkeeper. He succeeded in learning that the maintenance person was considered a "stubborn man" who cleaned only what he wanted to—and when.

Sam arranged to meet the man. "What's the problem?" he asked.

"Well," the maintenance man replied, "whenever I asked the director for good quality cleaning materials and enough help to keep this building clean, he just ignored me."

"What do you need to get the building clean? Write me a list."

Sam gave the list to the bookkeeper along with instructions on hiring temporary help. The result was a clean building and an admiring membership.

On his second trip to the Twin Cities, Sam dropped in on the health club, where JCC members, for a fee, could get a massage and a steam bath. He noticed that a man wrapped in a towel and occupying a deck chair was eyeing him.

"Who are you?" the man asked him.

"I'm the acting director of the center. And who are you?"

With a twinkle in his eye, the man answered, "I am the mayor of the health club. If you are the acting director, can I ask you a question? I already know the answer because I heard it for five years from the director who just left."

"Ask," said Sam. "I may surprise you."

"We've been trying to get a telephone jack in this room for the past five years. What can you do for us?"

"You'll have your jack as soon as we can get it installed, Mr. Mayor of the Health Club."

By that afternoon the jack was in, and Sam got a call from the president of the board congratulating him. At the next board meeting, twenty-five members gave him a warm reception. From then on, Sam was looked upon as a man of action. And when the permanent director was hired, the national office received a letter of congratulations for having sent such a competent and effective consultant.

Shortly after, Sam was promoted to assistant executive director of the Columbus JCC at $8,000 a year. The new post allowed him to use his talents to meet the needs of every age group, from children in nursery school to the elderly.

In all, Sam developed nearly six hundred family-directed programs that involved everybody in the Jewish community in one way or another, and volunteer participation was high. The JCC became known as *the* agency in Columbus. Everyone recognized it as a model for programs and facilities.

As the Stellman boys grew, they were greatly influenced by Sam and Mandy's values and commitment to fairness and justice. Even in daily routines, they reflected their parents' moral convictions and sense of responsibility. At seven A.M. the boys had piano lessons before going off to school. After school they attended Columbus Hebrew School and still had time for science club and other activities. There was little need for discipline, but when deserved, punishment meant not being allowed to practice piano. This they grumbled about.

When Mandy's volunteer activities occurred on a Sunday, the boys often accompanied her, and helped entertain by playing the piano and the violin.

During this period, the United States was growing increasingly conscious of racial issues. The Stellmans, outraged by the obvious injustices to women, minorities, and all disenfranchised people, campaigned for civil rights. In the days before open housing legislation, property owners could advertise their discrimination along with their real estate listings. In 1957, with twelve-year-old Steven and six-year-old Leslie in tow, the Stellman family joined in picketing the governor's mansion in Columbus in the cause of fair housing. And when Father Groppi came to Ohio in 1967 to support welfare mothers and their children, the Stellmans donated money and food for the marchers and joined the protest as it reached Columbus, the state capital.

Given their parents' leadership, it is no surprise the boys became ardent civil rights activists themselves. At an early age, they saw the effectiveness of letter writing as a means of making their views known. When Leslie was eight, he wrote to the *Columbus Dispatch* in defense of two sisters being harassed for advertising that the property they were selling would be shown to "everybody." Local people had reacted to the sisters' nondiscrimination declaration by making obscene phone calls, tossing garbage on their porch, and throwing rocks through their windows.

When Leslie's letter appeared, one of the sisters telephoned to talk to the little boy who had written it. She thanked Leslie profusely and offered to buy him a bicycle.

"Just a minute," he said, turning to Mandy. "Mommy, they want to buy me a bicycle. What should I do?"

Mandy replied, 'Well, I don't think you wrote the letter so you could get a bicycle, did you?"

"No," the eight-year-old agreed. He turned back to the telephone. "My mother and I don't think I should get a bicycle. But how about a pizza?"

When young Leslie decided to join the Future Teachers of America he was informed it was for girls only. Unperturbed, he persisted and became the first boy in his elementary school to join the organization.

At twelve, he wrote to the editor of a local newspaper to demand "full rights for Negro citizens."

Steven, at sixteen, wrote to both the JCC newspaper and the local paper lamenting the isolationist posture of the country. "When, oh when will the Republicans wake up?" he wrote. "I refuse to surrender my precious liberty because some uneducated politicians think it is still 1945."[36]

Steven also entered a newspaper contest about the U.S. Constitution sponsored by the conservative DAR, the Daughters of the American Revolution. He won the prize three years in a row. But he confided to his parents that he'd answered the questions exactly *opposite* to his own knowledge and beliefs.

"I knew then he was an okay kid," said Mandy, "and probably a feminist."

###

When the historic March on Washington took place in 1963, nothing could have kept Mandy from joining the protest against racial discrimination and the demands for civil rights legislation—although many of her Jewish friends were critical of her participation in the demonstration. Among hundreds of thousands of marchers, she stood before the

Lincoln Memorial and thrilled to the inspiring "I Have a Dream" speech of Dr. Martin Luther King Jr.

While the marchers waited, jammed together, Mandy struck up a conversation with a group of black teenagers from the South. They told her of marching for their rights and being attacked by the police. Realizing that these young people could have been killed by the high-pressure water hoses, she expected them to say how they hated the system. But not one talked of hate. They were excited about being in Washington, and they believed President Kennedy was going to realize their plight and make changes immediately.

On returning to Columbus, Mandy wrote a passionate defense of the demonstration. Thinking of the criticism she had heard, she addressed her letter "to the community" and sent it to the *Ohio Jewish Chronicle*, where it was published.

The newspapers and television spoke of 200,000 marchers. I was there [and] I must speak of 200,000 heroes. Anyone can march. But these were no ordinary people. I talked to teenagers from Mississippi, Alabama, South Carolina, Chicago, New York, and Detroit. They were the boys and girls who were subjected to fire hoses, police dogs, and indignities of all kinds. Yet they marched and sang and danced with hope in their hearts. I saw no fear, no malice, no hate. In fact, there were many moments when I could have substituted the song "Hava Nagila" for "We Shall Overcome." And these dedicated young people could have been one of our own Zionist groups fifty years ago who dreamed of Aritz [the land of Israel]. But this was Washington, D.C., August 28, 1963. We Jews have always had a feeling of belonging to a Jewish society. We all feel a bond with Jews from Africa, Europe, and Asia. But this was the very first time in the history of the American Negro that this type of bond was creat-

ed. Negroes from Alabama were embraced and kissed by Negroes from Ohio. As a Jew, I was overcome by emotion. For I had embraced and kissed Jews from Nazi Germany, Hungary, Egypt, and Iran. I had embraced them with my heart. Yes, there were 200,000 heroes. If B'nai B'rith is going to present its annual award to an outstanding American, I would like them to consider 200,000 names. They will have a difficult time trying to select a winner. I was there and I'm grateful.

Mandy was again criticized when she participated in the Poor People's March on Washington five years later, following the assassination of the Reverend Dr. King. Leslie, then seventeen, accompanied her. Friends asked, "Aren't you afraid to go to Washington? Aren't you afraid you'll get hurt? It's going to be dangerous." The Stellmans found it an eye opener to learn what some of their friends stood for.

Another time when they became involved with the open housing bill and a free speech bill, some friends said, 'You're going to get negative results. It's going to hurt Sam's career."

Mandy and Sam narrowed their list of friends considerably. Although they were widely known in Columbus, they counted only a small number as real friends.

###

During the years the boys attended school, Mandy felt fulfilled by her volunteer work, which was both relevant and innovative. "Our family is our greatest joy," Mandy often said. Still, she knew that some day she would pick up her career again.

"We had baby sitters, but one of us was always there when the boys came home from school," Mandy said. "It wasn't easy to do but that's what we did."

She involved herself in her children's schooling and was

not shy in demanding change from the educational system. The boys, however, did not always appreciate their mother's frequent intercession on their behalf. One day when she asked Leslie, "How was school today?" he replied, "I'm never going tell you again as long as I live, because you'll only call the principal and the superintendent."

The Stellmans' commitment to their sons' education occasionally involved some sacrifice. The summer Leslie was bar mitzvahed, he attended Interlochen summer music camp in Michigan, and on coming home begged his parents to let him spend his high school years studying music at the four-year college preparatory school. Attending the Interlochen Arts Academy meant he would have to board away from home. Even with scholarships, tuition represented a considerable financial burden for the Stellmans. And the thought of their younger child being away from home was unsettling. But particularly distressing to this egalitarian couple was the idea of their son's attending an exclusive school.

"Private school was for snobs. Public school was good enough for my kid," said Mandy, who referred to herself as a "reverse snob." She was fond of quoting Carl Sandburg: "*Exclusive* is the most detestable word in the English language. When you're exclusive, you shut out humanity."

However, as any parent of a teenager knows, a kid who is hell-bent on something often succeeds. So the Stellmans took out a six-year loan—meaning they would not retire the debt until two years after Leslie's graduation.

The boy went off to Interlochen, coming home on holidays carrying his violin with him on the bus.

When Sam received his Ph.D. from Ohio State University on June 13, 1963, he was forty-four. Although social work had been his major, he had switched to adult education for his doctorate, with minors in sociology of the family and in community organization and development.

At the graduation ceremony he was offered several teaching opportunities, and with mixed feelings he resigned from the JCC. After fifteen years of accomplishment, Sam felt he could make a greater contribution by accepting an offer to become an associate professor with tenure at OSU.

Remaining in Columbus, he began teaching classes that fall in community organization and administration. He also signed a contract as an instructor in the sociology department at Capital University to teach short courses in race relations and in marriage and the family.

His resignation from the JCC led Sister Miriam, with whom he had developed the Car Mechanics Program, to write to the *Jewish Chronicle,* praising Sam as a bridge builder with the non-Jewish community. She further wrote:

> *His admirable ability to express himself with gentle but firm frankness in support of a minority viewpoint in a community notorious for slow social change should not be underestimated. Moreover, his vision, his original thinking, his respect for creativity in others, his courage in initiating new projects are reminiscent of the characteristics of that brand of American willing to pioneer and to risk for the sake of progress rather than enjoy the security of the immediate present....*
>
> *Dr. Stellman has a hopeful optimism which reflects his own religious commitment and impresses those of other faiths.*[37]

The *Columbus Dispatch* called Sam "probably the best-known member of the city's Jewish community." Citing his "no-bench-warmer policy" among his many accomplishments, the article noted that a "large part of the Jewish Center is Stellman."[38]

###

With Leslie in boarding school, Steven enrolled at Ohio State University, and Sam—his graduate work behind him—teaching at the same university, it was Mandy's turn. She decided to enroll in OSU's School of Education for the September 1964 term. Deciding was easy; enrolling was not, requiring great persistence as well as a sense of humor.

Mandy needed to know if she could be granted credit for any of her early courses in education from the Toronto Normal School and the University of Toronto. So she tried to make an appointment with the dean of admissions. After several telephone attempts and no response, she simply showed up at the dean's office one day and asked the secretary what it would take to have someone review her transcripts and teaching credentials. Instead of getting an answer, Mandy was shuffled from one unpleasant secretary to another, from one indifferent faculty member to another, and from one recalcitrant administrator to another.

Thinking it couldn't be any harder to get an audience with God, Mandy tried another source, her husband, the professor. "Who is the dean of the School of Education?" she asked.

With the information in hand, she reached the correct office just as the assistant dean was putting on his coat to go to lunch.

"As you can see I am in a hurry, so state your business briefly. If it's about enrolling, we have a large staff prepared to handle that."

Mandy was shocked by the man's rudeness. "Before you go, could I ask you one question?"

"Okay," he replied. "One question."

"Do you believe in the separation of church and state at OSU?"

"Of course," he replied.

"Then how come everyone around here acts like God, including you? What does it take to get someone to look at my record?"

The dean started to laugh and took off his coat, and Mandy got her Canadian credits accepted.

By this time, however, she had become so fed up with the School of Education and its attitude that she decided to transfer to the School of Social Work—the reverse of Sam's path in moving from social work to education.

###

Once enrolled, it didn't take long for Mandy to begin re-forming the school. Much of the system, she realized, was operated for the benefit of those who ran it, with the 40,000 students a necessary nuisance to be tolerated.

Required to take three semesters of physical education, Mandy completed classes in golf and bowling and was en-rolled in Ping-Pong when she developed a painful ganglion on her wrist. She could be excused only with permission from the health center.

Mandy walked across campus and found the health cen-ter. "Do you have your fee card?" said the receptionist loudly, without looking up. "If you don't have your fee card, you can't get any service here; you will have to come back an-other time."

Mandy produced the card.

Still not looking up, the receptionist said, "Okay, sit over there and someone will see you soon."

"How soon?" asked Mandy. "I have a class next period."

"That's your problem."

After a wait, Mandy was ushered in to see Dr. St. John. She looked at Mandy's fee card, but not at her, and asked, "What's your problem, Mrs. Stellman?"

Mandy explained about the ganglion and asked if she could be excused from further physical education classes, in view

of her being middle-aged and having taught physical education classes for many years.

"Sorry, Mrs. Stellman," the doctor said. "If you can't take
table tennis this quarter you will have to take it another
time." As Mandy left, the doctor still had not looked at her.

That evening she asked Sam, "Who is the head of the
health center?" The next day she called Dr. Fancher's office.
Suspecting, correctly, that her call would not be put through
if she identified herself as a student, she introduced herself
as the parent of an OSU student—which, in fact, she was.
She described her experiences at the health center and insisted that no student, regardless of age, should be treated
in such a shabby manner. The doctor apologized and promised to take action.

When Mandy returned to the health center, the receptionist looked up, smiled, and spoke pleasantly.

Dr. St. John seemed chastened as well, though with questionable results. "I am sorry, Mrs. Stellman," she said, looking at Mandy for the first time. "I thought you were a
youngster." She pleaded guilty to a "misunderstanding,"
which suggested that younger students might continue to
be treated rudely and unprofessionally.

Although Mandy received her release, she was not satisfied. She had become determined not to take physical education classes ever again. A visit to her own physician
produced this letter: "Please excuse Mrs. Stellman from any
further physical education classes for the rest of her life for
gynecological reasons."

Dr. St. John read Mandy's note, then asked, "What's the
problem, Mrs. Stellman?"

Mandy answered indignantly, "I'm sorry, Dr. St. John, that's
between me and my doctor."

###

At different times when Mandy was required to wait in the health center's reception room, she observed other violations of students' rights, especially the right to privacy. On one occasion an office door left ajar enabled anyone in the waiting room to overhear a consultation between the school psychologist and a student. Another time an open door informed all within hearing of a young woman's problems with her kidneys. Mandy could hear the doctor ask the student about menstruation and urination, and could tell that he performed no physical examination before prescribing medication. Later on, Mandy phoned the doctor about the incident and found him flippant. So she simply contacted the student and took her to her own family physician.

It wasn't the first time Mandy had stood up to the medical profession—and certainly not the last. When pregnant with Leslie, she and Sam had been new to Columbus. "Everyone I met said I just had to go to a certain gynecologist. He 'did all the fancy ladies.' Just had to go to him."

At her first meeting with the highly regarded specialist, she answered all his questions as he took her medical history. She volunteered the information that she had a history of serious migraines. In fact, her mother and one sister suffered from severe migraine headaches as well.

"Mrs. Stellman," the specialist replied, "I'm only interested in the pregnancy and not in your head."

Mandy was shocked and then quickly became angry. "You know what? You can go to hell." She got up, put on her clothes, and walked out.

Sam was seated in the waiting room. Surprised, he said, "That didn't take long."

"I'm not using this fancy doctor," she responded.

Instead, the Stellmans found a general practitioner. At Leslie's birth, the doctor needed to call in a specialist, but he knew enough not to call "that one."

Some years later she again followed the recommendations of "everyone" in going to see the "best ear, nose, and throat man in Columbus." When she arrived for her appointment, she could not help but notice that every patient in the waiting room had some kind of long, thin rods up their noses. The nurse explained that it was a routine testing procedure, but Mandy declined to undergo such a test before even seeing the doctor.

Some time around 5:30 P.M. Mandy was finally ushered into an examination room. The specialist looked at her chart, and without looking at her asked, "How are you feeling, Mrs. Stellman?"

"Not so good. I had a three P.M. appointment, it is now after five, and my time is as valuable as yours, Doctor. Why was I given a three o'clock appointment if you weren't going to see me until five thirty?"

A surprised doctor and nurse looked at each other. "Well," the doctor replied, "we have a great number of appointments and some emergencies, and that puts us behind."

"I can only say, Doctor, that obviously you can't give me the attention I may need as a patient. So good-bye, Doctor. And I think you might want to give up that business of having those rods put up people's noses before you see them, unless they are all coming here with the same problem."

In the sixties, free speech on campus was a hotly debated issue. The late U.S. Senator John Bricker, a man considered the Jesse Helms of the sixties, headed the OSU Board of Trustees, which had approved a rule defining who would be allowed to speak on campus. Segregationist Governor George

Wallace of Alabama was deemed acceptable; Pete Seeger, internationally acclaimed folk singer, was not.

So the faculty and the students picketed the administration building to protest the gag rule. Among the picketers were Mandy, the middle-aged student; Sam, who joined the picket line between teaching assignments; and Steven and his girlfriend, Jeanne.

One day as Mandy and Sam circled the administration building, protest signs held high, they noticed a woman arguing with Steven and other students. The woman wore a hat with a veil, white gloves, an expensive dress, and matching jewelry.

Steve motioned to Mandy to join them, explaining, "This lady wants to know what my mother thinks about my picketing the university administration building."

Mandy replied, "As Steven's mother, I have never been more proud of my son for standing up for free speech."

Shocked, the woman departed so quickly that Mandy had no chance to discuss the First Amendment and the constitutional right to peaceful protest.

Neither the classes nor the instructors presented much challenge to Mandy during her first quarter at OSU. What shook her was encountering at least one sobbing coed curled up on a sofa in almost every women's lounge on campus. Whenever she asked, "Can I help you?" they opened up to her—seeing in her, perhaps, a mother image. She learned, between sobs, that one coed was afraid of being expelled because the dean of women had threatened discipline for some alleged violation of university rules. From another she learned that an instructor had told a class at its first meeting, "Nobody in this class can expect to get better than a C in the course"—when a B average often meant keeping a scholarship. Sometimes a first-year student was simply home-sick or having difficulty with a boyfriend. But sometimes it was because of sexual innuendoes by faculty—behavior not yet labeled sexual harassment. One student said that an instructor had told the class, "I would like to put the girls with the short skirts in the front."

Mandy spent considerable time providing emotional support to an ever-increasing number of extremely upset young women. When she approached several highly placed administrators, she found them sensitive to her concerns. Yet a year later she was encountering even more sobbing students. She suggested that the administration appoint a committee of females to study what she called "Revelations in the Rest Rooms." Nothing was done, and Mandy regretted not having taken the necessary action herself to establish such a committee. It was a lesson in self-initiated activism that Mandy did not have to learn again.

During the era of the Vietnam War, expulsion of a male student from OSU meant military service. But that was not the only reason Sam defended student rights at the state-run university. He believed education was the means to a better life. When he discovered that a number of students from rural backgrounds were about to be thrown out because their grades were poor, he went to bat for them.

"They are nice kids who don't cause any trouble," Sam told the dean. "If you kick them out, I'm going to make a lot of noise. If you don't understand that these kids come from a variety of rural schools, that they may lack adequate academic grounding, that they may need tutors, then you are in the wrong business. Something has to be done." As a result of Sam's intervention, a large number of disadvantaged youngsters were able to stay in school.

Many years earlier Sam had taken a stand on another issue of discrimination against students. Shortly after he'd
graduated from the University of Toronto, its alumni association contacted him to solicit a contribution. He responded by writing a letter asking about the school's policy on
admissions to the medical, law, and dental schools. He pointed out that a number of his friends with exceptionally high
grades had been turned away because, as he understood it,
they were Jews. He wondered if a quota system existed in
the three professional schools regarding Jews and other
minorities. If so, he had no intention of supporting the
university financially, or otherwise.

The letter of reply from the president of the alumni association emphasized the greatness of the university but skirt-
ed the issue of discrimination. Sam wrote back, pledging to
become a lifetime donor if he received a notarized letter
from a person in a position of authority stating that there
was not and never would be any discrimination against any
group because of religion, race, or gender.

No answer was forthcoming from his alma mater, and no
money was forthcoming from Sam.

At OSU in the sixties, Sam also became involved in the
issue of curfews, which existed for the women students but
not for the men. One couple asked Sam to intervene. The
young woman was facing discipline for having been in the
room of her fiancé after 11 P.M. Sam went to see the appropriate administrator, who bore the imposing title of Dean of
Disciplinary Investigation.

"He was an ex-FBI man with the typical crew cut," Sam
recalled. "We went into a little room where he had all kinds
of electronic equipment. I didn't know what the equipment
was for, maybe just to make an impression. He wouldn't

answer me when I asked him what he was writing, so I said, 'First of all, I don't know who the hell you are. You mean to say that nothing happens in a fraternity house or the back seat of a car before eleven P.M.?'

"When I said 'fraternity house' he got very mad. I said, 'This conversation's over. I can't talk to you. You don't belong on this campus anyway.' But this was the sixties and I guess they were going to discipline students no matter what."

Sam met with the president and threatened to resign if the two students were kicked out. At the disciplinary hearing, it came out that the dean of women had been using spies, such as cab drivers, to report the comings and goings of the coeds. A number of faculty members and heads of departments rallied to the support of the students and the policy was changed. Not long after, the dean of women resigned.

Sam was a realist. He understood when to act and how. He knew when an issue demanded swift and radical action because a university system practiced outrageous discrimination against the people it was suppposed to serve, and he recognized the issues that called for more patience and tact because the act of discrimination came from an individual's ignorance.

A situation reflecting the latter sorely tested Sam's patience one December. A philanthropically minded sorority on campus was planning a Christmas party for underprivileged children—its "project for the year"—and telephoned the School of Social Work for assistance.

"Could you find some orphans for us?" the sorority sister asked.

Sam deplored what he called the once-a-year charity syndrome, but he remained polite as he took the call. "I appreciate your wanting to help at this time of year, but I suggest you allow the professionals who work with children in need to run the parties. They are best equipped to run the kind of party the children would enjoy most."

The sorority sister was disbelieving. "But we've spent so many hours preparing! And we've already ordered the ice cream and cake and presents for every child."

"In that case," replied Sam, "I suggest you donate everything to the agencies. They really know what these children need and want. They know from experience that the children will be happiest if they have their party in a setting where they're most comfortable."

The persistent young woman continued enumerating the activities they'd planned and the music they'd rehearsed. Again, Sam patiently explained that the needs of the children should come first. But the young woman seemed determined not to understand. The conversation went back and forth for some time. Finally, Sam switched tactics.

"I've checked our records," he said, "and I regret that we are fresh out of orphans."

###

7. Morality and Economics

"**Y**ou're kidding," Sam replied when the receptionist in his department said the mayor was on the phone.

"No. It's really him, and he wants to talk with you."

Sam reached for the receiver.

"Professor Stellman? Maynard Sensenbrenner here. Columbus and Central Ohio are joining President Johnson's War on Poverty, and I'm calling to ask you to be the director of the program."

Sam was taken aback. It was late in 1964 and he had been teaching at Ohio State University only a little over a year. "Who suggested me for the job?" he asked.

"I appointed a citizen's committee to oversee the program and to pick a director," replied the mayor. "They unanimously picked you."

"With all due respect, Mr. Mayor," said Sam, "I can hardly picture being the only candidate in a city this size. I'm afraid I'll have to turn you down."

The mayor persisted. "I've talked to a lot of people in Columbus, and everyone who knows you says you're the perfect person for the job. Don't turn it down so quickly. What will it take for you to accept?"

The mayor, known for his persuasive powers, kept repeating, "What will it take for you to accept the job?"

Sam suggested the mayor talk with OSU President Novice Fawcett and with a leader in the business community, Ralph Lazarus of the Federated Department Stores. "They know my work in the community. If they think I'm a good choice, I will certainly think seriously about taking the job."

Within fifteen minutes, Fawcett and Lazarus each called Sam, expressing full support and urging him to take the job. They said his was the sole name submitted for the position.

So in mid-1965, Sam Stellman became the director of the Columbus Metropolitan Area Community Action Organization (CMACAO). Under Title II of the Economic Opportunity Act, this agency had as its main purpose the improvement of conditions of the poor at all levels. Sam would administer a $57,000 planning grant from the Office of Economic Opportunity.

Columbus, the capital of Ohio, was conservative. A predominantly white-collar community, it contained very few ethnic enclaves. But it did have its share of poverty, which in the mid-sixties was defined as an annual income of $3,000 for a family of four. More than 10,500 men, women, and children in Franklin County were eligible for aid under the federal Economic Opportunity Act.

Sam agreed to serve for six months and stayed two years. For the first six weeks he worked without pay, unable to hire an office staff because approval of the application was delayed.

Another setback occurred when the Community Services Building, which housed the poverty office, was gutted by fire on September 15. The entire operation had to be temporarily relocated. Bad wiring was the official cause, but arson was suspected.

Sam met the challenge. "On first impression," one columnist wrote, "Sam Stellman—scholar, athlete, conversation-
alist—seems ill-suited to the job of milling new people from
the grinding stone of poverty. Urbane and humorous in ca-
sual conversation, he assumes the air of an affable Rolls
Royce salesman."[39]

Sam enjoyed being likened to a Rolls Royce salesman.

"But his manner changes when he gets down to the brass
tacks of poverty," continued the reporter. He quoted Sam as
saying: "My first goal is to impress upon this community
that poverty is a *community* problem, that everything that
affects Columbus affects the poor, and vice versa."

The reporter, understanding the basis of Sam's purpose,
summed up his conviction in a few words: "He's talking
about morality as well as economics."

Similarly, a fellow sociologist at OSU, Dr. Simon Dinitz,
described Sam's organizing approach this way:

> *You know how he drags people in. He was a master at it*
> *[as a graduate student] and he hasn't gotten any poorer*
> *at it since. Sam had very little patience for pure theoriz-*
> *ing, then as now—it put him off. But he was tremendous*
> *when it came to the fieldwork.... Sam's methods are to*
> *call around, ask for referrals, get people involved. He has*
> *a penchant for putting people together. At meetings, he*
> *is a moderator, a facilitator; he doesn't let you off the*
> *hook until you reach some conclusion or plan.... He has*
> *infinite patience...[he] suffers fools very well.*

These are the techniques of someone who makes things
happen through community-wide involvement. Sam's moral convictions combined with his modus operandi made him
an effective organizer and activist, uniquely suited to his
new responsibilities.

Sam thought long and hard about how to meet those responsibilities. He was disturbed by comments against Medi-

care and other federal programs made by actor Ronald Reagan. Once a liberal Democrat, Reagan was becoming active in Republican politics during Barry Goldwater's campaign for president in 1964, and his viewpoints were getting a lot of press. In a number of letters exchanged between the two men, Reagan wrote to Sam, "You will get no argument from me about our moral responsibility to ease suffering and discomfort of our fellow man.... Alright [sic], I agree we should help. Now where we differ is in *how* to do the job." Reagan said he believed help should come from local communities, "not some bureau in Washington."

Sam knew that communities often needed a push from Washington and assistance with funding.[40]

He often said, "The most difficult part of a poverty program is, how do you get people out of poverty? To me, poverty is a shortage of money. You have to get money to them, but the federal program wasn't designed to give money away. It was designed for us to develop programs for them, which isn't easy."

He saw his function as laying the groundwork for the poor to eventually get money by giving them the job training, health, and education services they needed. Critical of programs in which people who didn't understand the problems were prescribing the answers, Sam had his own plan.

The heavy artillery in Columbus' war on poverty will be education and employment.... Stellman plans to meet with other groups and organizations that are concerned with poverty to discuss the problems that exist and what possible solutions might be. He also plans to employ some knowledgeable consultants—the poor themselves. This brings to life the old axiom about helping people to help themselves....[41]

Committed to involving people in planning the programs that would affect them, he hired and trained people from the community to become neighborhood workers. "It's funny," said Sam in retrospect. "I looked at what we paid them— a dollar fifty an hour for unskilled people. At that time it was considered high! Everybody was happy to have the job because it was better than most were earning."

Expecting Franklin County to receive between $1.5 million and $2 million of federal funds in the second year of President Johnson's War on Poverty, Sam planned an ambitious, all-encompassing program. He initiated an after-school remedial program for children in eight target areas of Columbus, convinced that the child having difficulty today becomes tomorrow's dropout.

At seventeen city schools, he developed Head Start programs that served about 500 four- and five-year-olds from adverse economic and social backgrounds.

And he asked church leaders to get involved, suggesting that the churches operate neighborhood centers, health programs, employment counseling, and programs for the young and the old.

Sam and Mandy drove to a rural area outside Columbus one day to see what was needed there. They came upon a poor all-black community that had been settled in the days of the Underground Railway and virtually forgotten ever since. The Stellmans were shocked to discover the community did not have the most basic of services—not even water and sewer.

"What do you do for water?" asked Sam.

"We go way down the road and haul it in," replied one of the residents.

"How do you keep your kids clean?"

"It ain't easy!"

Mandy observed that the children were well-groomed. "Just

a joy, and the people lovely. But poor—dirt poor, as we say."

"We felt something had to be done," Sam recalled. "We got 'em water. Don't ask me how. All I know is they needed water—otherwise, how the hell can you live? They had no money so you couldn't tax them. It took a lot of work—talking to Columbus city officials, state officials, federal officials. We got them water."

A year into the program, Sam gave this assessment of the progress of the Columbus War on Poverty:

> So far, the war has been rather static, limited to a few skirmishes. The Neighborhood Youth Corps program is reaching some 1,000 teenage boys and girls who are real or potential dropouts. About 300 men and women are enrolled in Adult Basic Education programs to improve their reading and writing.
>
> The Welfare Department has started its Title V program to provide work-training and work-experience activities for some 325 welfare recipients. Youths are being screened for training camps and centers for boys and girls. The Ohio State Employment Service is conducting job training for unemployed and underemployed people. And a work-study program on several college campuses provides part-time jobs for students who cannot afford their own college education.

One of Sam's visions that failed to materialize included a series of health service centers where, for three hours a day, physicians, dentists, and dental technicians would be on hand to meet the needs of children.

Though praised for his efforts, Sam felt the Columbus anti-poverty initiative could have been more successful had better assistance come from certain sources. Interviewed for *Ohio Schools* magazine, he criticized the attitudes of teachers toward the victims of poverty.

"Teachers must get out of their ivory towers and establish an effective one-to-one basis of communication with the parents of poor children," he said. "These children have had little education, and unless their parents motivate them at home, there's very little chance for them."[42]

In the end, Sam learned what many grassroots organizers learn: how politics and government affect the process of making change. He offered this postmortem of the War on Poverty:

My work off-campus was laying the groundwork to get people out of poverty, which we never really did when you look at it across the country. If I had stayed with it, I don't think it would have made any difference. There were too many things happening politically. People working in government are not always the greatest people either, in terms of their knowledge or commitment. Try to convince them about some of these things when their superiors are political people who don't see it as politically advantageous. It's very difficult.

He also learned, "This is a society which has a propensity for fighting the wrong enemy. The poor are looked upon as the enemy, whereas poverty is the enemy."

The following year, 1967, Sam was serving as president of the Central Ohio Chapter of the National Association of Social Workers when sixty members were fired for picketing the Franklin County Home and its affiliated Alum Crest Hospital. In their place, the county was having kitchen aides without health permits dispense patient meals and workhouse inmates disguised in white jackets operate as porters and orderlies.

Sam spearheaded a campaign that used letters to the editors of Columbus newspapers to chastise the county com-

missioners and defend the strikers. The strikers won, and
Sam discovered how powerful the pen could be. This was
the real beginning of the Stellmans' "literary" careers.

Racial tension was mounting across the United States,
and many large cities were experiencing race riots.

On a day early in May 1967, the receptionist for OSU's
sociology department called Sam to the phone. "The director of the Columbus Community Relations Council is on the
line. His name is Walter Tarpley and he wants to talk with
you."

Tarpley told Sam, "Ours is about the only major city in
Ohio that has not had a race riot. All the factors that have
been the riot igniters for these other cities exist in Columbus. Will you join us in trying to head off trouble?"

Sam agreed. But he pointed out that almost every riot in
the country had been set off by a police incident. Though
the police don't create the conditions that lead to riots, he
said, they're usually involved when things break loose, and
their behavior often adds to the troubles that follow.

So he proposed starting with a human relations program
to educate police about inner city residents. "But we have
to work at the other end, too," he told his caller, knowing
that many inner city residents held very negative attitudes
about the police. "Of course, in too many cases that's based
on how the police treat them during confrontations." Sam
believed that distrust was the biggest problem in the inner
city. He asked, "How can people be expected to trust a government that deals with *results* and not *causes?*"[43]

Sam's approach to this volatile situation was to bring about
change at the most fundamental and difficult level—a
change in attitude. He proposed a series of meetings in which
inner city residents and police officers would meet sepa-

rately, voice their grievances about each other, and come up with recommendations. Then, in a joint meeting, the recommendations of each group would be reviewed.

It was the first program of its kind in the nation.

The Columbus police department assigned some seventy police officers to attend four weeks of discussion about the problems of inner city Columbus. Walter Tarpley and Sam Stellman trained the police sergeants to be discussion leaders. Case histories were presented in which the police had behaved insensitively, and each discussion group was challenged to analyze that behavior.

The inner city residents also chose seventy people to meet for the same period, and their discussion leaders also received special training.

To provoke thoughtful discussion within each group, course materials were developed that included questions such as these:

> *(For the police groups) "Why do citizens in the inner city seem to show a large disrespect for the police?"*
>
> *(For the citizen groups) "Why does a police officer use his uniform as a means of excessive use of authority in the inner city?"*

At the end of four weeks, both groups came to joint meetings with their recommendations. The police were asked to wear street clothes, and one officer remarked, "You can't tell the good guys from the bad guys."

"That's the whole idea," said Sam.

Interactions among the members of the two groups produced some much-needed insights. "We won't call you colored if you won't call us cops," said one officer, which led to an intense four-hour discussion. "Brutality" was interpreted by the police to mean physical abuse; to the citizens, it encompassed a broad spectrum of police behaviors toward them, including how they were addressed.

In the end, the meeting produced positive feelings between the two groups, as well as twenty-two pages of recommendations, which were carefully studied and acted on. In addition, Sam interviewed all the major groups in the community and submitted his own comprehensive report. One of his recommendations called for the police department to receive training in methods that would avoid triggering a riot. The Columbus vice squad was to receive special training because riots in many cities had been set off by incidents involving vice squads. Sam developed the training along with others in the field of human relations, and he participated as an instructor.

He also suggested that inner city playgrounds be staffed by residents familiar with the culture of the area, and that neighborhood centers and settlement houses be granted money to offset people's entrance fees to area swimming pools. One recommendation to build several outdoor basketball courts in the inner city was fully implemented by the mayor within ten days.

But Sam had no illusions about the efficacy of such programs. Not for a minute did he think social issues could be solved by night basketball. He knew that no preventive measure could be considered a solution to urban problems unless it took into account basic problems such as inner city housing, segregation, and discrimination. He saw his Columbus efforts as simply buying time until the community could get all levels of leadership—politicians, educators, and citizens—to sit down and work together in resolving the underlying causes. The vision and ability to address a problem at its root cause and make changes that affect an infinite number of people from then on—these are the qualities that distinguish the activist from the providers of service to limited numbers of individuals.

###

Having established one of the largest War on Poverty operations in the nation, and having taken Columbus through two uneventful summers while Watts and other major cities smoldered, Sam returned to teaching at Ohio State University in 1968. But he maintained his ties with the Office of Economic Opportunity, and from 1967 through 1969 he spent his summers as an OEO consultant and technical assistant. This meant living in Chicago in the summer and coming home to Columbus on weekends—the reverse of his consultant's travels for the JCCs ten years earlier.

Not long after he returned to teaching, the city of Columbus once again requested the Stellman touch. Mayor Sensenbrenner had an interesting request: to use the university to study the inner city and methods for alleviating potentially volatile situations. Said the mayor, "I am asking you to appoint a committee of OSU faculty to meet and bring in recommendations for a better city."

Sam became chair of the "Brain Trust," as it was nicknamed. Sixteen members of the faculty volunteered; they represented specialties in economics, city planning, law, education, criminology, social work, psychology, race relations, political science, and disaster research. They came up with recommendations for developing jobs, helping consumers with housing, getting more people to vote, assuring representation of inner city residents in city government, and improving citizen access to government for voicing complaints. Recurring issues included police behavior and the quality of the public schools.

The mayor saw to it that many of the recommendations of Sam's Brain Trust were implemented.

As Sam's work resulted in social changes of ever-widening scope, during this period Mandy was reevaluating her options for doing the same. Immediately upon receiving her B.A. in Social Work *summa cum laude* in 1966, she applied for admission to Ohio State University's Law School. The same year Steven received his B.S. from OSU.

Using a manual typewriter and carbon paper, Mandy typed her application for law school. Where the application asked, "State in your own handwriting in a paragraph not to exceed 100 words your reasons for desiring to be an attorney at law," she wrote: "My desire to be an attorney-at-law is based on my conviction that the legal profession has a vital role to play in the alleviation of many urgent problems of society. Although my background is social work and teaching, I feel I can make a better contribution to my community through the legal profession."

OSU responded favorably, and Mandy made an appointment with an admissions officer for final review of her application.

"You appear to be well-qualified for admission to the law school," said the admissions officer, a woman. "Now, Mrs. Stellman, I have one very important question to ask you. If we admit you and if you succeed in passing all the courses and graduate, do you plan to practice law?"

Mandy shot back, "No, if you admit me and I succeed in graduating, I don't plan to practice law, I plan to do brain surgery. Now I want to ask *you* something. Have you ever asked that question of a man?"

The face of the admissions officer turned red. She stammered and reluctantly admitted she hadn't.

"Well," said Mandy, "I want to assure you that if you do ask any other female applicants that same question, and I hear about it, I will personally sue you for sex discrimination."

Mandy began her first semester of law school that September. The next semester she transferred from OSU to the

Franklin Law School of Capital University because it proved a better commute—ten minutes from home. There, her budding legal talents were rewarded in 1967 in the form of the Hornbook Student Award from West Publishing Company, and the year after by a scholarship from Franklin Law School for outstanding academic achievement. In addition, she received the American Jurisprudence Prize for excellence in insurance law from the Joint Publishers of the Annotated Reports System. In 1967 Mandy also became president of Kappa Beta Pi, a legal sorority.

For Sam, a new call to action came in the spring of 1968 from Madison, Wisconsin. The voice on the phone was that of Glen Pulver, Dean of Human Resource Development for the University of Wisconsin-Extension. "I've read about your work in Columbus and at Ohio State," he said. "Would you be interested in doing that kind of work in Wisconsin on a statewide basis?"

Sam thought for a moment. Facetiously, he asked, "Where's Wisconsin?"

The remark didn't faze the Dean. "How about coming up here and talking it over?" he replied. "You would head your own department, and you'll have an opportunity to develop what you think is significant without interference. You'll be working with a state that believes in bringing the university to the community."

Sam and Mandy talked it over. Leslie, seventeen, was about to graduate from Interlochen and enter Johns Hopkins University. Steven, who the previous September had married Jeanne, was living in New York and working toward his Ph.D. in chemistry at New York University.

The only Stellman whose education would be affected by moving from Columbus was Mandy, who would have to transfer in the middle of the school year. If she could get into law school in Wisconsin, Sam would accept the offer.

They also had to sell their house in Columbus. "A good 'liberal' friend of ours was a real estate broker," recalled Mandy, "so we engaged him." When he came to look at the house, which was in an all-white neighborhood, Mandy told him, "I want you to show it to everybody. If a black family wants to look at it, show it to them and sell it to whoever wants it. I don't want anybody to be discriminated against."

Her so-called liberal friend said, "I'd rather you give the listing to someone else, because I'll be blackballed."

"Fine, said Mandy. "Good-bye."

The Stellmans called in another broker they knew and told him the same thing. He showed it without restriction.

Among the black prospects to see the Stellman house, one, a county judge, mentioned to Mandy that he was having trouble just being shown houses in the neighborhood.

"A number of our friends became angry with us for showing the house to blacks and eventually selling it to a black family," Mandy recalled.

"How could you do that?" they'd asked her.

She'd replied, "I thought you were liberal yesterday. What happened to you today?"

But they'd responded "with all the trite crap," Mandy said, such as: "'You know all the other houses will lose their value.'"

Mandy had simply told them, "You're crazy."

###

PART THREE: ACTION

Do not follow where the path may lead.
Go instead where there is no path and leave a trail.
Muriel Strode

8.   On Wisconsin!

What reason on earth would induce the Stellmans to move to the snowy North, their Ohio colleagues wondered, especially when so many better-paying opportunities existed in states with warmer climates?

The reason was Wisconsin's reputation as "The Progressive State." It offered this progressive pair an unprecedented opportunity to carry out their roles in *tikkun olam,* repairing the world. They viewed their education and chosen careers as tools that would aid them in setting things right for people who deserved better than they had been getting from their government and from the public institutions whose reason for being was to serve people's needs.

As children of the Great Depression, Mandy and Sam were sensitive to the inequities all around them. What carried the fire for them in their efforts on behalf of others was their common feeling of outrage. What else could one feel when faced with evidence of so much poverty and injustice in a society that *had the ability to make things better but resisted doing so?*

Their interest in relocating was enhanced by Sam's learning about the "Wisconsin idea" of linking resources and brain power of the University of Wisconsin to progressive experiments and legislation.

Sam would head the University of Wisconsin-Extension Center for Social Services. He would also become a tenured faculty member, although his work would not necessarily involve teaching in the classroom. Tenure, he knew, would shelter him when he initiated controversial programs and stuck his neck out for high-risk issues.

Sam had been further convinced to take the job by Glen Pulver's explanation of how the extension programs in Wisconsin were unlike the strictly agricultural offerings available in other states. Wisconsin's extension programs operated as counterparts to the academic departments of the university but were separate from them.

"The Extension System is not an agency of state government," Dean Pulver had told Sam. "We're a part of the university, with some responsibility to do public service."

Sam would continue essentially the same work he had been doing in Ohio: developing programs in communities that would then continue those programs.

"That," replied Sam, "is the thing I like to do."

Since his work was to be statewide in scope, the Stellmans could live in either Milwaukee or Madison. They chose Milwaukee.

For nearly five years, from September 1968 to April 1973, Sam headed the statewide Center for Social Services, building it from two offices with a staff of five to five offices with a staff of fifteen.

He traveled a great deal, setting up programs in many locales to address current social problems affecting families. He trained professionals, introduced up-to-date methods and techniques, and initiated enterprises that affected whole communities. All these programs operated according to the principles of his philosophy, and all the offices thrived.

Despite a slim budget, Sam managed to construct a strong department.

"Look," he would say to his dean, "I know well enough you have a budget, but every year so many people retire and you don't replace them. I want some of that money for my new faculty." Most of the time he got the funds he needed. Sam believed it was because his center accomplished its mission, becoming probably the best known operation in the extension system.

Having seen how the administration and the male faculty at Ohio State had treated its few female faculty members, Sam intended to make sure this didn't happen in Wisconsin—at least not in his department. Although his job description did not include changing the system, Sam did not hesitate to do so wherever he could. In short order he arranged for five women to be hired for faculty positions, to the annoyance of many male colleagues. And Sam fought for the women when they applied for tenure.

###

As soon as Mandy arrived in Milwaukee, she, too, began fighting for the rights of women. Having been accepted at Marquette University Law School, this forty-four-year-old Jewish liberal had her work cut out for her at the Jesuit-based institution. But not over religious differences.

Because Mandy maintained her own set of values and her own convictions, Marquette's Catholic environment did not cause her any discomfort. Some law students had never met a "Jewish person," and their questions, which Mandy gladly answered, often led to conversations comparing Judaism and Christianity. For example, on returning to class after Yom Kippur, the day of atonement, she found herself explaining that Jews believe they can be forgiven for their sins against another person only if they get forgiveness from that person. Several students said they sought forgiveness of sins only from God. She explained that in Judaism, "the only forgiveness you get from God is for sins you commit against God."[44]

The discrimination Mandy experienced while attending Marquette was almost exclusively sex discrimination.

Only two other women were enrolled in Mandy's class. Because the school had no history of women as students, it was suddenly faced with the need to create a washroom for them. An old broom closet on the top floor of the law building was designated for the honor, and a toilet installed next to the original utility sink. This state-of-the-art "women's room" sat three floors above the library in a building that had no elevator.

Mandy asked for better accommodations, but the administration ignored her. So she began to use the lounge for female employees. Her audacity prompted the posting of a sign: "For Staff/Faculty Only." Mandy ignored it.

When the dean reprimanded her, she informed him that if better accommodations were not provided, she would start using the students' washroom for men—with appropriate notice to the males, of course.

At this, the faculty hurriedly called a meeting. Agreeing that the women did, after all, need better facilities, they decided that a proper women's room would be built in a "reasonable" length of time. Meanwhile, the three women began using the men's room. Construction of the women's washroom began promptly.

When Mandy applied for membership in a law fraternity, all four fraternities rejected her because their membership was restricted to male students. But she believed that if she and other women possessed the same educational qualifications as the men, attended the same classes, and took the same tests, they should be admitted to the associations that were professional in nature. The social activities of the fraternities did not interest her.

One day Mandy noticed signs posted on campus inviting students to a "beer blast" at one of the fraternities. The event was a recruiting effort for potential pledges, but the signs did not specify that attendees be male. So Mandy showed up, shocking the fraternity brothers. Wondering why she would want to enter their select group, they claimed she would ruin their social events.

"To hell with your beer blasts," Mandy told them. "I'm not interested in drinking your beer." She was interested only in taking advantage of every professional opportunity, aware of the solid professional benefits derived from membership in a law fraternity.

The fraternity brothers suggested, rather petulantly, that she join a law sorority. Mandy rejected that option, knowing that sororities would be less useful professionally. The fraternity then presented what it considered a handsome offer: associate membership, which would enable Mandy to attend all the fraternity's functions, with one small distinction—she could not vote.

"No, thank you," Mandy told them. "Separate but equal went out in 1964."

Like the attorney she was destined to become, Mandy turned to the landmark Civil Rights Act of 1964 and began to research related decisions that might apply to her own situation. She succeeded; the Supreme Court had previously found the American Medical Association guilty of discriminating against females and blacks in restricting membership.

Without threatening to sue, she presented her findings to the fraternities, pointing out that they had what she considered a legal duty to admit women. As a result, the local chapter of Tau Epsilon Rho, a Jewish law fraternity, voted unanimously to admit her. But its national constitution barred females from membership, so the chapter agreed to take Mandy's case to the national convention. There, in 1970, the word "fraternity" was reinterpreted to include women. Soon, other legal fraternities began to admit women, and five years later, Mandy became the first woman in the nation to gain membership in a law fraternity. She also became the first woman elected to the Supreme National Council of Tau Epsilon Rho. In a further move toward inclusiveness, "fraternity" was changed to "law society."

Her unwillingness as an individual to accept injustice not only benefited her, it also opened the door to other women from that time forward. Thus, her accomplishment represented truly radical social activism, for it tackled a discriminatory practice at its root and created ongoing changes in the system itself.[45]

Mandy did well in her studies, as usual, and her progress toward her goal was swift and sure—and characteristically contentious.

Some professors had difficulty accepting the invasion of their all-male domains and showed it in their treatment of the female law students in their classes. One professor pretended not to notice that three women occupied seats in his room. He would not call on them when they raised their hands to answer a question. And he began every lecture with "Gentlemen."

Undaunted, Mandy decided to respond with good humor. When the professor came to class one day and began with

"Gentlemen," there sat Mandy in her customary front-row seat—wearing a paper mustache.

By the end of the semester the professor had unbent sufficiently to acknowledge the presence of the women in his class and to call on them.

###

As a law student, Mandy usually dressed in rather plain student attire—skirt and blouse, flat shoes, and cloth coat. One winter her father gave her a gift of money to purchase a fur coat, so she went to the fur department of the Boston Store. The saleswoman took a quick look at Mandy's simple attire and said, with disinterest, "What can I do for you?"

"I'm looking for a mink coat," said Mandy.

The saleswoman offered to show her some less expensive furs.

"That's not what I'm looking for," said Mandy. "I want to see your better minks."

The saleswoman eyed her condescendingly. "I think our mink coats are not for you. I'll show them to you if you like, but they're very expensive."

"Forget it," said Mandy, and left. A few months later while visiting her family in Canada, she bought a full-length coat of dark ranch mink.

Most people experiencing a similar act of prejudice would be content to let the story end here. Not Mandy. She believed in eradicating prejudice, not walking away from it—whether it affected many individuals or just one. So she paid a second visit to the Boston Store's fur department wearing her new coat, and she asked to see the manager.

"My, that's a beautiful coat," the manager said. "Where did you buy it?"

"Not here," she said. "I would have bought it here, except your salesperson didn't think I was a legitimate customer."

She then told the story about her first visit to his department.

The manager was crestfallen. "I wish you had asked for me when you were here," he said.

Replied Mandy, "I assumed that your people were trained enough to understand that everyone who walks into your department is a potential customer regardless of appearance. I know when my parents were in the retail business many years ago, they treated everyone alike no matter what their appearance or their apparent ability to buy more expensive clothes."

The dejected manager apologized again and promised that employees would be trained better in the future. Mandy's determination to speak up and take a stand changed a policy and a practice that affected other customers from that time on.

Although Mandy entered Marquette University Law School with the class of '71, she received her J.D. degree six months earlier, in mid-semester, December 1970. She ranked in the top ten percent of her class. And she never let up in tackling discrimination by using a radical approach—as in seeking to make change at the root of a problem.

As graduation time approached and recruiters set up their appointments, she discovered they would be interviewing only the top fifteen percent of her graduating class. Although well qualified herself to be included in the interviews, she was concerned that many others, particularly minority students, would not have an equal opportunity to meet potential employers. When she questioned the dean of the law school, he said it had always been that way.

Among the recruiters intending to interview only the top fifteen percent was the U.S. Department of Housing and

Urban Development (HUD). Mandy found such discrimination by an agency of the government unconscionable, so she signed up for an interview. After answering all the recruiter's questions, she asked if he would answer a few of hers. He agreed.

"HUD is a department of the federal government, right?"

"Right."

"Then by what authority do you exclude tax-paying citizens on the basis of their standing in the class rank? Does that mean you have a policy of discriminating against people because of their grade scores?"

The recruiter looked uncomfortable but didn't respond.

Mandy went on. "Does the federal government have some indication that those who are not in the top fifteen percent of their class will not make good lawyers?"

The recruiter fumbled for an answer. Mandy concluded by saying that if the policy remained in place, he would be hearing from Wisconsin's senators and members of Congress, and from the local press, as well.

The next morning, a new notice appeared on the bulletin board for HUD inviting all students to sign up regardless of grades.

The concept of women in law school apparently gave the U.S. government as much difficulty as it had given Marquette University. At graduation time Mandy received an invitation to report to the Army recruiting station.

She duly reported, telling the startled recruiter, "I'm too old to start at the bottom, but I'll enlist if I can start as a general."

Having decided against a career in the military, the feisty forty-eight-year-old went looking for work, filled with the idealistic goal of using her new professional status as an attorney to help as many people as she could.

This time she found that most law firms, large as well as small, were not willing to hire women—even someone who had graduated in the top ten percent of her class. If a woman did manage to get hired, she ended up working as a "researcher" or the firm's "librarian." Rarely did a woman get an opportunity to go to court. Only a few women practiced law, and fewer still practiced trial law.

Undaunted, Mandy applied for a job with the Milwaukee District Attorney's office. Entering the interview room at Marquette, she found herself face to face with the D.A. himself, E. Michael McCann.

"I understand," said Mandy, "that you assign women to prosecute cases only in family situations and in the juvenile court. If you hire me, I would like to handle all kinds of cases, including criminal cases."

"But Mrs. Stellman," replied McCann, "it can be a touchy situation for a woman handling criminal cases. I think you would be embarrassed hearing all the foul language that so many of the defendants use in court."

"Well," replied Mandy, "I think most of us, even women, have heard foul language at one time or another in our lives. It's almost impossible to grow up without hearing such words."

The D.A. shifted uncomfortably in his chair. "I'm sorry," he persisted, "but I do feel that in the best interests of my department I have to protect women from being exposed to the kind of violent defendants who use that sort of language. It even embarrasses me at times. Women have to be protected from those situations."

"Like f___ they do," replied the usually staid and proper Mandy Stellman. It was the first and last time she was ever heard to use such language.

###

Only one attorney came forward and offered Mandy space in his office and a chance to learn the business.[46] That was Alan D. Eisenberg, famous—or infamous—throughout the state as a flamboyant, controversial individual. Mandy ignored the criticisms leveled against her mentor, grateful for his patiently teaching her the practice of law and for taking her with him into the courtroom so she could experience the "real thing."

Eisenberg wanted someone creative who would be fair to women and minorities, who was not primarily interested in money, and who would not be hired away from him by a corporate firm. He admired Mandy's academic record and her willingness to stand up for principle. He was impressed, he said, by her "extremely flexible mentality." He added, "She is an original thinker, and few law firms want that."

He believed Mandy gravitated into family practice because it was a better forum for espousing the causes of women's rights and human rights. "She is a feminist because she is a humanist. She's smart—a tough, competent, brilliant lawyer and person. She is much more than a lawyer. She has the maturity and depth to see beyond the courtroom. In family work that's important."

It was Eisenberg who chose Mandy to be his co-counsel in the Jennifer Patri trial, which gave the neophyte attorney national exposure. It was a wise choice all around. Though Mandy's role in the trial was not large, it was pivotal. Her awareness of women's issues, in particular the battered woman's syndrome, directly affected the outcome of the historic trial.[47]

If Alan Eisenberg helped mold Mandy's career, so, too, did Mandy's feminism mold him. She got him involved in her causes and wasted no time in recruiting him to membership in the National Organization for Women.

Eisenberg has said that Mandy would have made a good judge but was too controversial to be elected. "If she didn't like something, she said so. She didn't take shit from anybody, and, better than that, she gave a lot of it back."

Whenever Mandy was asked if she would like to be a judge, her answer was, "Yes, I would. However, I'd prefer to be a U.S. Supreme Court Justice—I'm too old to have to work my way up. I have to start at the top."

A familiar sight around Milwaukee in the seventies and eighties was the business card Mandy developed for herself. Women passed it along to others looking for feminist legal advice, and it appeared in all the program books that sold ad space for worthy causes. It featured a reproduction of a well-known painting, *The First Reading of the Emancipation Proclamation Before the Cabinet.* A close look at the reproduction reveals the figure of Mandy Stellman sitting among the men of power and position in Lincoln's cabinet, a cutout of her photograph superimposed over an empty chair at the right-hand side of the prestigious group.[48]

When handing someone her card, Mandy was likely to say, "You can find me on the far right, though for the record, my political leaning is more to the left."[49]

In the late spring of 1971, Mandy's first year out of law school, she fell on some slippery stairs and broke her leg. Ironically, the accident occurred inside the county's Public Safety Building.

During Mandy's hospitalization following surgery, the chief social worker paid her a routine visit. He stood by her bed and went through the usual small talk about his desire to help. Then, in a misguided effort to comfort, he said, "I know this was a bad accident, Mrs. Stellman, but you will be a better person for it."

"I was a damn good person before the accident," Mandy retorted, "and I can't see how a broken leg will make me a better person. I want you to take your social work gobbledygook with you and never show your face in this room again." He left quickly.

At the time that Mandy was rushed to Milwaukee's Mt. Sinai Hospital, the orthopedist on duty had never met her before, and he spoke to her only briefly before her surgery. After, he stopped by her room. "Just because you're a lawyer, don't make a federal case out of your accident," he told her.

Mandy, her right leg in a cast, was too weak from surgery to summon a retort. But from that moment on, their relationship was all downhill. She found him arrogant and sarcastic.

As the days passed and Mandy complained of pain, she was ignored, along with her record of allergies, which she'd reported when she arrived in the emergency room. As she continued having pain, her allergist stopped by to see her and mentioned that tight bandages or a cast could cause a bad reaction.

But whenever Sam tried to get the orthopedic surgeon to come look at the situation, he was never available. During the day, he would not return Sam's calls. If it was evening, he was at a meeting, or out riding his bike, or too busy to talk to anyone. When the nurses suggested to the doctor there might be some problem with the leg, Mandy had the impression they were told to ignore her because her complaints suggested she was a "malingerer."

When the pain became intolerable, Sam called Mandy's sister in Toronto. A registered nurse, Sandy and her physician-husband took the next flight to Milwaukee. They arrived to find a hospital extern about to remove the cast—his own decision, contrary to the surgeon's orders. As the cast came off, the extern's face turned white. Sandy tried to get a pulse in the leg but there was none. Sandy's husband, Dr. Morris Spring, came rushing back to the room from the nurses' station, where he had been reading Mandy's charts. A phone call was quickly placed to the surgeon—again not available. But his senior partner answered and hurried over. He, too, turned white on seeing the leg. He called in two experts in hematology, one of whom ordered an angiogram to determine the reason for the loss in circulation. He warned Mandy that she could lose the leg. Fortunately, the angiogram indicated the source of the problem and the leg was saved. The nurses were informed that the surgeon was not to be allowed in Mandy's room ever again.

After returning home, Mandy used a wheelchair for many months. From then on, she had to use a cane because the cartilage in her knee was destroyed, occasionally causing her knee to buckle without warning.

Mandy did not sue the surgeon for negligence, although she could have. She would, however, sue for negligence on behalf of a client who wanted to bring a lawsuit in a similar situation. Her reason for not taking legal action on her own behalf? She has never favored litigation except as a last resort. It is a tactic that fits her history of activism, in which the *threat* of legal action usually has been sufficient to bring about desired change.

###

Seventeen years after Mandy graduated from Marquette, she endowed the university with a scholarship for law students, the Samuel D. Stellman Award.

"I decided not to wait until one of us died. I wanted to honor Sam while he was alive."

Jews believe in "giving *covet,*" she explained—letting someone know you're honoring them, "because when they are gone, there is no enjoyment for them. My husband had the privilege of knowing that someone was being educated in his name every year."[50]

One year she received a letter of appreciation from a recipient of the scholarship who assumed Sam was no longer alive. The student wrote: "Thank you.... It's a nice way for you to honor the memory...."

Mandy replied, "Well, I just talked to my husband and he appreciates that."

###

The Stellmans became grandparents in 1974 when Andrew was born to Steven and Jeanne. Two years later, Emma arrived. When she was seven she won a New York City-wide contest held as part of Women's History Month. Her winning essay told about her grandmother—the same subject she chose years later when she wrote the following as part of her college entrance application to Bryn Mawr.

During winter vacations, when other kids would be visiting Disneyland with their grandparents, my grandma would be taking me and my brother to the Milwaukee courthouses. By the fourth grade, I knew almost all of the judges by first name, and a whole lot of lawyers, too.

I loved going to Grandma's office. Every wall and surface would be covered with anti-smoking and feminist paraphernalia. Grandma's male secretary would let us type on his typewriters. I don't remember Grandma ever telling me to be a feminist, but I know that many of my thoughts and ideas about the nature of justice and the importance of equality among people can be derived from her influences.

My grandma is, however, conservative in some respects.

She looks like practically every other grandma. She is
short and round and wears her hair in a little bun on the
top of her head.[51]

###

Christmas Eve can be a difficult time for estranged parents, and for one of Mandy's clients, it became even more difficult one year when a couple disagreed over visitation. The dispute involved a child for whom Mandy had been appointed guardian ad litem by the divorce court. Although the father had been granted visitation, it was stipulated that he should never be alone with the child. Usually, this was no problem, because the father had remarried, but on this particular night his new wife would be working late. She would not get home until ten thirty. The child's mother refused visitation.

Mandy had a suggestion to resolve the mother's concern about the child being with its father. "How about if I stay with them until his wife comes home? Since Christmas is not our holiday, we're available."

So the Stellmans arranged to take the little boy to his father's house. On the way to pick up the child at his mother's, they stopped at a toy store and bought a small stuffed toy. "It's Christmas," Mandy said.

Sam waited in the car as Mandy went up to the mother's door and disappeared inside. Ten minutes passed. Then half an hour. When nearly an hour had gone by, an impatient Sam went up to the house and asked for Mandy. She came to the door, carrying a very happy child.

"Is that in the job description of a guardian ad litem?" Sam asked.

"I wanted him to get used to me first," explained Mandy. "Besides, once a mother and grandmother, always a mother and grandmother. Lawyering can wait."

The rest of the evening the Stellmans spent at the father's house. They got home close to midnight.

For fifteen years Mandy had been banking at the same location, making deposits several times a week, sometimes daily. One day as she entered the bank she noticed a change. All the female tellers were wearing bright yellow jumpsuits embroidered with their first names. The male tellers were wearing their own business suits, and their nametags were printed with the courtesy title "Mr." and their last names.

Upon inquiry, Mandy learned from a female teller that the women employees had not been consulted about what had become required dress. That same afternoon she telephoned the bank president for an appointment, and the next day both Mandy and Sam went to call on him.

Asked about the uniforms, the president explained that the bank's officers thought it would dress up the appearance of the bank.

Not so, the Stellmans told him. "Aside from the fact that the uniforms are ugly, I hope you realize you are discriminating against the women by allowing the men to dress as they wish. That includes having the women's first names emblazoned on their uniforms while the men wear name tags with *Mister.*"

"I hadn't thought about that," admitted the president.

"What we suggest," Mandy told him, "is that you get rid of the uniforms. They don't enhance the image of the bank. At the same time you won't be leaving yourself open to a lawsuit based upon discrimination."

The next day the uniforms were not in evidence, and it was a very happy teller who greeted Mandy.

A small change? Perhaps, but it was an institutional change that affected both current and future employees, and it came about because two people decided to use a very simple tactic and inform a decision-maker of some facts.

Five years later Mandy encountered a different form of sexism at the same bank.

One day, just as she had done on many others during her twenty years of doing business with the same institution, Mandy walked up to the commercial counter to make a deposit. A young male teller, not looking at the deposit but looking only at Mandy standing before him, shook his head and pointed toward the tellers handling other customers.

"Sorry, lady, but you'll have to get in that line," he said. "This line is for business people only."

Mandy looked him in the eye. "And tell me, young man, what does a business person look like?"

A long silence followed. The teller looked at the deposit, looked at Mandy, and then, without ever replying to the question, completed the transaction.

One more discriminatory practice was ending, the result of another very simple act on the part of one person to correct one employee. But this time Mandy went further. She told the story to Alex Thien, columnist for the *Milwaukee Sentinel*. When his retelling of the experience appeared in the morning paper, thousands of readers throughout the state had their consciousnesses raised as well.[52]

###

In Wisconsin, as elsewhere in the seventies, crime was on the rise. It came to affect Sam's career when Governor Patrick Lucey[53] grew nervous over the publicity. At a cocktail party one evening, Lucey, ever-sensitive to voter issues, button-holed John Weaver, president of the state's university system. What, the governor wanted to know, was the university doing about crime?

"I'll get back to you," said Weaver.

Although the university system offered some courses for police, no comprehensive program existed. But it didn't take long for the Board of Regents to put the issue on the agenda for its next meeting. On April 23, 1973, the Regents authorized the creation of the Criminal Justice Institute within the UW-Extension System. Unfortunately, the Regents failed to authorize any operating funds.

Dean Harold Montross telephoned Sam, whose organizing and directing abilities had become evident in the five years since he had moved from Ohio to direct the Center for Social Services.

"Sam, we're launching a new Criminal Justice Institute," said the dean, "and I'd like you to consider directing it. You could try it on a part-time basis and see how it goes."

Two weeks into the job Sam called the dean and told him it couldn't be done part-time. So Dean Montross authorized him to direct the Institute, also known as the CJI, on a full-time basis. Sam was able to acquire enough money from the dean's office for one full-time assistant. William F. Winter turned out to be an outstanding grant writer—a decided asset for an institute that depended on grants from state and federal government, as well as from an occasional local funding source. Winter became the chair of the CJI when Sam retired fifteen years later.

A statewide media campaign was launched in 1977 to educate communities about their roles in reducing crime and to get them to make use of the CJI in developing new criminal justice programs to meet community needs. The media campaign was called "Arrest Crime—Live Without Fear." The title quickly became a motto for the Stellmans, who had an artist design a logo for it. The framed motto hangs in their home.

The Institute had a statewide mission to respond to the professional training needs of people working in criminal justice and in related fields, while at the same time addressing ever-changing community crime problems.

The CJI was designed to reflect contemporary thinking, which viewed criminal justice as a system made up of three interrelated components: law enforcement, the courts, and corrections. To fulfill the CJI's mandate, Sam worked with judges, police, prosecutors, politicians, and others concerned about the increase in crime.

"We're working with business and industry along with law enforcement," said Sam when interviewed for the extension system's newsletter.[54] "We think we have some responsibilities as part of the university community to make some impact on social problems."

Sam took note of what he felt was an important difference between the disciplines of social work and criminal justice: "Criminal justice is far behind social work in terms of dealing with root problems," he said. "Many CJI programs deal with crime after the fact. The study of criminal justice evolved out of what I call the 'lock-up' philosophy, which is now revived."

Some of the more prominent programs developed under Sam's direction offered alternatives to incarceration for certain nonviolent offenses. The CJI also provided technical assistance to other organizations dealing with mentally retarded offenders, perpetrators of sexual assault, and batterers of women and the elderly. Sam went to great lengths to make CJI resources available to those it served, including developing courses in different formats—such as brown bag minicourses offered at lunch time.

Though many programs were later handed off to other groups, the CJI continued its training of law enforcement officers. After Sam retired, general funding cutbacks led to severe downsizing throughout the university system, and by 2000, the CJI staff consisted of Dawn Drellos. But certain programs will find a home because a great many judges and organizations want them kept running.[55]

Among the many who came to like and respect Sam and his work was the Reverend Donald Olson, court chaplain for Milwaukee County. Operating from a small office in the courthouse, the chaplain had the job of providing spiritual relief to offenders in the city and county courts, and placing them in roles whereby they could make restitution for their crimes.

Once when Rev. Olson had to be hospitalized and someone was needed to fill the gap for about a month, Sam Stellman stepped forward and volunteered to use his personal vacation time to fill in for his friend. It didn't take long for those he counseled to begin calling him "Rabbi Stellman."

After about a week on the job, Sam looked up from his temporary desk one day to see a young man poke his head in the door. Addressing Sam as "Reverend Olson," the man asked for a prayer.

"I'm not Reverend Olson," Sam replied, "and I regret I don't have an appropriate prayer for you, but I think we pray to the same God. Shalom to you, and I wish you the best in court."

The young man appeared comforted as he headed across the hall to the courtroom.[56]

While Sam made use of his educational mission to create the kind of social change that would improve the community, Mandy made use of her legal expertise to take community action that would create social change.

As an attorney, she knew that women were not considered equal to men under the law—a double standard that made it possible for women to be treated unfairly by the criminal justice system, employers, credit lenders, the telephone company—even a local restaurant.

Changes to such systems *can* be brought about by individuals—as each of the Stellmans proved over and over. However, many individuals have a hard time challenging the powers-that-be. Even the *thought* of action can be inconceivable to some people, especially women, who are further hampered in challenging the status quo because of a long history of isolation and powerlessness. Although the role of women in society has been changing, powerlessness is often reinforced by media images, by the economic realities that force many women to be dependent on men, and by cultural myths that tell women to mistrust other women. Even the housing patterns for middle class families in the fifties had the effect of isolating married women in their own homes. There were no women's ghettos or locker rooms that threw women of different social strata together where they could share their experiences, frustrations, and anger—not until the women's rights movement, that is.

When NOW, the National Organization for Women, was born in 1966, hundreds of thousands of women flocked to local consciousness raising groups and began to discover something important about themselves: the unequal treatment each woman had experienced in her own life did not result from some personal flaw or character defect. Rather, inequality had been rooted in tradition and codified in the laws, which remained on the books for centuries, out of which grew social institutions that had a stake in preserving the status quo.

Multitudes of women discovered through consciousness raising that agitating for reform was not "unladylike." And they liked discovering how banding together through NOW gave them power they lacked as individuals.

Of course, Mandy had known these truths all along. Never one to feel powerless or to be intimidated by false assumptions of inadequacy, she demonstrated what one person could do. Further, she and Sam together had demonstrated what two could do. Still, some types of reform are most effectively accomplished through large-scale community action and grassroots mobilization.

Mandy joined the National Organization for Women in 1970, a few years after the Milwaukee chapter began. With women and men banding together, a number of local institutions began to change as a result of a larger number of outraged citizens taking group action.

Heinemann's is an old Milwaukee institution. Formerly situated in the heart of the downtown office and shopping district, one of its restaurants had long enjoyed great popularity among the business lunch crowd. In the sixties, only its front room served the general public; its back room was reserved for businessmen. On the theory that it was important for men to get back to their offices, Heinemann's made sure that the tables in the back room received prompt service.

One day when a woman attempted to sit in the back room, she was refused service. "The men have priority," the owner told her. That was in 1969.[57]

The incident galvanized NOW members. They met to plan strategy. First they would meet with the owner; if discussion failed, they would then organize a sit-in of the back room. Mandy was active in the campaign.

To the women's surprise, the owner refused to alter his policy. The unreasonableness of his position made the women all the more ready to unite behind Plan B, and the sit-ins began. Each day before lunch, NOW members arrived at the restaurant and occupied all the tables in the back room. Each day they were refused service. But the businessmen were not able to be served either, because the women would not vacate their seats.

One day Mandy brought her younger son with her, and another activist, Sue Deutsch, brought her son. The boys entered the restaurant first and took seats. Then the women came in and sat beside them. The boys ordered for their mothers. "They wouldn't serve the women," Mandy recalled, "but they had to serve the boys. My son loved it! The owner said he was going to call the cops. We said, 'Call 'em.'"

After weeks of sit-ins, the owner became increasingly upset. He was losing money, yet he refused to change the policy. So the women took the next step. They brought a discrimination suit against Heinemann's Restaurant, and the owner finally capitulated.

Other restaurants in Milwaukee with similar policies took note of Heinemann's difficulties and decided to bend with the winds of change. Thus, the group action brought about more widespread, permanent change that went well beyond the immediate benefits to those taking part in the original action. Moreover, the gradual escalation of action-reaction tactics demonstrated that radical change can come about via peaceful methods, enabling participants to further maintain their beliefs in the justice of their cause and feel comfortable about acting *en masse*.

###

NOW's ability to promote grassroots activism on a large scale appealed to Mandy, who always saw the value in maximizing the outcome of any effort. It was just such a grassroots action that succeeded in getting the names of married women into Wisconsin's phone books. The effort was spearheaded by an active NOW member, Florence Dickinson, owner of the Cliff Dwellers, a resort hotel in Door County. She became one of Mandy's all-tme idols.

The year was 1974. Dickinson noted the irony that the busiest day of the year for the telephone company was Mother's Day, but mothers couldn't have their names in the telephone directory if their husbands' names were listed. The phone company insisted that it was impossible to print two names in one listing. Thus, someone using the phone book either had to know the first and last names of the husband, or telephone everyone listed with the same last name. The wife was invisible—but for a fee she could have a separate listing in addition to her husband's.

In March 1975, many chapters making up Wisconsin NOW came together for a state conference, at which they resolved to take action against the phone company. They nicknamed their action DIAL, an acronym for Directory Identity Action League.[58]

Mandy came up with the idea that NOW take out a statewide newspaper ad saying, "Don't call Mom on Mother's Day, she isn't in the phone book." When the ad appeared it created a furor among women throughout the state. Many took up the campaign, writing letters of protest to the Wisconsin Public Service Commission and testifying at hearings.

Eventually the message got through, and the directory was opened to married women.

Before 1978, girls in the Milwaukee Public School System (MPS) were not offered the same opportunities and privileges offered to boys. For example, when the boys and the girls basketball teams both wanted to use the gym on the same night, the boys had first choice.

Reacting to this discrimination against girls, Milwaukee NOW filed a complaint with the Department of Health, Education, and Welfare (HEW) against the Milwaukee Board of School Directors. The complaint alleged sex discrimination under Title IX of the Educational Amendments of 1974.

MPS had been about to cut its gender equity budget, but "NOW showed up in force. "We said 'No way,'" recalled Mandy, who was among those testifying at open hearings.

NOW was prepared to go to court. However, after dozens of hours of hard work, an agreement was reached that would begin the work of eliminating sex discrimination in the public schools.[59]

"We achieved our goals because we got our facts together and had our position very clear," Mandy explained. "We knew what we were doing and we negotiated what we wanted."

The victory demonstrated that change could come about in a major institution without a protracted court battle—provided the laws against discrimination are already in place.

To ensure compliance, MPS agreed to submit reports to NOW, and for the next several years, Attorney Stellman received those reports on behalf of NOW. The reports documented the school district's affirmative action programs, its annual athletic budget, its handling of complaints of discrimination, and the results of mandated school surveys of the participation and interest of girls in various sports.

According to a spokesperson for the U.S. Department of Health, Education, and Welfare, this agreement by the Milwaukee Public School System was the second in the nation in which a women's organization played a major role in negotiating an end to sex discrimination in the schools. It was the first in which such an organization was involved in monitoring a school district's compliance.[60]

The *Milwaukee Sentinel* declared this arrangement the "Wrong Role for NOW." An editorial questioned the propriety of having the task of monitoring turned over to "the complainants, a group of activist feminists."[61]

Mandy immediately responded with a letter to the editor:

How dare the Milwaukee Sentinel, *a prominent newspaper which purports to monitor political and civic leaders in order to protect the public interest, unfairly criticize another group for doing the same thing?*

...Since when is the Milwaukee Sentinel *the ultimate authority on the "Wrong Role for NOW"...?*

Where was the Sentinel for the last several decades (at least since Brown vs. Board of Education, *1954) while girls and women have been treated as second-class citizens in the Milwaukee Public Schools?*

Where were the men's civic groups?

Where were the nonmilitant citizens?

NOW and its civic-minded members, both female and male, both militant and nonmilitant, should be applauded by the entire community and should be awarded recognition for seeking and obtaining justice in our schools.

As an active member of NOW, I invite all men's civic groups to challenge every injustice in our society. I would be more than willing to share the glory as well as the hard work as long as justice is obtained.[62]

###

Mandy's activism in NOW added to her visibility. Articulate, knowledgeable, and witty, she was much sought after as a speaker. Whenever an honorarium was offered to her or to Sam for speaking, the host organization would be asked to make out its check to the Milwaukee Women's Crisis Line.

During the national push to ratify the Equal Rights Amendment, Mandy spoke before the Lions, the Elks, the Kiwanis, and almost any group that asked Milwaukee NOW to provide a speaker. Ordinarily, she turned down a request if it meant simply filling a slot on a program. But during the ERA push, if she felt she could "maybe move that clogged society mem-

bership to do something," she didn't mind being speaker of
the month. She also took the opportunity to speak before
organizations that asked NOW to simply provide "a speaker
on the ERA." She understood that in some cases, the audience did not care who showed up, only that it would be fun
to bait a "women's libber." Her presentation style surprised
them.

One wintry evening, Mandy and Sam made their way to a
restaurant near Milwaukee's Mitchell Feild where a men's
service organization held its meetings. As usual, Mandy's
hair was perfectly coiffed and her suit expensively tailored.

"I do own a full-length absolutely gorgeous dark ranch
mink coat, and I decided to wear it to the meeting," she
said after the event. "I may be a feminist but I ain't stupid."

Not only was it a cold night in February, but also Mandy
was well aware that the organization would be expecting to
see a "dungaree-clad young woman with long hair who believed in the bra-less look—in other words, a stereotypical
hippie-type radical feminist—which in their minds was a
negative."

The Stellmans entered the meeting room and encountered
the person handling name tags. Mandy described what happened next.

*I said, "I'm your speaker"—and I think the guy almost
died. I made sure he saw my ring—it's a whopper. Someone graciously asked, "Can I hang up your coat?"*

I said "No thank you. I never hang up this coat."

*I draped it on my shoulders and went to the head table
where I knew I was supposed to sit, with Sam on one side
of me and the head of the organization on the other. I
took a whole long time to sit down. Sam knew* exactly
*what I was doing. Then I just put the coat over the chair,
but everybody could still see it. This night the wives had*

been invited, and the women loved the way I looked.

When I got up to speak I said, "I'm Mandy Stellman, I'm an attorney, and I'm a radical feminist. I'm married to a wonderful man and I just love being married, and I'm a grandmother, and I have two children and two daughters-in-law, and I just love the whole thing. But I'm a radical feminist. So perhaps you'd like me to tell you what that is." They all started to giggle and it put everybody at ease, and the men were no longer abrasive because they were sitting with their wives and here's a mother, a grandma, and a loving husband.

I think I said at the beginning, "What did you expect, blue jeans? I don't own any and they probably wouldn't even look good on me. I don't think they make them big enough." You do it with humor but you have to catch them first.

Parents themselves, the audience paid attention as this well-educated, highly articulate professional talked passionately about the need for their daughters and granddaughters to prepare for a place in the work world.

I gave my usual on the ERA and talked about what's fair: "You got a daughter, you just paid a lot of money, at great sacrifice, so she could get a degree, and you're so proud of her, but your best friend is a corporate personnel manager and he doesn't hire her. He hires this male, this young kid who doesn't know anything, while your daughter is perfect for the job. Why didn't he hire her? Because she's a girl. Is that fair?"

The women are sitting there with their husbands getting upset. By the end of the evening there were a lot of questions. Women were standing in line to talk to me and tell me about their lost chances. "I wish I had done this...I wish I had done that," and some of the men were saying, "I've got a daughter who just graduated from the

university. You know, you're right."
No one had ever thought of it that way before.
Mandy received a standing ovation.

###

Among the hundreds of speeches Mandy delivered during
the seventies and eighties, many were to feminist groups.
But the feminist perspective has never meant unanimity on
all issues. Possibly the most divisive issue among women
during those years was smoking. With Mandy's asthma and
her allergic reactions to the chemicals in cigarette smoke,
she experienced some vexing episodes.

A room on the UW-Milwaukee campus had been booked
by a feminist group hosting one of her speeches, and about
fifty women were present when Mandy walked in. She took
off her jacket and immediately wrote on the blackboard in
large letters, "Please, No Smoking."

One member of the audience loudly announced that she
would not put out her cigarette for anyone, and would Mandy
please proceed.

Mandy walked over to the coat rack, put on her jacket,
and walked out the door. As far as she was concerned, she
was on her way home. Two group members came racing after her, apologized, and explained that the smoker was willing to put out her cigarette if Mandy would go ahead with
her talk.

Mandy returned to the room and without further incident
delivered a dynamic speech.

###

The lobby at Children's Court Center is always crowded,
and until a few years ago it was as smoke-filled as one of
Milwaukee's corner taverns. As the social workers, probation officers, and police officers waited for their cases to be

called, many smoked. And many of the juveniles who waited also smoked, as did their parents. Not surprisingly, foul
air infiltrated the hearing rooms.

"Your Honor," said Mandy, interrupting a hearing, "this
has nothing to do with my case, but the place is so bad I
just can't breathe." The commissioner hearing the case
agreed. So Mandy wrote a letter to the chief judge and threatened to sue if something wasn't done. Finally a "no smoking" sign appeared in the lobby, affording some relief.

One day Mandy arrived for a hearing, meeting the twelve-
year-old boy she was representing and his mother in the
lobby. On a bench directly underneath the no smoking sign,
a lawyer sat smoking his cigar. He was, in Mandy's words,
an "old-time lawyer who should have known better."

She said to the attorney, "Are you aware that this area is
now no smoking?"

The twelve-year-old pointed to the sign.

Without hesitation, the attorney responded, "Go f___
yourself."

Even the street-smart kid was offended, because he whispered, "Mrs. Stellman, he shouldn't have said that to you!"

Mandy decided to deal with the situation by simply telling every lawyer she encountered for the next three months
what this man had said to her. Instead of filing a complaint, she saw to it that whenever the attorney appeared
among his colleagues, they would remember this was the
attorney who had said those words to Mandy—and in front
of a child.

Today, the courthouse has a more effective no-smoking
policy, and city and county ordinances restrict smoking in
all public buildings. So if Mandy were to find the same attorney smoking in the lobby now, she wouldn't hesitate to
call the police and have him arrested.

###

Sam resigned from the board of the Milwaukee Council on Alcoholism because of smoking at board meetings. He couldn't see that much difference between the addictions. "I accepted being a member of the board of directors because I thought I could make a major contribution to the problem of alcoholism in our community," he wrote to the president of the group in his letter of resignation. "But when I attended board meetings and half the board members were smokers, aside from the difficulty in breathing, I concluded that I could not be part of a board in which so many members are addicted, possibly not to alcohol but to tobacco."

Shortly after he resigned, Sam learned that the board voted to eliminate smoking at all its meetings.

###

Mandy's strong sense of civic duty led her to run for a position on the school board of the local high school, Nicolet. It was 1974, the only time she ran for public office. As a mother, former schoolteacher, and a college instructor on such subjects as marriage, family, and adolescence, she believed local voters would find her an appealing candidate.

She campaigned on the slogan, "A Vote for Mandy means More"—more value for the educational dollar, more community support for teachers, more personalized education for students, more opportunities for adult education programs. But she was defeated by a businessman who talked about less—how to spend less of the taxpayers' money on education. The fact that Nicolet High School spent more money per student than any other public high school in the state seemed to elude many voters.

What caught the attention of some voters was her position that no one should smoke in the schools. Any smoking ban would affect teachers as well as students.

"Some of the teachers were furious," she knew. "They asked, 'Do you mean *nobody?*' and I said, 'Yes—you're examples, aren't you?' I taught school and I always thought I owed it to the kids to set a good example."

It took another fifteen years before smoking was eliminated altogether on the Nicolet campus.

###

Both Stellmans fought to keep smoking out of school buildings and schoolyards long before mainstream support convinced President Clinton to take a strong stand on the issue—and long before any municipality, restaurant, or airline even thought to limit the practice. Mandy was as tireless and aggressive on this issue as on any other, even though her stand made her unpopular with many groups, including at times her own NOW chapter.

She also had little patience with the process of group consensus, which a number of women's liberation groups at the time regarded as basic to the empowerment of women.

"If eighteen people were there, they needed eighteen people to agree or they didn't make a decision," explained Mandy. For someone who already had a string of victories dangling from her belt to attest to the efficacy of independent action, consensus seemed painfully slow and unproductive. "They would not call someone the chair or the president, because 'we're all equal.' If you disagreed with the majority in a meeting you could be criticized for blocking progress. Well," observed Mandy, "you get no progress unless someone directs the meeting. Someone has to take the heat."

In the courses Sam taught on community organization, he also defended individual leadership, pointing out, "Risk-takers sooner or later get their noses bloodied. But it is only through risk-taking that important changes take place."

Despite differences of opinion, Mandy was highly respected by the women's community, and her contributions to the growth and development of many local and state feminist institutions were valued. So much so that she was honored by the Milwaukee Chapter of NOW as its Woman of the Year. The celebration was held November 12, 1977, at the historic Villa Terrace on the city's East Side.

Because of limited space, not all who attempted to make reservations for the banquet could do so. Many who were turned down came after dinner, sitting in chairs set up around the room to accommodate the overflow.

More than two hundred people, including Mandy's sons, their wives, and relatives from Toronto, turned out to applaud her achievements as they were enumerated from the podium.

Letters and telegrams poured in from well-wishers, including former Wisconsin Acting Governor Martin Schreiber and State Supreme Court Justice Shirley Abrahamson.

The most prominent personality to mount the podium that night was Gene Boyer, a Wisconsin activist who was among the twenty-eight founders of the National Organization for Women.[63]

A witty and dynamic speaker, Gene cited a few of Mandy's firsts in opening up jobs and law fraternities to women and changing the way police and courts handled rape victims. Then she spoke about the honoree herself:

I guess I should have known there was a woman of substance somewhere in the Milwaukee area, for I met Sam before I met Mandy—that was at the University of Wisconsin-Platteville where we participated in a program on the women's movement. And there was Sam, shaking a finger at one of the panelists telling her that men opening doors for women or helping them in and out of automobiles had nothing to do with the women's movement.

Although the evening was Mandy's, Sam's role was acknowledged frequently during the evening and their partnership of thirty-four years applauded.

"And then I met Mandy," Gene continued.

Probably I should start by talking about her contrariness. Everyone knows she's not a docile person.... If you ask her how she likes being a professional woman and has she given up being interested in homemaking, she will tell you how much she loves her work, and then she'll give you her recipe for potato pancakes and chopped liver. Then she will pull out her knitting and tell you about the dozens of afghans she has made, and all the ski hats, and the one she's proudest of, now being worn by Federal Judge Reynolds.

If you say to her, "Mandy, how come you are so critical of the police, of the district attorney's office, of other attorneys in your articles in the press? Won't you antagonize them?" she'll say, "But I'm not mad at them. I love them all. Besides, Chief Breier just shook my hand today; Mike McCann gave me a big hug, and the president of the Milwaukee Bar is my attorney."

Then Gene asked the audience:

Every time NOW has a new task force, who volunteers to be on it and give free legal advice? When a newsletter needs funds or it won't publish, who can be counted on to provide the means to assure publication? When members of NOW can't afford to attend a conference, who makes sure they participate?

###

Publicly, Mandy has said, "My biggest criticism of the women's movement—and I have to take some of the blame—is that we have told women, 'There's a better world out there, come join us,' but we haven't stood beside them while their

house is falling apart and their world is caving in. Not all
women can safely leave an unhappy situation after hearing
a lecture."

This is where men come in, she told a reporter in 1981.

*We need to literally recruit men who are sympathetic
but not active.... After all, they're members of this society, too. They'll be raising daughters. Their wife or mother could be the next rape victim.... The burden of changing
society is also on men.... When someone is raped, I'm
always disturbed when there is little or no reaction from
prominent men in the community.*[64]

A few months earlier, Mandy had recruited the Democrat-
ic party's gubernatorial candidate to join NOW, telling him
he had a better chance of being elected with the women's
vote. Tony Earl, father of four daughters, won the election
and served as Wisconsin's governor from 1983 to 1987. In a
handwritten note dated August 2, 1982, he told Mandy,
"Joining NOW was one of the best steps I've taken. Thanks
again."[65]

Earl's appointment of women to the bench became one of
the most significant steps forward for Wisconsin women.

###

9. Money, Money, Who Controls the Money?

Chicken Littles have been predicting the end of the family throughout modern history. In the twentieth century alone, sky-is-falling fears paralleled every hint of change in the status of women. Fears escalated as the fifty-year battle for voting rights was achieved in 1920. Concern mounted again at the end of World War II as women showed a reluctance to retire gracefully from the workforce when returning servicemen were embraced by the nation's employers. In the late sixties as the women's rights movement gained attention, fears rose to a frenzy and continued escalating with every social change. Everything from juvenile delinquency to AIDS to the rising rate of divorce has been blamed on the women's movement. Among the few males who sought opportunities to clarify the issues, Sam Stellman did not hesitate to explode such myths.

"The family as an institution in American society is not ending," he told a suburban women's organization shortly after the 1972 Christmas holiday. "Look at the number of remarriages following divorce or widowhood."

But Sam distinguished between the family as an institution—which was enduring—and the family unit—whose forms were expanding. In addition to the traditional mother, father, and children, society was increasingly being made up of single parent families, couples as well as singles adopting children, foster care families, and those who decide not to have children. Sam's all-encompassing definition embraced households in which same-sex couples as well as opposite-sex couples established family units, whether or not their commitments were recognized under law.

"If you don't want to accept that these are families," he told the suburban women's group, "then you're out of the ballgame, for this is the situation today."[66]

Sam believed the strength of the family and its ability to meet the needs of its members were more important than its structure.

He also believed the women's movement *was* having an impact on changes in the family, but he never lost his conviction that this impact was positive. He credits Mandy—and her clients—with raising his consciousness and making him speak out for the rights of women.

"Marriage isn't what it used to be," he would say. "And that's a good thing!"

He observed that the so-called Ozzie and Harriet marriages of the fifties and sixties kept women and children economically dependent upon the husband and father, who controlled decisions for the whole family by virtue of controlling all the finances. That sort of control was not what Sam meant when he talked about strong families.

Strength, as he defined it, came from all family members respecting each other equally. His own family had been headed by a widow from the time he was four, yet he never doubted that he was, like Mandy, the product of a strong family.

Sam often said that respect for the family must go beyond lip service. It must be reflected by the actions of all of society's institutions, because such institutions can perpetuate discriminatory conditions that go beyond the ability of individual families to overcome them. Such conditions might result from the biases of certain elected officials in drafting family laws and of certain judges in interpreting them.

As for divorce, when it came to that, Sam was adamant: *Society has a responsibility to ensure the right to dependable child support, to adequate maintenance or alimony when needed, and to realistic job training if a former stay-at-home mother lacks marketable skills.*

He insisted that society also has a responsibility to eliminate barriers to jobs that pay decent wages, that provide a measure of job security, and that enable people to perform meaningful work so they can maintain their self-respect and dignity. Additionally, he and Mandy often called for affordable quality child care for working parents.

To those who say that keeping barriers to divorce in place keeps families together, Sam always replied: "That's foolishness. People do what they want in spite of the law. Believe it or not, money, not sex, is the biggest cause of divorce."

Decisions about money—how to spend it, who would earn it, who would control it—were the basic issues.

The need to inform women about their rights to credit increased when the Equal Credit Opportunity Act passed Congress in 1974.[67]

The largest audience the Stellmans drew was made up of

"suddenly single" women desperate to learn their rights following divorce or the death of a spouse. They crowded into an auditorium at UW-Milwaukee one night in 1974 for a discussion entitled "Suddenly Single."

"The cultural lag hasn't caught up with the fact that we are really here," Mandy told the women, most of whom did not realize that until recently the law had considered them the property of men. "Our banks, lending institutions, and employers haven't quite accepted the fact that the law has changed, and many are acting as if the law doesn't exist. Businesses are hoping the women's movement will go away, but it won't."

Women faced discrimination in three areas, she said: insurance, employment, and housing. "If you're a single woman and want to buy a house, they think you're going to run a house of ill repute."

The life of a married woman, Mandy told the women, was in many ways like that of a teenager. The wife had to "wheedle, manipulate, and pout for money from her husband, even to run the household." Mandy's listeners nodded, and some hung their heads.

Knowing that some of her own female clients had never paid a bill or handled a checkbook, she told her audience: "If you are single, for heaven's sake go out and establish credit *immediately*. Borrow money from a friend if necessary to establish collateral for a credit account, then pay the money back. Remember," she added, "you're having to be sixteen again—you're manipulating those crummy banks. *Maybe* your savings account plus your job will get you credit. A year or so ago you wouldn't have stood a chance."

The dumbest thing for a widow to do, Mandy advised, was to tear up the credit cards in her husband's name. A widow should continue to pay the bills for about three years, then inform the company that it was she who had been paying and demand credit. A divorcee could use the same technique with utility bills, Mandy pointed out.

Pay your bills, and in three years march in and say, "Now look, I've been divorced, or widowed, for three years. I've been paying the damn bill, and I demand that you change it to my name. Don't make trouble for me because my lawyer says _____."

If denied credit, she added, threaten to sue. "Yell and scream bloody murder."

Mandy often handled cases for female clients who had been denied credit or who had suffered some form of gender-based economic discrimination. At times she had to do battle for herself.

She and Sam were shopping at Lord & Taylor's in Northbrook, Illinois. "If you take out a credit card with us you can get ten percent off," said the clerk as she prepared to ring up a purchase.

Mandy began to fill out the credit application and paused at one line. "I'm not putting down my Social Security number," she told the clerk. "Under the law I don't have to do that."

"I'm sorry," the clerk said. "If you don't you can't get a credit card."

Mandy repeated that she did not have to provide that information under the law. "Besides," she added, "I am a lawyer and I deal with this subject many times in my practice."

"No," said the clerk, "you are wrong. My brother is a lawyer, and I know you have to fill in your Social Security number."

Exasperated, Mandy asked, "If your brother were a brain surgeon, would you be able to operate on your customers?"

A letter from Mandy produced two apologies from the store's general manager—one by phone and another by mail. It also produced the ten percent discount and an assurance that the staff would be made aware of the correct procedure so a similar mistake would not occur again.[68]

###

Leslie Stellman, the younger son, and Judy Cohen were getting married, so Mandy went shopping for a dress to wear to the August wedding. On finding a lovely pale green chiffon with a scattering of small rhinestones, she arranged to have the dress delivered. First it had to be altered. Gesturing to her five-foot stature, she laughed. "What long dress is going to fit me?"

Invited to open a charge account by the salesclerk, Mandy duly filled out the application in her own name. The credit card arrived before the dress. It bore the name Samuel D. Stellman. So Mandy cut up the card and mailed it back to the store with a letter.

"I want you to know," she wrote, "that Samuel Stellman didn't buy the gown, and he doesn't plan to wear it to the wedding. Pale green chiffon doesn't look good on my husband; he plans on wearing a blue suit."[69]

She assured the store that they would not get paid if they continued to bill Sam, and since the store evidently wanted her husband's business and not hers, she was canceling the order for the dress.

Her letter drew an immediate response. The store manager called with apologies and explained that the store always issued credit cards in the husband's name.

"If you want my business, you won't do that again when a woman applies for a card in her own name," said Mandy.

The manager agreed to change the store policy. A new card in Mandy's name arrived in two days, and she wore the pale green chiffon dress with rhinestones to the wedding. She looked stunning.

###

A number of the financial seminars Mandy presented with Sam included special advice for parents and grandparents. Parents either go overboard for their children, the Stellmans observed, or become unnecessarily tightfisted. If the latter, the children tend to go to the grandparents for money, and the grandparents indulge them, flattered to be asked.

Because people seldom talked about these family secrets in the seventies, the Stellmans' outspokenness caught the attention of Jane Bryant Quinn, well-known financial advisor. She devoted one of her nationally syndicated columns to reprinting the practical tips that Mandy and Sam Stellman shared in their joint workshops and lectures. In August 1979, newspapers coast to coast carried the Stellmans' views on financial relationships between parents and their adult children.

Don't lend money to adult children unless you can afford to not see that money again, they advised. Although the child may very well pay it back, the parent has to be prepared to lose it. "Even an honest child may fall on hard times—divorce or job loss—that may make repayment practically impossible," the Stellmans noted. "When you do lend, get the protection of a signed promise to repay."

Oral promises are the hardest to enforce, either in or out of court. "If you lend money to help buy a home, consider putting yourself down as co-owner," they recommended. This method would afford some protection to a parent in case of a divorce in which one spouse, the child, gives the house to the other spouse, the in-law.

Some children continue to need the loan for a second and even a third home, and they justify their acquisitiveness by saying, "Don't worry, Ma, you can always live with us."

But this, cautioned the Stellmans, may not be the form of loan repayment the parent wants.

With their own sons married and living on the East Coast, Sam and Mandy knew it could be healthy for parents to live at a distance from their grown children.

In one of Mandy's conversations with Leslie, who also became an attorney, he mentioned some legal work he was doing *pro bono* for a Jewish retirement home. His mother urged him to do a good job because she and his father might be living there some day.

When Les protested Mandy's view of the future, she responded, laughing, "Well, I'm not going to live with you, kid."

Added Mandy, "We adore our sons. But we love it that they live far away in Brooklyn and in Baltimore."

Money—who controls it, who divides it, who awards it?

In a divorce case, there are no public defenders as in a criminal case. Whatever the judge decides, the couple lives with, unless one of them wants to spend more money on appeals.

Sara D____, a client of Mandy's in the late seventies, was in no position to appeal an unfavorable ruling. Although she and her three small children had a roof over their heads, only a small welfare check met all their other needs.

Sara's back tensed as the judge cleared his throat and pronounced his decision. "And considering the plaintiff's argument that his continuing to pay the mortgage on the house would be a financial hardship for him," the judge announced, "the court hereby orders the home be sold."

Sold! The woman was as stunned as if someone had punched her in the stomach.

"Your Honor," Mandy began, standing to address the judge, "if that happens, my client and her children will have nowhere to live. With what she can afford on her monthly welfare payment, she'd never find a decent apartment that accepts children."

The judge removed his reading glasses and glared at Mandy and Sara. "Then I suggest," he said, drawing out the words with icy precision, "that instead of sitting at home all day watching soap operas, she ought to get herself a job."

Mandy was outraged. She had seen so many divorce settlements that had been equally unjust, especially when judges blithely advised lifelong homemakers raising their children to "go out and get a job." But she could do nothing.

"It's a horrible decision!" fumed Mandy at supper with Sam that evening. "Cruel, totally cruel. It's as if what these women had been doing for the past thirty years—taking responsibility for the home, raising the children, sometimes even 'raising' a husband who acts like a child—is worth *nothing.*" Mandy grew even more agitated. "Any money the couple saved was because she *did* stay home, kept a careful budget, and supported her husband as he moved up in *his* career. A lot of judges won't take any of that into consideration."

Seething, she added, "It's as if they're saying, 'Well, lady, if you want this divorce, we're gonna give it to you. You're really gonna pay for it.'"

###

Even when money caused no problem during a marriage, it nearly always became one for the woman in a divorce. Isabel V_____ was represented by Mandy in a child support action in which the husband, who worked for his brother, made good money. But every time Mandy helped Isabel get a court order for child support, the husband's brother would lay him off. He should have been held in contempt, but he wasn't. Mandy never found a judge who would hold a husband in contempt for lying.

Linda M___'s husband had been vice president of a high-tech company, and the couple owned a comfortable house in the suburbs. But he lost his job, and according to court records did not work regularly after that. When the couple separated in 1979, the former executive was ordered to make child-support payments of $800 a month. Over time he fell behind by some $1,100. Although Linda believed in staying home with her boys, ages six and eight at the time of the divorce, she had to get a job. Even so, she couldn't keep up with the bills, and the second mortgage on the house demanded much more than the low wages her job paid.

All that a judge could do when an executive remained unemployed was to order the husband to pay something from his unemployment insurance.[70]

With her debts mounting, Linda lost the house in a sheriff's sale. She felt the legal system had failed her. And there was little Mandy could do for her client.

###

By the early eighties, Mandy was finding cases of this kind affecting her whole outlook on the law. "I used to be able to go home from my office and enjoy my home and family," she told the media after one of her clients experienced a particularly unfair divorce settlement. "Now I am upset. I am not enjoying my practice the way I used to."[71]

In some of her divorce cases, however, she felt she had been able to make some positive impact on the lives of her clients, even though the financial settlements for the women were usually terrible.

I have dealt with people, mostly women, who were at the point where they were depressed, even suicidal, and I have been able to help them not only stop thinking about the end of the world, but think forward, in a positive direction. They can go back at age forty and get a high school diploma, or change careers. It can be done—though they may not be able to see that right away.

When the outcome of a case upset her, or a judge's unfair, punitive decision outraged her, Mandy knew that Sam shared her feelings. She would say, "Society has been able to place a dollar value on everything from aircraft carriers to paper clips. It's time to place a value on the services performed by mothers and wives!"

Sam would agree. "There should be a definite economic value placed on women's services. They have paid their dues and should be compensated."

Over the years, the Stellmans came to know several fair-minded judges who realized that a woman needed time to be reeducated or to sharpen her skills to compete in the employment market. But not all judges understood that buying this time took money.[72]

In cases in which the husband made $100,000 a year but her client had just gotten a job as a nurse's aide, Mandy was known to say to the opposing attorney, "Wonderful. Trade jobs—she'll be *happy* to give him two hundred dollars a week."

Whenever she felt opposing counsel had uttered a sexist remark about a client she was representing, she would turn to the judge and say, "Your honor, I think that's the most sexist comment I've heard in a long time, and I think that attorney ought to apologize to my client."

Mandy's outspokenness often caused the opposing attorney to back off a little.

###

As divorce became more widespread, Mandy was deluged with cases. It became apparent that many women were not only suffering from the effect of unfair divorce laws, but also experiencing unfair economic and workplace practices.

Sam and Mandy each decided, as they put it, "to jump into the issue with both feet." Mandy became more involved through the cases she worked on, and Sam took it on as a criminal justice issue. Their variation of the popular sentiment, "Don't get mad, get even," became, "Get mad, then get even"—through legal recourse.

The Stellman strategy involved educating people in how to help themselves when the system was not working for them. But Sam and Mandy went far beyond education, as they did with many of the issues they took on. Each time they stood in front of an audience or gave an interview, they maximized the opportunity to catalyze others to take action and make their own changes in the system.

In this way their personal convictions became transformed into a force capable of bringing about larger change—especially in the legal system. With such methods the Stellmans were able to see themselves as two small people making big changes.

###

One fact became obvious to Sam from the divorce cases Mandy handled: "So many of these women had no future. They'd all been homemakers and had never entered the workplace." He wondered where they were going to go. If there hadn't been that much money in the family to begin with, any alimony they got—or maintenance as it was called—didn't amount to much.

Mandy said, "Alimony was often a big joke. It may have been ordered, but the woman rarely received it."

Such abuses led her to help formulate Wisconsin's divorce

reform bill, which recognized that women had a right to half the marital assets in a divorce. Popularly known as no-fault divorce, the bill also sought to eliminate the requirement that one spouse had to blame the other for the break-up of the marriage.

Sam testified on behalf of the bill before the state legislature, identifying himself as someone who did research in the marriage and family field and provided training to marriage counselors in methods for dealing with clients who were divorcing. He then attacked the testimony given by opponents of divorce reform:

> *Many people seem to take special pleasure in seeing that when couples are miserable in a marriage, they be forced to stay together no matter what. I assure you I have yet to meet a divorced couple who were sorry they'd gotten divorced. Their greatest difficulty had been trying to convince the court that their spouse was a rotten person and therefore responsible for the break-up of the marriage, as the law demanded. As you might suspect, a lot of the 'reasons' were fabricated.*
>
> *I don't think the law intended that people in divorce cases lie during their testimony. And can you imagine their relationship after the divorce when these nasty statements were made in the courtroom?*

Not long after, Wisconsin's no-fault divorce reform legislation passed with little opposition. It went into effect in 1978—the same year Congress voted to extend the deadline for ratification of the Equal Rights Amendment.

The Stellmans' attitude toward divorce differed considerably from the prevailing sentiment in the sixties and seventies. "No matter how many times you hear that the stigma attached to divorce has been reduced," Sam said in 1973, "don't believe it. Divorce is still not accepted and won't be for years."

Even when the social climate gradually became more tolerant, the Stellmans maintained a philosophy more progressive than most people, including most professionals in the field of marriage counseling.

[Counselors] have been told that you try to hold the marriage together no matter what. We believe totally contrary to that. Once the marriage is gone, it's gone. Counselors must stop working on the premise that the marriage has to be saved. Divorce is not a bad thing. It's one of the best things to happen in this country in terms of people's mental health.

People should not have to live in unhappy marriages. Divorce may be a painful experience, but it's better to get out than to live in a situation where there is little hope of enjoyment. If a couple has to 'work hard' to make a marriage work, chances are that the marriage isn't going to work at all. Divorce should be looked upon as a new life beginning for both parties.

To ease the transition to that new life, the Stellmans realized that divorcing couples needed help in many parts of their lives—financial, social, and personal. "Solutions don't come at the wave of a magic wand," Sam said. "While divorce is a solution to an unpleasant situation, it poses some dilemmas of its own."

Sam gave Mandy credit for suggesting a way to help the hurting men and women she saw in her legal practice. He contributed by mobilizing the resources at his disposal, and together they created numerous outreach courses offering practical skills to people dealing with issues of single parenting and other post-divorce realities. In the mid-seventies, these classes and support groups were ahead of their time.

They took their well-attended "Suddenly Single" presentation to Madison in June 1974, shortly after its debut in Milwaukee, and led a session each of three days during College Week for Women.[73]

###

Despite their emphasis on women's needs, the Stellmans offered their first courses in divorce for men. Sam pioneered this idea despite the skepticism of his colleagues, who thought men would never go for it. "But we had a hundred calls when the course was announced, and once it started, we had inquiries from all over the country."

Called "Successful Divorce for Men," the classes they began in 1974 were the first group counseling effort in the nation aimed solely at the divorced man.

Those who gathered for the initial session ranged in age from their early twenties to their mid-sixties. Most were educated and outwardly successful. Several were doctors and lawyers. Yet Sam described the men to a fellow professor the next day as "the most lost people you ever saw. If you've been married for fifteen years and now it's over, where do you go from here?"[74]

When one of Sam's discussion leaders, a well-known psychiatrist, began by asking how many men had contemplated suicide, "Mandy and I were shocked to see every hand in the room shoot up." When they were asked how many had thought about suicide recently, half the hands stayed up.

Mandy and another lawyer were on hand to discuss legal problems, such as child custody, support payments, and visitation rights. Those attending the first class were so intent on what they were learning they refused Sam's offer of a coffee break.

The Stellmans found that the typical divorced man lived alone in one room. "They come home from work and don't know what to do next," said Sam. "When we asked them who their best friend was, almost all of them said it was their former wife. This means they don't have an emotional support system."

The Stellmans faced a daunting task in convincing the men who enrolled in the course that divorce could resemble the course description; that it had "the potential for being a dynamic and creative step toward a future of personal satisfaction and fulfillment." To foster that potential, the Stellmans led the men in discussing what to expect and how to cope with the emotional trauma.

Soon an announcement went out for a new course called "Successful Divorce for Women," starting "at the request of a great number of women following the success of the nationally acclaimed course 'Successful Divorce for Men.'"

Fees for both the men's and women's courses were reasonable—ten dollars or fifteen dollars for three or four sessions lasting several hours apiece. The Stellmans led both courses.

Mandy and Sam not only saw the need for such classes before anyone else, they also saw them in the context of the entire community of changing social conditions. Because Sam never created a program simply for the purpose of having a program to offer, these classes represented another dimension of the Stellmans' multipronged effort to address issues they recognized as significantly interrelated: divorce, women's low economic status, discrimination in employment and credit, counterproductive attitudes about the roles of men and women, and the need for economic counseling.

The Stellmans were not newcomers to issues facing single people. Having initiated the nation's first Jewish single parent group in Columbus, Ohio, in the fifties, they started a similar group in Milwaukee in 1976 to facilitate discussion of the problems of raising children alone.

The following year the Milwaukee section of the National Council of Jewish Women sponsored a free series of discussions, announcing that "nationally known family experts, the Stellmans, [would] act as group leaders."

Wisconsin law at the time required everyone filing for divorce to participate in at least one session of counseling to determine what the couple really wanted, divorce or reconciliation. The Stellmans already knew that reconciliation, which rarely occurred, was not the big issue to surface during such counseling of women. The big issue was what each woman saw as her future after the divorce.

While the seventies saw a rise in the divorce rate, this was a period in American family life in which most married women had been exclusively homemakers. Most were untrained and inexperienced in the work force, so they were at a great disadvantage after divorce. To educate them about the various educational and social offerings available to them, Sam next began organizing group sessions on planning for a future in the workplace. Mandy dubbed these programs "Life Coping."

According to the Life Coping slogan, the program aimed to assist the divorced woman "from the courthouse to a career." About thirty to forty women, mostly middle class, attended the monthly sessions.

Mandy explained the law, and Sam brought in social workers from the court who talked about personal issues and gave the women advice and direction for their economic futures. Educators and employment experts proposed ways that women could move into the marketplace no matter what level of work skills they possessed.

Sam estimated that about eighty percent of the participants took advantage of the educational opportunities they heard about through Life Coping. They became aware of psychological and job aptitude testing, literacy classes, placement services for skilled and unskilled workers, and financial aid from scholarships and loans.

After spearheading this course for three years, Sam got the Milwaukee Area Technical College (MATC) to take it over. The Stellmans continued to present it on a *pro bono* basis, and were still doing so through the spring of 1979 at four locations of MATC.

###

It took a few more years before enough public awareness of the economic issues facing suddenly single women brought legislative action. After intensive lobbying by women's groups, in 1978 the Wisconsin legislature recognized the job training needs of women who found themselves out of a job as a homemaker as a result of divorce or death of a husband.

Shortly after, despite heavy opposition from conservative groups such as Phyllis Schlafly's Eagle Forum, $5 million was designated nationally for comprehensive training programs for displaced homemakers.

###

The Stellmans seemed an odd couple to be taking a positive view of divorce, having been happily married more than thirty years at the time they entered the field.

Mandy pointed out that the Jewish religion allowed for divorce. "I don't see any problem with these values. If you don't live to your full potential you have every right to a change." Her slogan was: "You don't have to cope with crap."

Whenever the Stellmans' divorce-related programs were

In June 1943, Sam was the first and only male among sixteen women to graduate with a degree in physical and health education from Toronto University. (Page 82)

As soon as Sam received his draft notice, the couple moved their wedding date up a month to July 11, 1943 — quicker than a shotgun wedding. (Page 86)

With an army buddy (right), Sam visited London during his 1945 overseas tour of duty with the Canadian army. (Page 88)

"Green Cabs" sponsored one of many teams that Sam coached in the 1950s as director of physical education for the Columbus (Ohio) Jewish Community Center. (Page 94)

Mandy (foreground) clowning around with a hockey teammate made up for Purim, a Jewish celebration of freedom. Both Stellmans were very talented in many sports.

For thirteen years, Mandy directed women's physical education at Columbus (Ohio) Jewish Community Center. (Page 97)

According to the expectant father stationed in Europe, Steven Dale was born on V-E Day, 1945. A second son, Leslie Robert, completed the family in 1951. (Pages 88, 97)

Mandy joined Dr. King's 1963 March on Washington for racial equality despite the criticism of some friends and acquaintances. (Page 102)

Sam leading a session at the Federation of Jewish Women's Organizations Conference of Women, March 1976, in Toronto, at which he and Mandy also were keynote speakers. (Page 185)

Videotaping training for police in how to handle developmentally disabled offenders. L-R: Kim Baugrud; Lt. Grant Furman, Racine County Sheriff's Department; Sam; Judge John Ahlgrim; John Lindars, Racine Police; Susan Perry, director, Developmental Disabilities Information Service; Ron Spitz, Southern Wisconsin Center for the Developmentally Disabled. (Page 277) (Photo by Media Services, UW-Parkside).

Handing off the MRO program to the governor for use in police training throughout Wisconsin, 1984. L-R: Sam, Gov. Tony Earl, Chancellor Patrick Boyle, Kim Baugrud. (Page 277)

Jeannetta Robinson (left), founder and executive director of the Youth Development Commission, talking with Mandy at an event Oct. 30, 1997. (Page 304) (Photo by Cy White, Photo Action USA. Used by Permission.)

Edmund G. "Jerry" Brown, governor of California 1975-1983, stayed at the Stellman home during his 1980 campaign for the presidency.

Visitors to Mandy's law office could not miss the women of accomplishment pictured on her wall, including Golda Meir and Betty Friedan. (Photo by Dan Johnson, reprinted from *Marquette Magazine,* spring 1993. Used by permission of Marquette University)

A familiar sight around town was this business card depicting Attorney Stellman sitting among Lincoln's cabinet. (Pages 144, and 334 note #48)

announced in the newspaper, they received phone calls from a few members of the clergy who inferred from the titles of these programs that the Stellmans were promoting divorce.

On the contrary, said Sam. "I contend that for a long time the ministry was promoting bad marriages. Of *course* we weren't promoting divorce. Our view was, 'You're getting divorced. That's a sure thing. Now what?'"

Mandy added, "We moved from a save-the-marriage posture to viewing divorce as a positive thing. You have your whole life ahead of you to enjoy." For the first time, many professionals were hearing that it's not necessarily better to hold a marriage together.

"We firmly believe in marriage and the fact that marriages should last as long as they can," Sam often said. "However, we take a strong position that if with effort, thinking, maybe counseling, two people still fight all the time and are miserable, they should not stay married. Women who may have been dependent can have a new, good life."[75]

In early 1973, the Stellmans began a series of training sessions for professional counselors and social workers. They traveled throughout Wisconsin presenting their three-session program on the finer points of divorce counseling. In time, more than five hundred professionals in ten cities around the state participated in their innovative "Divorce Counseling." It was the first such course presented in the Midwest for professional counselors, and, as far as Sam could learn, the first in the country.[76]

"Our purpose was not to inflame emotions but to offer practical advice and motivation for those beginning life on their own," Sam explained. He and Mandy recognized that divorce was a volatile topic. That's why he enlisted a Catholic priest, Father Labi of Racine, to help him plan the course. Eventually, the priest gave it his stamp of approval.

But not all members of the clergy were so responsive.

###

In one Wisconsin city, the audience consisted entirely of ministers, several of whom came up to Mandy during a coffee break to say how much they were getting out of the evening. The last minister waiting to speak to her handed her the notes he had been writing during her talk. He looked unhappy.

"You're all wrong, Mrs. Stellman," he said. "The husband is the head of the household. I've made a few notes. Perhaps they will help you."

Politely, Mandy took the pages and said, "Thank you. I appreciate it." As the minister turned away she scanned the handwriting, and the words leapt out at her:

"Man is made from dust in the image of God, and woman from man's rib.... Woman is temptress and instigator of disobedience.... Women are inferior and unclean...."

There was more. One cited Leviticus chapter and verse; another made reference to Paul's instruction to women, in the New Testament, to cover their heads, be silent in worship, and obey their husbands. Yet another referred to women as property, as chattel.

Mandy's reaction of the moment was to grit her teeth.

Later, the minister complained that the class wasn't at all what he expected. Sam offered to return the man's money.

The dean, on learning of Sam's method for dealing with the situation, remarked, "What a simple solution. The university would have had a committee meeting."

###

When J. Lester Johnson took office in 1972 as the family court commissioner of Racine County, he found he had neither the time nor the training to counsel divorcing couples as required by law. Neither were the local social service agencies equipped to handle the increasing volume. Racine County, which lies just south of Milwaukee County, recorded 231 divorces from January to April in 1972, but for the same quarter one year later the number was 309—a one-third increase.

Few families had the resources to seek private counseling. Black families found most marriage counseling beyond their economic ability, as well as insufficiently tailored to their environment and situations.

Johnson called Sam. "I've been told by judges and others here that you are the person to solve a major problem I have."

The need for some kind of counseling to supplement professional help was evident, and Sam knew it would take more than a three-session "Divorce Counseling" series to deal with the phenomenon Commissioner Johnson described. Sam suggested a meeting with the Racine County Bar Association and the Pastors Association. From that meeting came the idea for a corps of volunteer counselors made up of professionals: psychologists, clergy, attorneys, and social workers. Already well-trained in their professions, these volunteers were to receive specialized graduate level training, which Sam developed for the purpose. The training course spanned seven two-and-a-half-hour sessions

When Racine County sounded the call, Sam expected twenty people to enroll in the new course. To his surprise, seventy-two professionals turned out; sixty-eight completed the course. They went on to serve as advisors for the county, taking some of the burden off the family court commissioner.[77]

"We trained the volunteer counselors to recognize cases where a marriage no longer existed. And we trained them in how they could help couples prepare for divorce. First," Sam said, "the husband and wife had to reduce the hostility between them. Next, they had to realize that money would continue to play a crucial role in their relationship. There is never enough. Then they had to realize that they had to begin leading independent lives—immediately."

The program Sam started did not simply set up a referral service so divorcing couples could find counselors. Sam believed that traditional referral by itself was "the enemy of the client, because too many times the client gets lost between the cracks." In this program, couples seeking help could exercise some choice, selecting counselors they wanted by name or by religious affiliation—though it was made clear to the counselors that religion was not part of the program. Significantly, area attorneys encouraged their clients to participate.

The program expanded and evolved into the Family Life Center, a place that people experiencing the breaking up of a marriage could go for help in putting their lives back together. Programming included job training for women who had never before worked outside the home. The state's local job services department helped place them in paying jobs.

The results went beyond the individuals who were helped: the entire community was enriched by the ongoing economic benefits.

Unexpectedly, the program improved the working relationships among clergy, counselors, and lawyers. This, too, benefited the entire community.

Shortly after the center became established, Sam helped the Racine family court commissioner expand it to include walk-in premarital, marital, divorce, and post-divorce counseling, all provided by trained volunteers. The program kept growing, with additional specialized courses developed under Sam's supervision to help families with successful step-parenting and second marriages and to help single parent families with their growing teenagers.

As the social stigma of divorce began declining with the growth in the number of divorced couples, so too did the stigma of "living in sin." By 1977, the number of unmarried cohabiting couples was estimated at between 1.5 million and 5 million—and growing.[78]

Observers who were not busy denouncing such living arrangements were touting it as a preventive for divorce.

However, as Sam pointed out, "It is now known that the divorce rate is just as high for couples who lived together before marriage as it is for all other couples." The Stellmans advised against unmarried couples cohabiting, but not because of any moral objection. On the contrary, they advised women who wanted such arrangements to spend nights or weekends with their boyfriends while still keeping their own living quarters. The Stellmans' opposition came from knowing the legal complications that could arise, particularly if the couple had children, and they knew that the partner with the most to lose from such an arrangement was the woman. So whenever possible, the Stellmans spoke out on the risks versus the benefits in starting a household without marriage.

Cohabitation captured the nation's attention in May 1979 when a California judge ordered actor Lee Marvin to pay $104,000 to the woman he had lived with six years. Although the sum represented a small part of the actor's worth, it marked the first time a U.S. court of law had recognized *any* financial claim on a relationship outside the bonds of matrimony.

The media dubbed the award "palimony." Mandy called the settlement "peanuts."

In Wisconsin when the Marvin decision hit the news, the Stellmans were immediately sought out for their opinions. Sam decided to put together a panel of professionals to discuss the impact on the American family of the unprecedented legal ruling. More than thirty educators and attorneys assembled. No consensus on the issues emerged, but panelist Mandy Stellman made an important observation: "The point is, if the woman had been married to Lee Marvin, I am not so sure she would have been any better off."

The fact was, under the laws of most states, Wisconsin included, even a married woman had no rights to property or income acquired by her husband. As many women had already discovered, only if the marriage was *ending* would the courts step in and take a role in settling a family's financial disagreements. *During* the marriage, the courts refused to intervene.

The Wisconsin Governor's Commission on the Status of Women, under the leadership of Kathryn Clarenbach, had been collecting stories from married women since 1974, and mounting anecdotal evidence was exposing a number of hazards of choosing homemaking as a career. Thus, the question of property rights within a marriage was already an issue in the heart of the Midwest at the time of the 1979 "palimony" decision on the West Coast.

The Stellmans were part of the growing movement on behalf of marital property reform, as they had been with the state's divorce reform bill that became law in 1978. For both bills, Mandy and Sam were among a number of supporters who lobbied legislators, gave interviews to the media, accepted invitations to speak before all kinds of organizations, and testified at state hearings.

Opposition to property rights for married women was strong, and the Wisconsin Bar Association spent some $70,000 attempting to defeat it. Almost ten years in the drafting, the bill passed on its second round through the state legislature and went into effect in 1986.

The new Marital Property Act presumed that unless a couple established a different arrangement, their joint assets belonged to each partner fifty-fifty because each spouse made contributions to the marriage of equal value, whether or not both were earning money.

This legal presumption not only treated the divorcing woman's contributions fairly but also solved problems related to her ability to get credit and to will her property as she wished. It also reflected a new egalitarianism in the law, which most spouses thought their marriages already represented—and were shocked to learn did not.

"If we'd just left all the male judges and the all-male legislature to make the decisions," Mandy said, "it never would have happened. Why would they give up what they've got?"

Years after passage of the legislation for equal property rights in a marriage, controversy continued, but Mandy still felt it was a good law. "Sure, there may be some men who won't marry because of the law. I say, 'Good riddance.' Who wants him? What kind of husband would he make?"

Wisconsin's new law set a precedent. It became the model for other states, reinforcing Wisconsin's reputation as a progressive state.

Over the years Mandy came to feel that she had made some impact on a number of judges as a result of litigating hundreds of divorce cases in their courts. Her handling of one such case set a precedent in Wisconsin.

It involved a middle-aged couple. "She wanted to divorce him because he had been abusing her for years," recalled Mandy. "One day he took a wooden crucifix and hit her in the ear—isn't that ironic? It caused permanent damage."

In addition to filing this woman's divorce papers, Mandy filed a civil lawsuit over damage to the woman's ear. The simultaneous legal action was a first in Wisconsin.

"When the divorce was set for trial the husband admitted everything," said Mandy, "so we settled the civil lawsuit out of court. The woman ended up with a settlement for the battery, plus an equal share of his pension."

As Mandy's activism increased, so did her law practice. She developed a reputation for representing women in divorce, but at no time did she or Sam ignore the men—especially when issues threatened their need for fair treatment.

One of her male clients suffered from the same ailment affecting Mandy—asthma. The man's doctor told him he needed a smoke-free house or his asthma would become worse. But his wife smoked and wouldn't give it up.

"They got a divorce, of course," explained Mandy. "It wasn't that she wouldn't give up smoking. It was that she didn't respect him."

###

10. Above and Beyond the Job Description

Respect for others played a quiet but unmistakable role in shaping Sam and Mandy's values. They believed that respect for each other was the key to any successful marriage, and they were acutely aware of the fundamental disrespect toward women that discrimination represented. Just as society's outrageous practices led the Stellmans to take action to reform laws governing marital property, divorce, and credit, the outrageous acts of sex and age discrimination in employment motivated reactions that propelled them into the public arena even more dramatically.

"As recently as 1975," observed Mandy, "it was often routine for an employer to say, 'Sure, I pay a man more than a woman for the same job. He has a family to support; she is just working for pin money.'"

"False!" declared Sam. "More single-parent families are headed by women who need to work than there are intact families headed by men."

Nevertheless, the "pin money" myth continues to prevail today. The difference is that "employers are much more careful about discrimination today because we've got laws against this sort of thing," Mandy noted. "But not that long ago, many bosses weren't the least bit embarrassed to reveal such attitudes. In fact, if such men were called 'male chauvinist pigs,' some took it as a compliment."

Thus, Mandy brought lawsuits against major corporations and municipalities on behalf of her clients.

One case involved the Wisconsin Electric Power Company (WEPCO). Although employees who had vasectomies got time off from their jobs, employees who asked for maternity leave did not. In 1975 when one WEPCO employee was denied leave despite her obstetrician's advising her to take time off from work, the woman retained Mandy.

The company argued that its employees "voluntarily" joined the health insurance plan offered by Employers Mutual Benefit Association (EMBA), although EMBA's was the only health plan employees were offered. The power company claimed it had no ties to EMBA, arguing that the insurance carrier was a beneficial association and therefore not subject to federal Title VII prohibitions against sex discrimination.

"I had suspicions about the relationship of EMBA to WEPCO," Mandy said. "Was EMBA strictly an independent operation with no ties to WEPCO, as claimed? Something looked fishy to me."

So she spent hours doing her homework for a hearing before a state examiner. In a deposition prior to the hearing, she asked the director of EMBA to show her his paycheck. "That check and my client's check from Wisconsin Electric were signed by the same person." Mandy explained that a corporation sometimes "puts a veil on other corporate entities, such as a subsidiary, when Papa is really directing the traffic."

At the hearing, Mandy interrogated the director and succeeded in establishing that EMBA's offices occupied a floor in WEPCO's main building in downtown Milwaukee.

"Does EMBA pay rent for these offices?"

"No," the director had to admit.

Mandy's detective work paid off, and the examiner ruled in favor of Mandy's client. But WEPCO was not through arguing. It appealed, sending the case to a judge in Madison. Finally, in 1979, this judge also ruled in favor of Mandy's client and ordered the company to change its policy. In addition, because Mandy had shown that the corporation and the insurance entity were one and the same, the judge pronounced the words she had been hoping to hear.

"He said I had 'pierced the corporate veil.'"

The Milwaukee Chapter of NOW filed a number of lawsuits on behalf of women discriminated against in the workplace, and Mandy represented the chapter in many of these. In 1974, NOW brought a sex discrimination suit against Allis-Chalmers (A-C), at the time one of the largest employers in southeastern Wisconsin.

The complaint was filed on behalf of Doris Schermer, a translator who worked in four languages. A-C classified her as a secretary, which enabled it to pay her $5,000 a year less than it paid a man in her department performing the same work. Doris referred to it as a "corporate gang-bang."

The complaint pointed out manifest sex bias: the corporation's top eight hundred employees were men, only one female held a middle management position, and no woman held a policy-making position.

After Schermer filed her lawsuit, Mandy received nearly two hundred phone calls from other women who felt they, too, had been discriminated against in their jobs. Members of the NOW Task Force on Employment Discrimination, which Doris Schermer formed, interviewed the callers and screened out cases that were not provable. The women were told, "If you do file a complaint, you need to be psychologically tough enough to see it through. You may encounter petty harassment at work, unpleasant scenes, verbal attacks from other employees, or even the threat of physical attack." In fact, a man had followed Doris home and made a scene.

"I *never ever* did not believe the complainant," Mandy said. "But I always told a client, 'Not everything that's unfair is illegal. I don't think you'll win this and you'll spend a lot of time and emotion. You'll have to live with this.' Some of the cases we lost—I couldn't get enough proof. But most of the cases I took got settled eventually."

Everyone involved on the task force worked without pay, including Mandy. The Allis-Chalmers sex discrimination suit was the first of about 124 sex discrimination complaints filed against Milwaukee employers. Mandy brought more than one hundred of these suits altogether, and had some thirty sex discrimination cases in various stages at one time.

Not long after a settlement was reached in Doris Schermer's sex discrimination suit, another suit was brought against the same employer, Allis-Chalmers, this time for age discrimination. Mandy described what happened:

In 1974 they put a male employee on permanent layoff about a year before he would have been vested in his twenty-year pension. We checked and found they were taking back younger employees, so we got a court order allowing us to see all their personnel files. The files were voluminous. I recruited another lawyer to help me, and we went to the factory to see the files.

They wheeled out carts with boxes and boxes of computer printouts, hundreds of files. I'm sure their lawyers were laughing and saying, "We'll show Mandy. She wants files? We'll show her files. What's she going to do with all this?" I'm sure they thought that when I saw the boxes I'd say forget it.

But they didn't know Mandy.

We went through all the files. We wrote by hand the names of everyone born before a certain year so they'd be over age sixty by then. It took time. You drop everything in your office and you spend eight hours a day for two days just going through boxes of records and you're not getting paid. It had to be a fire in your head to do it. But we did it.

Mandy discovered a pattern.

The company had been laying off people, men and women, before they had twenty years of service. This meant their pensions wouldn't be vested, according to Allis-Chalmers' pension plan at the time. With that evidence, we went back to court. The company settled, and my client received his pension intact. It had taken three years.

As a result of this legal action, untold numbers of other employees were in a position to benefit as well—the true measure of an effective action.

###

Other corporations discriminated just as blatantly but were not so obstinate about changing their policies. In the early seventies, Kohl's, the state's largest supermarket chain,[79] had different pay scales for comparable positions of responsibility. For example, female department heads earned ten cents an hour more than their subordinates; males, $1.80

an hour more. Schermer asked management to review the situation, and changes in store policy grew out of a series of meetings she, Mandy, and other NOW task force members held with the store's lawyers and personnel director.

"I always prefer to negotiate rather than litigate when possible. Unfortunately, that wasn't too common in those days."

One tactic Mandy found effective was the task force's picking one or two local corporations at a time and calling up the personnel manager or the president.

"We'd say, 'We want to meet and talk about your affirmative action plan. If you don't have one, we'll help you get one. We don't want to sue you.'"

She added, "A lot of changes were made quietly."

Some job discrimination suits in the seventies required different strategies. The Stellmans were always ready to respond with whatever action it took.

Sears Roebuck, the national retailer, became the target of a campaign brought by NOW nationwide. Here is Mandy's explanation of the issue:

> Sears did not place women in sales positions in the "big ticket" departments where salespeople made big commissions. Men were selling TVs, refrigerators, stoves, and freezers; women were selling needles, thread, pantyhose, and children's socks. Salespeople were on a base salary plus a commission that depended on the dollar amount they sold. How many needles and spools of thread would you have to sell to match a big ticket item?
>
> The lawyers for Sears used the fact that many women worked part-time to explain why they weren't in higher-paying positions. They said, "Women don't want full-time jobs. They want to go home and take care of the kids and

make supper for their hubby. They love to come in on a
split shift from ten A.M. to noon and then come back in
the evening from six to ten." But I knew that nobody
likes split shifts. It kills your whole day. And the lawyers
didn't mention that these part-time positions didn't pro-
vide benefits like health care or maternity leave.

When Sears management would not agree to stop discriminatory practices, NOW's early strategy involved picketing a
high-profile store. Demonstrations took place in cities across
the nation, embarrassing management; in Milwaukee, members of the Milwaukee and Waukesha County chapters of
NOW, Sam and Mandy among them, picketed the main entrance to one of the area's busiest stores for several Saturdays.

Soon, the local personnel manager agreed to a meeting,
which led to several more meetings at which the activists
used the powers of persuasion and the subtle threat of a
lawsuit. Continued Mandy:

Sears didn't want us picketing and they didn't want to
be sued. Someone in another state was suing, but the
local Sears management didn't want it to happen in Wis-
consin. We didn't want litigation, either, if we could get
our demands met.

"Just put women in the departments selling big ticket
items," we insisted. Someone from Sears' headquarters
in Chicago, where NOW members had demonstrated at
the company's 1975 stockholders meeting, came to Mil-
waukee to meet with us in person. Eventually we worked
out a satisfactory solution, which meant that the Wis-
consin stores stopped their discriminatory practices sooner
than they would have otherwise.

Mandy was certain that the Wisconsin action made a difference in getting the largest retailer in the country to
change its employment policies nationwide.

At the time, Mandy participated in a panel discussion sponsored by NOW and held at the Downtown YWCA. She won the biggest burst of applause of the night when she said, "We will know we have equal rights when we have an incompetent woman as president and incompetent women as senators...but today we have to be superstars."[80]

Sam often said every woman who is a member of the police department in Milwaukee owes her job to Mandy.

Being a female police officer for the City of Milwaukee was not the same in the early seventies as it is today. Women were not called police officers but police*women*, and they were paid substantially less than police*men*. Unlike the male officers, policewomen were not allowed to carry guns. In addition, they received fewer benefits, were not eligible for promotion, and could not work overtime for additional pay. If a policewoman became pregnant, her options boiled down to resigning or being fired.

Yet these women were graduates of police academies where they had received the same training as their male counterparts.

An article in the *Milwaukee Sentinel* noted in 1974 that of the city's approximately 2,230 police officers and aides, only 58 were black and 16 were women (seven-tenths of one percent). Of approximately 1,120 fire fighters, only six were black and three were Latino. None were women.[81]

Such discrimination was common throughout the nation. At the same time, the federal government had affirmative action programs in place representing an attempt to end such unfair job situations for women and minorities.

Mandy described the situation:

The federal government was telling police departments all over the nation, "You have to start taking in minori-

*ties and women." So city police departments would pub-
lish ads saying how women could come in and take the
qualifying tests.*

*The women were thrilled, of course. They went to the Y
to practice. All the women were in good shape, because
this job was something they wanted. Several were body
builders who pumped iron or played baseball.*

*A higher percentage of women passed the written test
than the men. Then it came time to take the physical
agility test, which the men didn't even have to think
about because most would be hired anyway. The women
took the test—and not one got a passing score. That's
when they called me.*

*I invited them to meet with me in my office one evening
after work hours so we wouldn't be interrupted by phone
calls. Some twelve women crowded into my office, which
was so small they had to sit on the floor.*

*The women told me about the test, how it was deliber-
ately set up so no one in the world could pass it. And
there were no standards. It's not like arithmetic where
two plus two has to equal four. It was subjective, and
they all flunked.*

Mandy recognized that the police department was obey-
ing the letter of the law in letting women apply, but "they
were testing these candidates and then saying, 'Well, they
don't fit.' The discrimination was outrageous!"

So Mandy got the Milwaukee chapter of NOW to join the
women in filing a complaint with the U.S. Equal Employment Opportunity Commission (EEOC) against the City of
Milwaukee Fire and Police Commission. They also filed a
class action suit with the equal rights division of the Wisconsin Department of Industry, Labor, and Human Relations
(DILHR) on behalf of all women in similar situations.

The case attracted national attention. The U.S. Justice

Department joined Mandy's EEOC complaint and sent two lawyers to Milwaukee from Washington. Another action against the Fire and Police Commission had been filed by Milwaukee attorney Lloyd Barbee on behalf of minorities, so the federal judge consolidated Mandy's case and Lloyd Barbee's, and the Justice Department then joined as plaintiff.

"This was a *big* case," recalled Mandy. "We started with discovery, but it was like pulling teeth to get the information. Chief Harold Breier wouldn't give it to us, so we had to go to Judge Reynolds, who would order Breier to give it to us."[82]

The federal judge, John W. Reynolds, chastised the city's handling of the lawsuit. "You've been fooling around...with a lot of dilatory tactics," he said. This was in March 1975.

Breier was not a cooperative witness. Judge Reynolds had to warn him several times that he was to cooperate. Even when asked to state his name, Breier would turn to the city attorney and ask if he had to answer the questions of the opposing attorneys.

When the FBI entered the picture to investigate employment practices in the police department, they found that Chief Breier had a tight gag rule; police department employees could be fired if they talked to the public without the Chief's permission.

The city attorney tried to block a subpoena for the department's employment records. It came as somewhat of a shock to the city when Judge Reynolds ruled that Breier's gag rule "improperly and illegally" interfered with the government's accumulating facts needed to determine whether discrimination existed in hiring. The FBI had contacted some thirty employees, but only three would consent to interviews; the others would not talk to the FBI for fear of reprisal. A member of the Justice Department investigating the case said that the gag rule "held employees in serf-dom."

Motions filed by Mandy demanded that the police and fire departments create a legitimate, replicable, objective physical agility test. Part of the suit also asked that female matrons receive pay equal to that of male jailers in the city jail.

Mandy described the situation affecting the matrons:

These were policewomen, but their job title was matron, and they got paid less than the men who took care of the city jail. They did everything that the males on the other side of the wall did. Plus they had to make sandwiches, coffee, and clean up the kitchen after everyone else. After all, they're "girls."

I remember the argument we got from the assistant city attorney. He was trying to prove that women working in the jail didn't have equal responsibilities to the men. He said, "Well, what if a big, buxom woman inmate got out of hand in the jail? How could a female matron handle her?" We all started to laugh, because he used such a stupid example. You'd think that even in the seventies he'd know better!

After two and a half years of court appearances, briefs, and depositions, Judge Reynolds ordered that twenty percent of all new vacancies had to be filled by women and minorities, and he established deadlines for compliance. But that wasn't the end of the work. To ensure ongoing compliance with the law, a monitoring system had to be put in place. Judge Reynolds ordered the city to send quarterly reports to Mandy, Lloyd Barbee, and the Justice Department. These confidential reports were to indicate the number of applicants by sex and race for positions in the police department, the number who failed the written and physical tests, the number appointed.

Mandy reviewed these quarterly reports for at least six years. She said:

> From time to time we'd get requests to bypass the court order. But the Justice Department and Lloyd Barbee and I would say, no way! Then they'd file a motion giving reasons, like: "There are six vacancies we want to fill right away but we're having a difficult time finding enough minorities. So can we fill them with white men?" And we'd say, "Hell, no. You're not doing a good enough job of recruiting." We forced them to recruit.
>
> One time the fire chief was interviewed by the press during the litigation and said, "I don't think it's a job for a lady. Maybe a woman." He was admonished for this remark by Judge Reynolds.[83]

In 1974 at the time the lawsuit began, the names of some women had been on the list for two years. When they'd applied they had been told there were no vacancies. Prior to 1975, more than ninety had applied to both departments. Fifty had passed the written exams and thirty-eight had shown up for the physical fitness tests. Yet the department claimed it could not find enough applicants.

The only monetary compensation Mandy received for her years of work on this momentous case was $1,000. The judge ordered that she and Lloyd Barbee were each to receive this token amount, which barely covered Mandy's cost of paper. Her office had supplied copying services, paper, and postage for years, but no expenses were reimbursed, not even the cost Mandy bore for her secretary's time on the case. The clients were never billed for the legal work performed on their behalf. The countless unpaid hours Mandy spent in court appearances, briefs, and depositions over the years came from her conviction that someone had to do it.

"So I did it."

###

Just outside the City of Milwaukee in the City of Greenfield, a cleaning woman employed by the school system sought Mandy's help in filing a complaint. A male janitor who performed the same work—from washing floors to scrubbing toilets—was being paid at a higher rate than she was. Moreover, she received a salary for the school months only; the man received his salary for the full year.

Even though this discrimination was blatant, the school district was advised by its attorneys to fight the case. Litigation dragged on for years. Finally, in 1983, the school district settled. The complaint had been brought in 1974.

Winning cases such as this brought no satisfaction to Mandy, because the Greenfield taxpayers had to pay many thousands of dollars for what she regarded as terrible legal counsel. To Mandy, fighting an unwinnable case of outright sex discrimination at taxpayers' expense is not only outrageous—"It's the closest thing to malpractice I can think of."

###

Having flunked a physical agility test in 1979, Mary Pat Foley was later sworn in as Greenfield's first woman police officer—but only after filing a complaint of sex discrimination and having it upheld by the EEOC. So the police department's physical agility test had already been changed when Laurie Kay Tollifson came to see Mandy some two years later after flunking the *new* physical agility test.

"They gave her a grip-testing device so large she couldn't get her hand around it, and she had a big hand," noted Mandy. "She was a body builder who had competed successfully in a number of contests."

Attorney Stellman knew right away it was another case of sex discrimination. "You'd think the City of Greenfield would learn."

Mandy described what happened next:

The city wouldn't settle. We made a very reasonable offer because she didn't want a whole lot of back pay; she just wanted to be a cop. The city attorney recommended that the city take the offer.

One of the city aldermen said to the press (they just never learn), "Well, we want to meet her first."

So I said to the press, "What is this, a horse? You want us to check her teeth?" So that got in the paper.

Eventually the city settled out of court, and Tollifson was accepted as a Greenfield police officer. But this settlement came only after Mandy filed a federal lawsuit against the Greenfield Fire and Police Commission.

She told the press at the time, "This could cost the city several hundred thousand dollars by the time this is settled. It is an outrage to ask taxpayers to pay to continue discrimination."

Mandy also filed suit on behalf of jail matrons working for the Waukesha County Sheriff's Department. These women, said Mandy, like those in the City of Milwaukee, were being paid less to do the same jobs as their male counterparts.

The Justice Department came in and settled it, but my clients did not agree with the settlement set up for some of the other women. So we continued the case, taking a risk in doing this. Fortunately, it was well worth the risk, because eventually the jail matrons received interest on their back pay and a lot more than what the Justice Department was going to accept.

Another gain occurred in the form of a changed job title: "matron" became "deputy."

In some cities after a sex discrimination suit was filed, women experienced retaliation on the job. In Waukesha,

Mandy recalled, "There was resentment at first, but it didn't last long. When the women showed they were good deputies, they were accepted. These women were very serious about their careers."

###

Mandy never solicited clients for discrimination suits. They always sought her out, for she developed a reputation as a champion of women's rights. When the people with legitimate grievances had no money, Mandy's generosity in providing time and talent for clients who could not pay a retainer fee echoed her family's Judaic sense of values and quiet charity: You shared what you had, and you didn't brag.

Despite her heavy caseload of discrimination suits, Mandy never neglected her other clients. "I didn't put any case on the 'back burner.' I used to come in at seven A.M. and work till six-thirty or seven P.M. I got fired up. It was great."

She estimated that of the hundred or so civil rights cases she filed on behalf of women and men, most were settled without trial. She preferred the class action suits because they made the greatest impact, benefiting large numbers all at once and into the future. She got her greatest sense of accomplishment from intervening to open up employment opportunities faster than would otherwise occur.

Mandy explained what happens in suing a big corporation:

> It changes the way they do business. Part of the settlement, called the consent decree, gets them to say, "I ain't done nothing wrong, but I ain't gonna do it no more."
>
> With the big companies, it wasn't until they were involved in big class action suits that things started to change. Before that, they could figure that "crime pays,"

*because they'd weigh the risk of having to pay off one
woman against the millions of dollars saved while violating the rights of other women. But when they were sued
in these class action suits, they were ordered to reveal all
their policies.*

However, when Clarence Thomas was director of the EEOC,
"the situation was horrendous," recalled Mandy. "I would
tell women who came in to file—who had good cases—to
forget it, because the present administration has an unwritten policy that no case will get anywhere."

In October 1991 as the nation watched the televised hearings on Clarence Thomas's appointment to the Supreme Court,
Mandy found certain allegations against him "absolutely
true from my own experience—that many thousands of discrimination cases had been put on back burners. They either lost your file or it took so long that the statute of
limitations ran out, and people lost their cause of action. I
know it was deliberate. *Nobody* could be that negligent."

Among the various forms of job discrimination that wom-
en continue to struggle against, sexual harassment is one
of the greatest challenges. Mandy often represented women
subjected to pornography and graphic sexual material at
work. In a few instances it appeared that the women had
been targeted. The materials left at their desks and work
stations were extremely gross—repulsive.

One such client was an executive secretary employed by a
major brewery. When offensive pornographic cartoons were
placed on her desk, she complained and was fired for making a copy of the evidence.

The company in its defense claimed the employees were
merely exercising their right to free speech.

Countered Mandy, "It's not free speech when the woman

is so upset she can't work. Free speech might be putting the controversial cartoons inside one's own locker."

The secretary won back pay, a letter of reference, and a clean personnel file. She didn't want her job back.

"I can't work with those creeps," she told Mandy.

For a while, Mandy was so busy with age and sex discrimination cases she had little time for any other kind of case. Her files show that during the late seventies and early eighties, the Wisconsin agencies and companies she either brought suit against for discrimination or negotiated a settlement with included:

- Arrowhead High School, for denying maternity leave to women teachers and other employees
- Blue Cross Blue Shield, for paying black women less than other workers
- Continental Insurance Company, for advancing young men ahead of the female employee who trained them
- Deaconess Hospital, for treating black female employees differently from whites in salary and job classification
- The Milwaukee office of the Internal Revenue Service, for not promoting a female investigator because she had not handled "tough" cases and for deliberately not assigning her such cases (the complaint had to go through the IRS's own procedure—"a lot of federal red tape," said Mandy)
- Joseph Schlitz Brewing Company, for sexual harassment
- Miller Brewing Company, for sex discrimination in pay, working conditions for women, and sexual harassment
- Milwaukee Department of Public Works, for limiting the number of hours women lifeguards could work by

not allowing them to work when men were swimming in public pools

- North Central Airlines, for making flight attendants give up their jobs when they married or became pregnant
- *Waukesha Freeman* newspaper, for paying men more than women in the same job of selling advertising
- plus a number of trade unions, for not representing women who brought legitimate workplace grievances to the union.

###

In 1975, Mandy once again became the object of job discrimination, this time when she applied for the post of assistant chancellor at the University of Wisconsin-Milwaukee. She was one of fourteen women rejected—and not one of these applicants had been interviewed.

When the post became vacant, the chancellor, Werner A. Baum, was asked if he would consider hiring a woman. As related in an article in the *Milwaukee Sentinel*, the nominations of the women:

>...came in response to an alleged statement by Baum that it would be impossible to find a woman qualified to perform in a job that required extensive knowledge of state politics and public administration.
>
>Through a university spokesman, Baum denied later that he had used the term "impossible," and was observing only that there were, for whatever reason, probably few women with the experience the job required.[84]

When women heard about Baum's alleged remarks, they became outraged. But by the time he denied having used the term "impossible," women's groups had begun circulating the job description, and a number of highly qualified candidates began applying for the position—several with considerable experience in the UW system.[85]

Mandy recalled that a member of the advisory committee in charge of nominations, who declined to be quoted by name, revealed at the time that the committee had decided it was not necessary to interview these applicants before turning them down, because "they were already known to the university."

"The advisory committee didn't know me," said Mandy. "I applied but they didn't talk to me. Isn't that something?"

So she filed a complaint of sex discrimination with the state and with the EEOC, charging that UW-Milwaukee had discriminated against her because of sex. The complaint also alleged that the university discriminated by "failing and refusing to appoint females to higher positions in the administration of the university."[86]

Ironically, the *Milwaukee Journal* carried the story of the class action lawsuit in its "World of Women" section.[87]

The state issued a determination of no probable cause.[88] The EEOC, under the direction of Clarence Thomas, conducted no investigation, ordered no change in the system, and merely adopted the State of Wisconsin's finding of no probable cause. Satisfied that she had made her point, Mandy dropped the suit.

Some eighteen years later she received further vindication. The U.S. Justice Department investigated a lawsuit filed by faculty member Ceil Pillsbury, who had been engaged in a bitter struggle for tenure.

The much-publicized result? The U.S. Justice Department released a finding of sex discrimination throughout the university system.

Prompted by the Pillsbury case, Mandy wrote a scathing letter that appeared in the *Milwaukee Journal*:

> ...Shame on the males in the UWM School of Business Administration who permitted their antiquated, sexist attitudes to interfere with Pillsbury's right to tenure....

I keep asking where was—and is—the university leader-ship...?

Where was the Board of Regents who are supposed to lead in making sure that discrimination does not occur on UW campuses?...

Where was the UWM Faculty Senate when such an injustice was being perpetrated on one of its members?

And where was UWM Chancellor John Schroeder? He certainly owes a public apology to Dr. Pillsbury as well as to all women in the UW system for his ill-advised defense of the original decision of the school of business faculty who illegally denied Dr. Pillsbury tenure. Schroeder's Old Boys Club defense of his male colleagues has now cost the university over one million dollars.[89]

###

11. The Power of Words

For a woman to become a university dean or a police officer, or for a man to become a nurse or "house husband," such a role has to exist—if not in actuality, at least as a vision, concept, or expectation.

"Nontraditional role models are scarce even now," Mandy observed. "But in the sixties they were absolutely invisible." Overlooked in the backlash against gender-neutral language were the well-documented studies of sex-bias in educational materials, so important in molding children's life expectations. In these books for children, boys starred in all the action and solved all the problems, from rescuing kittens stuck in trees to rescuing girls—equally pathetic victims of their own weakness and ineptitude.[90]

Mandy noted, "Kids' schoolbooks pictured women only as housewives and mothers. Sure, a nurse or teacher showed up here and there, maybe an airline 'stewardess,' but kids could see for themselves that the jobs with power belonged to the 'fireman,' the 'policeman,' and the 'postman.'" Any feminist who objected to such narrow terminology or to the limited options this language represented was accused of being anti-marriage, anti-motherhood, or anti-male—and that was just for starters, Mandy pointed out.

Progress began when the U.S. Department of Labor revised its classification of job titles in 1972. "Now we have firefighter, police officer, letter carrier—even flight attendant, meaning that men benefited, too."

Nevertheless, the concept of gender-neutral language continued being attacked on all fronts. No other women's issue has been accused of such irrelevance or been subject to such ridicule. "That shows how much resistance there was," Mandy said.

By the mid-seventies, guidelines for nonsexist language had been issued by the National Council of Teachers of English, a few other organizations, and major publishing houses. Market-savvy publishers knew better than to exclude half their audiences.

Not all wordsmiths fully understood this principle, of course. The editor of one corporate magazine acknowledged that the whole gender language controversy could be resolved by simply using only female pronouns. "But that, we submit, would be a blatantly sexist usage."[91]

He wasn't trying to be funny. But others were. One journalist joked that we would soon be seeing "personhole" covers and tropical "hisicanes."

Some critics, on the other hand, managed to become comical by their very seriousness. One member of the Syracuse city council objected to a proposal to adopt the title *councilor* in place of *councilman,* announcing that losing the suffix "man" from his title of office amounted to a loss of his manhood.

A local activist advised him to avoid seeking higher office where he would have to submit to being called senator, governor, or president.[92]

Was it a similar fear of emasculation that threatened the many staunch defenders of the courtesy title *chairman?* "Look at all the chairwomen who insist on being addressed as *chairman,*" Mandy said. "They just prove the point that roles associated with men have higher status and greater power." Without a doubt, the hapless Syracuse councilman had unwittingly proven that the wording of a job title does indeed affect the self-perception of the job holder.

While public attention focused on the war of words, "opponents conveniently overlooked the reason *why* feminists pushed for these changes," said Mandy. Language determines how people define reality. Job titles can affect the make-up of the labor pool. That in turn affects the distribution of income, and earning a low income reinforces the second-class status on which much gender bias is based.

Recognizing these larger economic, social, and psychological principles, Mandy Stellman enlisted in the "war of words" with the same determination she brought to any conflict that diminishes women.

At committee meetings whenever she addressed the "chair," she knew what to expect—laughter and the exasperated tone one uses as if saying to a child, "Oh, come on, you're just being picky." But Mandy was not intimidated by such attitudes nor fooled by the argument that *man* includes *woman,* and that *he, him,* and *his* are "generic."

Her response was always a congenial: "Fine, if *chairman* is inclusive, so is *chairwoman.*" Having said that, she would begin to address the chairperson as "Madam Chairwoman," even when the person was male. To the man's predictably startled reaction, Mandy would explain, "Well, I consider the word generic. You've had it for a thousand years and now it's my turn for a thousand years. Let's make it even."

A little humor, Mandy believed, helps people get the point.

###

Moving from the boardroom to the courtroom, efforts to make the language of the law inclusive encountered more opponents, who dug in hard. Mandy dug in harder.

The Wisconsin legislature dragged its heels for years, cowed by vociferous objections from conservatives who opposed sex-neutering the state statutes. "They claimed it would lead to integrated bathrooms," recalled Mandy.

Patiently, she and the other proponents of change pointed out that inclusive language would enable all veterans, male and female, to qualify equally for benefits given only to "ex-servicemen." Similarly, a man would benefit by being included in the term "surviving spouse" rather than falling outside the narrow definition of "widow." And the state's power to regulate the hours of labor for women would also be extended to benefit men.

To demonstrate the need for changing the existing language, as well as to minimize the work that would be involved in implementing the legislation should it pass, a number of lawyers, Mandy included, agreed that each would take different sections of the three volumes of statutes and write changes in the margins of its more than 4,000 pages.

Opponents argued that adding words such as "he and she" would make the law books even longer. Not quite—when marital property reform came about thirteen years later, numerous extra words had to be added to Chapter 246 of the state statutes just dealing with the property rights of married women. "There's no similar law for men because they always had property rights," Mandy noted. "Words would not have had to be added at all if the rights for men and women had been equal."

To illustrate her point, she identified the supposition on which the statutes had been based. "The law put woman in her place years ago by saying 'you are not a person, you are property,' which is a thing, and a 'thing' can't sue for damages. Only male adults had legal status. If you were married, you belonged to your husband. If you were single you belonged to 'daddy,' no matter how old you were."[93]

On October 19, 1973, hearings were held on the issue of making the language of the Wisconsin statutes gender-neutral, and Mandy went to Madison. She testified that although the State Constitution *appeared* to give everyone equal status before the law, equal status was not a fact.

"The worst offenders are the lawmakers themselves," she told the lawmakers. "Running second...and perhaps trying harder to offend is my own profession, that of lawyer." Two examples she cited out of dozens were: "Milwaukee County has no woman judge and the Wisconsin Supreme Court has no woman justice."

Mandy called for strong legislation to spell out specific laws against discrimination on account of sex, and she demanded that women have a part in writing, considering, and interpreting laws which affect women.

Once the bill to change the language of the statutes reached the floor of the State Senate, it passed by a wide margin.[94]

But getting it to the floor meant getting it through committee. And the committee was chaired by Senator Gordon Roselip.

A large man weighing well over 250 pounds, Roselip had a tendency to belittle the women at the hearing. As he asked Mandy questions having little to do with her testimony, his negative attitude was palpable.

"Do you believe a woman ought to play football?"

"If she's big enough to play football, let her go to it," Mandy replied, adding that she had taught physical education for many years.

"Would [the proposed legislation] mean women would be required to work in a foundry?" continued the senator.

Mandy held her temper. "They would not be required to work there, but could if willing and qualified." Enough of being on the defensive; she turned the tables on the portly senator. "Do you think we should have a law that says men who weigh more than 250 pounds should be excluded from being a senator?"

The hearings lasted until well past midnight. Afterward, at a restaurant on State Street, Mandy and Sam got together for a late-night coffee session with about a dozen women who had also testified. The group was made up of women who were soon to be—or were already—known and respected throughout the state for their leadership on women's issues: Gene Boyer, Midge Miller, Mary Lou Muntz, Barbara Ulichny, and Kathryn Morrison. The chauvinism of Senator Roselip had gotten to them all, and they were angry.

"The nerve of him saying he's always felt that women should be treated with respect and honor and dignity," said one. "What about equality? *That* would be respect."

"We've got to get rid of him," said another.

They looked around the table, and all eyes fell on Kathryn Morrison, a professor at the University of Wisconsin-Platteville.

"Katie, don't you live in Roselip's district?"

"Katie, you've got to run against him!"

No woman had ever before been elected to the Wisconsin State Senate, but Morrison ran against Roselip, and she won.[95]

More than twenty years after the Wisconsin Statutes were made gender neutral, a proposal "to remove unnecessary masculine gender pronouns" from the State Constitution was sent to the voters in the form of a referendum. Supporters pointed out that the Constitution had been written seventy-two years before the law allowed women to *vote*. It was rife with pronouns referring to voters and state officials as male, whereas women in 1995 were both voting and holding office. But in 1995 the country was also experiencing backlash against so-called "political correctness," and the amendment was defeated.[96]

Observers also attributed the defeat to an "ornery" voter mood over other issues, such as a sports lottery.[97]

###

An advertisement appeared in the *Milwaukee Journal* in 1973 under the banner: "Boys 12 years old or older...earn a steady income with a *Milwaukee Journal* newspaper route." At the time, Wisconsin's labor laws prohibited little girls from selling newspapers.

"It was probably because of some old-fashioned view that you were a whore if you were out on the streets," theorized Mandy. The more she thought about it, the angrier she got. "If I had a daughter, why couldn't she deliver newspapers?"

Another local attorney, Ted Warshofsky, filed a lawsuit against the *Journal* because his daughter wanted a job delivering papers. The father won his case in court. And the job title "paperboy" was changed to "paper carrier."

Although Mandy did not have to take action on this issue, she did write to the *Journal* objecting to its ads that continued to depict only boys. The circulation director sent Mandy copies of the new ads to prove the paper's compliance, and he reported that more than 1,300 girls had been serving on newspaper routes throughout the state in a period of less than a year. "The girls have been doing a good job for us," his letter concluded.[98]

###

Mandy always believed that if women were to get equal attention in the workplace and everywhere else, language had to reflect that equality. No more would "Dear Sir" be acceptable. Every letter that came into her office addressed to "Mr. Stellman"—and there were many—was answered immediately, and each reply offered instruction in what it would take to appeal to the professional woman.

Because Mandy was not a typist, she usually handwrote a note directly on the piece of offensive mail and returned it to sender. Letters were typed by her husband or by her male secretary of many years, Robert M. Thompson.

When Sally Pray Ayers was Mandy's secretary in the seventies, she had a special way of handling salespeople who arrived at the office to see "Mr." Stellman—no matter what they were trying to sell.

"Uh-oh, are *you* in trouble," Sally would say. "Mandy will never buy what you're selling."

Then when the poor fellow looked properly dejected, Sally would add, "Wait a minute. If you join NOW and take a vow of feminism, and get your corporation to elect women to its board of directors, *Ms.* Stellman *may* order a dozen of your typewriter ribbons."

###

"As a professional man..." began the solicitations, flyers, advertisements, and other announcements that began to cross the attorney's desk as soon as she went into practice. These invariably depicted a male as the professional and the female as the secretary. Mandy would send back the piece with only the briefest of lines written thereon: "Please, no more 'male' mail!"

One legal research service, The Research Group, solicited "Mr." Mandy Stellman's business by assuring prospective customers, "our staff understands what you want." Mandy replied by letter and returned the solicitation, writing across it: "Next time research the attorney. I happen to be a female lawyer...."[99]

A similar blunder by a well-known manufacturer of postage meters prompted this advice: "Pitney Bowes obviously needs help. I suggest you read your letters prior to using your own postage meter."[100]

###

A solicitation from an insurance company began, "Dear Ms. Stellman: As a young professional, especially as a young lawyer, you realize the value of a well-planned program for savings...."

Mandy wrote back, "Finally, the correct sex but the wrong age!"[101]

###

Around the mid-eighties, some vendors began catching on that a large number of women were graduating from law school.

Mandy observed, "There are many young female attorneys now, more than ever, thank goodness. So someone must have gotten the idea to get the list of lady lawyers just assuming they were all of reproductive age, because I got a card in the mail offering me—as "a professional woman"—ten dollars off on a maternity dress. I called Sam and said, 'Do you know something I don't?' We had a good laugh over that one."

###

When representing a woman in a real estate closing, it was not at all unusual for Mandy to object to the phrase on the standard deed that reads, "Know all men by these presents."

It was also not unusual when a banker or other attorney laughed at her objection. "We do these by the hundreds, by the thousands!" said one banker.

"Well, I'm asking you to change this one," Mandy replied. "Take out the word *men* and have it say, 'Know all by these presents.' Otherwise I'm not having my client sign it."

They changed it.

To an astute listener such as Mandy, the subtleties of gender-biased language go beyond mere pronouns. Such bias can have major consequences when the speaker is an officer of the court. An example can be found in the outcome of a hearing to increase child support, in which the family court commissioner—a woman—kept referring to Mandy's client as the *ex-wife,* but to the opposing attorney's client as *Dad.* There was no mention of either *ex-husband* or *Mom.*

"It's very suspicious language," observed Mandy. Not surprisingly, the family court commissioner decided in favor of the former husband. Thereupon, Mandy requested a review of the decision. She also subpoenaed the man's employment records and, fortuitously, discovered he had lied about his income and presented falsified tax returns at the hearing. The circuit court judge who conducted the review reversed the decision of the family court commissioner, and child support was increased.

In corresponding with other attorneys, Mandy did not hesitate to correct the misuse of gender references in their letters. But she often did so with humor.

Deliberately calling a male corporate attorney "Madam" in responding to a letter of his, she quipped: "Your last letter to me was addressed, 'Dear Mr. Stellman.' I guess we can consider the score even. Actually, I found it amusing to be addressed that way—especially since the issue in the lawsuit is sex discrimination. I am sure you did not notice the error, and you are hereby forgiven."

Mandy received a letter of apology.[102]

###

Inclusive language in the practice of law represented one of the gender issues Mandy brought into the courtroom, thereby raising the consciousness of judges and other attorneys, as well as newspaper readers of every description who chuckled over such incidents with their morning coffee. For many years, Alex Thien's column in the former *Milwaukee Sentinel* reported these anecdotes—such as the time Mandy's opposing counsel, Donald Haberman, answered a judge's question by saying: "I think I'd like to ask for a six-man jury, Your Honor." (In a civil suit, judges leave it up to the attorneys to decide whether they want six or twelve people on a jury.)

Attorney Stellman spoke up. "You mean a six-*person* jury."

"Six-*person*," agreed the judge. "You won't get six *men* as long as Ms. Stellman is on the case, Mr. Haberman. Watch yourself."

"I'm sorry," said Attorney Haberman. "I'm still from the old school, Your Honor."

"Very old," Mandy interjected.

"Touché, Ms. Stellman," the judge replied.[103]

###

After this story was publicized, most judges and lawyers were heard to be asking for six-person or twelve-person juries. Such evidence of Mandy's continual reminders for gender-neutral language in the legal profession occurred even when she was not present, attesting to her effectiveness.

When the executive committee of the Milwaukee Bar Association met to update a brochure, Mandy was later told by a committee member that its president had said of the proposed rewording—which contained a male pronoun—"We'd better not say that because Mandy Stellman will send us one of her famous letters."

It took time and effort for such awareness to develop, of course, and the initial stages of this awareness had less to do with creating a level playing field for women than with avoiding correction by Mandy.

Yet her professional status was not diminished by her activism. In fact, her name was placed on the ballot as a candidate for the Milwaukee Bar Association's executive board—the first woman ever nominated.[104]

###

The Milwaukee Bar Association heard from Mandy many times. For three years in a row she objected to its invitation to members to attend its annual summer golf outings.

"Wives and guests welcome!" proclaimed the invitation. And what would the wives do? Attend a fashion show and the health club.[105]

Each year Mandy sent back a copy of the announcement with a reminder that "many members of the Bar are women," and asking if husbands were included. "My husband resents being left out of this invitation."

###

Mandy also corrected the American Bar Association on many occasions. It took an extensive letter-writing campaign to both the local and national bar associations for the term *law wives* to eventually disappear.

And when the ABA wrote its members in 1973 requesting nominations for *chairmen* of the family law sections in each state, this wording did not slip past Mandy. What caught her eye in particular was the statement: "It is important to those who practice in [the area of family law] that qualified men be members of the Section."[106]

To the attorney who had sent the request, Mandy wrote: "Please note that your attempt to increase membership...has failed to recognize the fact that women not only achieved the vote, but also managed to pass the Bar in every state of our Union." On the form letter itself she wrote: "If *lawyers* are not aware of the fact that women have an equal interest in the judicial process, then heaven help us."

The contrite attorney wrote back: "Your criticism is merited and appreciated. I will try to improve."[107]

Objecting to an article entitled "The 'Queen Bee' of the Office is No Honey," which appeared in a 1978 issue of an ABA publication, Mandy pointed out that its author "obviously appears to have written this article based not upon scientific data, but upon his own sexist perceptions.... I am very much disturbed that you would even find such an article worthy of publication in the *Bar Leader* since we pride ourselves in the legal profession for our ability to sort out *valid* causes from *frivolous* ones."[108]

Having been active in the American Bar Association for many years, Mandy ultimately resigned in protest when the ABA paid a huge speaker's fee to General Alexander Haig, Secretary of State under President Reagan. No one giving a political speech should be paid, she felt. Moreover, no speaker was worth $25,000.

At the time that the ABA invited General Haig to speak, the organization was run by men. It took until 1994 for

Roberta Cooper Ramo to be elected the first woman to lead
the ABA. Martha Barnett filled its second most prestigious
post, chair of its House of Delegates. These were the first
leadership positions held by women since the organization's
founding more than a century earlier.

Perhaps everyone at one time or another has wanted to
write the president of a company after receiving poor service or seeing an offensive advertisement, but how many
actually do so? Where did a busy attorney find the time and
energy to do what others just think about?

For one thing, Mandy never wasted energy in negative
self-talk and unproductive "should haves." If she heard something inappropriate, she didn't walk away and think, "I
should have said...." She said it.

For another, no matter how many times she encountered
the same examples of sexism, her energy was renewed by
the outrage that arose in her. It was not sapped by pre-
sumptions of futility. Resistance was a challenge, not a defeat.

In her office she kept separate folders with the names of
the companies she wrote to, copies of the offensive ads or
letters she objected to, and the replies she received. Ninety
percent of the time, according to her estimate, she received
an apology—often in writing, sometimes by telephone.

When "Mr." Stellman was invited to speak to high school
students interested in careers in law, Mandy wrote across
the top of the invitation: "The first message for students is:
Law is for women as well as for men."

She received a telephone apology.

As early as 1972, the president of the Bank of Commerce
in Milwaukee replied to a complaint of Mandy's by assuring
her that its future letters and publications would use a uni-

versal form of reference. He added, "By taking the time to write your letter, you are being helpful to the business community in bringing this type of error to their attention."[109]

"I almost purchased some of your equipment," learned the Dictaphone Company, "until I read your brochure. Surely you must know that women have entered the business and professional world." Mandy called attention to the photos showing men dictating letters and women transcribing them. "Not all of us are secretaries. Until Dictaphone comes out with non-sexist advertising, I shall avoid doing business with your company."[110]

She received immediate assurances that Dictaphone was an equal opportunity company and that it would "try to do better with our advertising material in the future."[111]

Nevertheless, one year later, Mandy had occasion to write a similar letter to the same company. "It is precisely advertisements such as [this one] which perpetuate the 'sexist' business policy and attitude of Dictaphone." Copies of the letter went to Betty Ford, two members of Congress, "Dear Abby," and others. Mandy knew not only the value of a letter of complaint but also the effectiveness of well-targeted copies.[112]

This time, a company vice president called to apologize, saying they were changing their advertising and probably hiring a new agency. A little while later, her mail bore proof of the new ads. "They said they would change and they did." So she bought two of their products and wrote to let the company know why.

For some time, a local television station had been conducting political talk shows called *Your Men in Washington* and *Your Men in Madison.* Mandy wrote the station a letter requesting a more appropriate title. "I want the record to show that my elected officials are not 'My Men.'" She sent copies to four U.S. Representatives.

The station agreed that her point was well taken and said that when her letter arrived, "we were in the process of changing the title." One program would be called *Your Voice in Washington;* the other, *At Issue.*[113]

###

A full-page ad from the Chicago Title Insurance Company described how to choose the right lawyer: "He should be someone you like…. The law is his business…he took years to learn it…. He will openly discuss his fee…" and so on. That was bad enough. But when the Wisconsin Bar circulated copies of this fine example of advertising to its members, Mandy was irate and wrote a letter. She received two apologies.[114]

Other companies not only apologized but hastened to send Mandy advance copies of their new non-sexist ads.[115]

But some accompanied their apologies with feeble disclaimers: "While my name appears as a member of the committee, I have not attended any meetings and had no part in the planning."[116]

And one company's apology cited an example that it mistakenly believed showed its understanding of what women were experiencing. "We at Callaghan are no strangers to gender misidentification in written communication," wrote the company's president. "Our Chairman of the Board is Rae S. Smith…." Might this name mean a woman held such an important position? Did the company really understand how gender misidentification affected women? No such luck. The letter continued, "…and at least 70 percent of the mail he receives from strangers is addressed to Ms. Smith."[117]

###

Of the stream of letters that poured from Mandy's pen and Sam's typewriter, many were addressed to elected representatives to voice strong opinions on every public issue that concerned the Stellmans: lifting the ban on gays and lesbians in the military, protecting safe and legal abortion, opposing "Learnfare," "Bridefare," and other punitive proposals to replace welfare with one or another unworkable scheme, and on and on.

Mandy usually began her letters by saying, "As a female attorney...." Regardless, the replies she received appeared to be form letters, for they almost always began, "Dear Mr. Stellman."

When even her U.S. Senator, William Proxmire, replied in this fashion, Mandy composed another letter pointing out the senator's oversight. She added, "It is obvious you failed to read my message to you."[118]

Proxmire wrote to apologize.

It didn't end there, for she wrote back, "I accept your apology."

###

"When you see something you object to," Mandy firmly believed, "write a letter. It works. They're not all male chauvinists. They're just behind the times and need a little encouragement."

Even women of accomplishment were not beyond learning.

When Barbara Walters demanded and got a salary comparable to men for doing the same work in television broadcasting, it made headlines for months—even though men had been getting that kind of money for years. Mandy sent a letter of congratulations to Barbara Walters for "showing the business and professional world that 'talent' is not based on gender.

"I represent dozens of women in sex discrimination charges against their employers," she added. "You have given the working woman a shot in the arm, as well as hope for a better world."[119]

The reply thanking the attorney for writing began, "Dear Mr. Stellman."[120]

Mandy penned a quick response, acknowledging that Ms. Walters was a very busy person and suggesting her staff find a new greeting, "since it is a mistake to assume that all professional people are male." Mandy also sent a copy to Abigail Van Buren, with whom she had developed an interesting correspondence.[121]

###

12. From Dear Abby to Dreadful Eve

It started in 1973 when Mandy's favorite personal advice columnist advised a reader to "ring up your lawyer and ask him what to do...."

Mandy shot off her first Dear Abby letter. "As a long-time fan of yours I wish to point out that there are many competent women lawyers. Your reference to a lawyer should not automatically assume a 'man.' You have been liberated longer than most Americans—so I was rather shocked at your use of the masculine pronoun in your August 15, 1973, column in the *Milwaukee Sentinel*. Even my husband was shocked. Keep giving advice—and I shall continue to practice law."

The typewritten reply addressed to Ms. Stellman read, "Yes, I was aware that there are women lawyers...if my father had his way, I'd have been one. However, with newsprint as tight as it is, I write with an economy of words, hence I omitted the "her" along with the "his."

The note was signed, "Forgive me. Abby."[122]

Some months later, a reader's plea for legal information resulted in Abby's advice to engage a lawyer "and pay him (or her) for what he (or she) knows."[123]

A delighted Mandy dashed off a "Bravo! Many thanks."

Abby replied, acknowledging Mandy's nudge as the reason for ignoring the need for economy of words. As a result of her new inclusive style, Abby heard from several other grateful lawyers.[124]

Some two years later Abby's column once again used "he" to refer to all lawyers.[125] Immediately, Mandy expressed her disappointment. "Surely you have not taken a step backward! Please, Abby—I have publicly applauded your sensitivity to the concerns of women. Don't let me down."[126]

Abigail Van Buren wrote back.

Good Lord, don't you ever miss a 'he' when it should have been "he/she"? All right, forgive me, again, will you? I assure you I have NOT taken a step backward. I'm still very much aware that we have women lawyers, but if I slip again I can count on a sharp-eyed watchdog like you to catch it. All good wishes,

Sincerely, Abby.[127]

The next slip came from a doctor's secretary, whose letter was quoted in the Dear Abby column of September 22, 1976. Abby not only caught the slip but also included this instruction in her published reply to the secretary: "Although your letter referred to doctors in the masculine, let's acknowledge that there are many women physicians, too."[128]

An ecstatic Mandy penned a quick letter of congratulations, and Abby wrote back:

I was hoping you'd catch that item! And if it makes you feel any better, Mandy, I thought of YOU when I wrote it! See? I do learn. And you have taught me.[129]

Only a week later, however, the popular advice columnist referred to doctors as "he," and the sharp-eyed watchdog wrote to ask, "What happened?"[130]

Abby handwrote her reply on Mandy's inquiry.

Good Lord—don't you miss anything? I'm improving (gradually) but it may take me a while longer to he/she, him/her, etc., and besides some editors still think the masculine pronoun is all inclusive, and so do most readers. But not Women Libbers. Forgive me?

Abby signed her note "L&K"—for love and kisses.

Before 1976 ended, Mandy had an opportunity to send Abby a copy of one of her many "Dear Mr. Stellman" letters. This one came from the woman who was showing the world "that 'talent' is not based on gender."

Dear Abby: I thought you would enjoy the enclosed letter[131]...from Barbara Walters in response to a letter I sent her congratulating her on her new job. Need I say more! Best wishes for a Happy Hanukah and a Happy New Year.[132]

"Dear Mandy," Abby wrote. "Nu? So she's too busy to know what's going on in her own office. Poor kid! Everyone isn't as conscientious as you and Ms. Van Buren. Love, Abby."[133]

When "Worried in California" had a question about rape,[134] Mandy let Abby know about the new sexual assault laws in Wisconsin. And she caught another "he" reference to a lawyer in the same column.[135]

Good-naturedly, Abby scribbled at the bottom of Mandy's letter: "My God—not again. So *sue* me! Warmest, Abby." Around the margins of the letter these words were added: "Thanks! I really should have been a lawyer!"[136]

A few months later, Abby replied to another of Mandy's reminders, writing: "Well, you don't miss a thing, do you?" followed by a mild protestation about the space consumed by equality in language. She ended with: "It's good of you to keep me on my toes, and I am grateful.... You are quite a woman. I hope one day we will meet." Then, as many people were saying at the time, she added: "When the ERA passes, let's get together and have tea. Warmest...."[137]

A year and a half later, the May 1, 1979, column advised someone to "consult a lawyer and pay him for what he knows." This time Sam wrote his first Dear Abby letter, beginning with an explanation of why he was stepping in:

> Mandy is too busy in court...and in the community, fighting the endless battles of trying to find justice—particularly for women—battered, raped, divorced, or divorcing, charged with "crimes" for which men would never have been charged.[138]

In revealing what else was taking place in Mandy's life at the time, Sam mentioned that she was one of four women who had been considered for a federal judgeship in Eastern Wisconsin—but the selection committee was instead recommending five men for President Carter's ultimate decision.

For these reasons and others, "I am requesting that you refer to lawyers as both 'hims' and 'hers,' [because] there's little hope for judgeships for women lawyers if the press doesn't recognize there are women lawyers available and important enough to be recognized by a feminist like you."

Noting that the column of May 1 was also Law Day, Sam added that Mandy "is one of the few women lawyers who have made it as independent practitioners—she, all by herself in her own office. That makes her rare and special. Your recognizing women professionals in your column, when appropriate, will help all women in professions—and women generally. Abby, we are both avid fans of yours, even when you goof."

By this time, six years after Mandy had sent her first Dear Abby letter, enough consciousness had been raised among the general public to generate letters from other watchdogs about the advice columnist's most recent "goof." One of these was reprinted in the column carried by the *Milwaukee Sentinel* on July 18, 1979. The column itself bore the headline: "Lawyer can be 'she' as well as 'he.'"

The reader, a Ms. Perlman, wrote: "Today, when approximately 25 percent of the graduating classes of most law schools are women, your readers could wind up paying a lawyer for what SHE knows. And it would still be a good investment."

Abby's published reply to Ms. Perlman read: "Thanks for keeping me on my toes. Mandy Stellman, a lady lawyer and vocal feminist in Milwaukee, has been chastising me for years for referring to lawyers as 'him.' Sorry. Old habits die hard. But I'm learning."[139]

This was the first time Abby had mentioned Mandy in her column.

Some weeks later Abby printed a letter from a man who insisted that 'he' and 'him' referred to both sexes, and allowed as how "Mandy Stellman of Milwaukee and Ms. Perlman of St. Paul should not object to being known as Mandy Stell and Ms. Perl after removing the 'man' from their names."[140]

Abby's public response revealed that she did find it "a nuisance to write 'he/she,'" et al. Such an admission apparently vindicated the feelings of at least one copywriter, because that day's column was exuberantly headlined: "Abby's voice cries out again in the Wide Wilderness of Pronouns."[141]

After Mandy's name appeared in the July 18 nationally syndicated column, Abby received this letter from her:

> *I am not sure whether I should thank or criticize you for mentioning my name in your [column]. At first I was extremely pleased to see your reference to me as a "vocal feminist." However, my phone did not stop ringing for several days. I heard from friends in Toronto...Baltimore... New York City...Columbus [Ohio], and other places.*

Adding, "I can honestly say I am in agreement with your advice and comments 99.9 percent of the time,"[142] Mandy also mentioned having just celebrated 36 years of marriage.

Abby's reply thanked Mandy for her warm letter, adding, "We (Mort and I) have you and Sam beat by four years. We just made 40. Sorry the publicity inconvenienced you. But wasn't it fun?"[143]

In November of that year, Mandy sent Abby a newspaper clipping about the 1979 Toast and Roast dinner held annually by the Milwaukee Women's Political Caucus. Mandy had been "toasted" for her "ten-year letter-writing campaign against sexism in the language and in the media." Her cover note to Abby explained: "Because of your 'name-dropping' (my name) in your column, I was awarded the first annual 'Dear Abby Award.'"[144]

In fact, Mandy had ended the night's event with laughter as she read from her vast collection of letters, roasting the businesses that had repeatedly addressed her as "Mr. Stellman."[145] Abby's handwritten reply read:

> *Dear Mandy Stellperson. Mazeltov. You're great. Abby.*[146]

Over the next thirteen years, a few male-only pronouns slipped into the popular syndicated column, and Mandy continued to prod, gently suggesting, "Did your staff goof?" and "I hope the editors are at fault."

On Valentine's Day 1992, Abby's column carried this introduction:

> Some years ago when I was less savvy about equal rights for women, I unabashedly wrote a St. Valentine's column on "how to keep your man happy." I called it the Ten Commandments for Women—and soon it was followed by a Ten Commandments for Men.
>
> Then an early feminist, Mandy Stellman of Milwaukee, wrote, demanding equality for the sexes and insisting that there should be only one set of commandments for both genders. Well, Ms. Stellman won....

The rest of that day's column was devoted to reprinting Mandy's gender-neutral "Ten Commandments for a Successful Marriage."[147] Since then, Mandy's list has been reprinted many Valentine's days. It reads:

1. *Put your mate before your mother, your father, your son and your daughter, for your mate is your lifelong companion.*

2. *Do not abuse your body with excessive food, tobacco or drink, so that your life may be long and healthy, in the presence of those you love.*

3. *Do not permit your business or your hobby to make you a stranger to your children, for the most precious gift a parent can give his or her family is time.*

4. *Do not forget that cleanliness is a virtue.*

5. *Do not make your mate a beggar, but willingly share with him or her your worldly goods.*

6. *Remember to say, "I love you." For even though your love may be constant, your mate yearns to hear those words.*

7. *Remember always that the approval of your mate is worth more than the admiring glances of a hundred strangers, so remain faithful and loyal to your mate and forsake all others.*

8. *Keep your home in good repair, for out of it come the joys of old age.*

9. *Forgive with grace. For who among us does not need to be forgiven?*

10. *Honor the Lord your God all the days of your life, and your children will grow up and bless you.*

###

In keeping with her 99.9 percent agreement with the content of her favorite advice column, Mandy wrote only two letters after that to challenge specific recommendations Abby made to readers seeking advice.

"It is *never too late to protest!*" shouted Mandy's handwritten response to a column about a woman who had stayed in an unhappy marriage for her children's sake. Abby had advised the woman to try to keep the peace.[148]

If the writer who signed "Confused" happened to be in her teens or early twenties, you might advise, "Get rid of the bum." Why should "Ms. Confused" put up with her husband's cruel treatment even after forty-six years? I recently represented a seventy-one-year-old woman who divorced her mean, nasty, insensitive husband after a marriage of forty-nine years.... She feels like a new person. Her married children tell me they wish she had left their father years ago.[149]

The only other time Mandy disagreed with the substance of Abby's advice came in defense of a papergirl whose plea described how it made her feel to be called a "paperboy." The girl had decided not to attend her employer's awards banquet because the invitation read, "Please wear a shirt and tie."[150]

Mandy wrote:

I believe you should apologize to "Palm Springs Paper Girl" for treating her serious problem so lightly. As a female lawyer I was annoyed and angered by my own Milwaukee Bar Association which requested all members to "wear a shirt and tie" for formal photographs to be used in a directory.[151]

###

If anyone understood how to turn the emotions of anger and annoyance into action, Mandy did. Her unflagging campaign to protest unequal treatment is a model for action by anyone, from women married many years to girls still in school.

Letter writing is the easiest way to get started as an activist. To ensure that the recipients of such letters pay attention, the activist may want to borrow another of the Stellmans' tactics—sending copies to the local press, to national organizations concerned with related issues, to high-profile politicians at all levels of government, and to governmental departments such as consumer affairs and the attorney general.

In the Stellmans' letters to companies, they usually promised to take their business elsewhere if an issue was not resolved satisfactorily. When a credit card was involved, they cut it up and mailed the little pieces back to the issuing company.

Their effective letter-writing tactics were not limited to championing only the rights of others. As consumers they experienced the same kind of commonplace problems most people do with subscription renewals, airline cancellations, and tax refunds. At those times, their letter-writing strategies worked just as effectively. Unlike most people, however, the Stellmans always went right to the top, and they didn't give up.

"If this is the way *Time* magazine is going to conduct business, you may cancel my subscription forthwith and send me a complete refund," Mandy wrote to the magazine's president about the handling of a subscription mix-up. That wasn't all. "For my office time and postage in responding to your billing, I am herewith billing *Time* magazine $7.50. Please pay this amount promptly."[152]

The magazine not only corrected the mix-up, but also extended Mandy's subscription to "compensate for the $7.50 charge for time and postage you mentioned in your letter." Persistence paid off, literally.[153]

###

Persistence paid off again when Mandy complained about the poor service and great inconvenience she and Sam experienced because of a flight's mechanical problems and subsequent cancellation.

Mandy addressed her letter to the president of Republic Airlines, and she sent copies to her travel agency, her credit card issuer, the Federal Aviation Administration, and her senator.

A reply came not from the president of the airlines but from an underling. Undaunted, Mandy wrote again to object.[154]

Since I addressed Mr. Wolf, a reply from him directly would seem more appropriate. As it is, there is no assurance that your president has read my letter or is even aware of problems such as we experienced.... Please advise [me] of your president's correct address so I may send my correspondence directly to him and receive direct replies.[155]

Although the next reply also did not come from Republic's president, the airlines' consumer affairs director apologized for addressing Mandy as "Mr. Stellman" and explained why there could be no refund—the tickets had been part of a low-fare promotion in which all restrictions had been waived. Nevertheless, "in view of the hardship created for you on this occasion," the director enclosed a voucher worth $216 to be applied toward future travel.[156]

By that time, however, copies of Mandy's original letter of complaint were already being acted upon. Senator Proxmire promptly notified the Civil Aeronautics Board, and that agency advised Republic of the senator's interest and asked "the carrier to send our respective offices an explanation of the manner in which this matter was handled."[157]

###

Whenever possible, Mandy spoke for the rights of others even if her letter of complaint dealt with a personal issue. For instance, there was the time in 1978 when the State of Wisconsin adjusted the way it collected and apportioned real estate taxes. As a result, the Stellmans were among many who received a refund. But the refund check was made payable to Sam, even though the original filing had been made in both names. A letter was quickly dispatched to Governor Lee Dreyfus.

"My husband and I believe the check should have been made payable to both of us," Mandy wrote, "since we are both owners of the real estate involved. Please have the check reissued properly."[158]

The reply from the Republican governor shifted blame to the state's income tax system and failed to acknowledge in any way the second, broader point Mandy had raised in her letter of complaint, as follows:

> As an attorney, I represent hundreds of female clients who also have joint ownership in real estate with their respective husbands. I have received many complaints and objections to the...refunds being automatically sent to their husbands.

This discriminatory practice ended when the state's marital property laws went into effect seven years later. Until then, however, Mandy could offer no help to the tearful women who came into her office telling of their husbands' cashing the refund checks and spending the money on girlfriends or in gambling.

"If the marriage wasn't going too well," Mandy explained later, "the husband took the money and the wife never got a damn cent. If a divorce was pending, we'd go to court. But the husband would say he'd already spent the money. What are you going to do—put him in jail?"

One of Mandy's acquaintances had been treated poorly when she needed her car repaired. A black woman, she had been made to wait at the dealership an entire day and was then told she might as well go home because her car wouldn't be ready until the next day.

On learning of this "service," Mandy fired off a letter to the dealer.

This is one of the most blatant cases of discrimination I have ever heard of.... You may be sure I will be investigating every legal action possible to support my client in her contention that she was discriminated against because she is a black woman.

Copies of this letter went to the governor's office, the state Department of Motor Vehicles, both U.S. senators from Wisconsin, the Wisconsin Department of Consumer Affairs, and the local district attorney.

The response from the car dealer was rapid and gratifying. The owner himself called Mandy and apologized profusely. They hadn't discriminated against her intentionally, the dealer said; still, he assured Mandy that never again would a customer be treated in that way, regardless of race or gender.

###

Like Mandy, Sam intervened on behalf of those unable to obtain justice by themselves. A slick, fast-talking salesman had used high-pressure tactics to sell insurance to a black woman, but when the woman realized she had been misled and attempted to cancel the policy, she was unable to get the agent to return her calls. The insurance company, one of the largest in the world, would not come to her aid either, insisting that she call the agent. She called Sam instead.

He wrote immediately to the local and head offices of the insurance company. The salesman, he said, had deliberately taken advantage of a minority woman by selling her insurance that she did not need, want, or understand. If Sam and the woman did not receive an immediate response, he would ask for an investigation by the state attorney general and the local district attorney. Moreover, he would pursue the matter further with other governmental offices.

Within a few days, the woman received a full refund from the company. No letter or explanation was ever offered.

How does a complaint get noticed by a big impersonal corporation that depicts men as executives and women as secretaries in their advertising? "You write letters," said Sam, "and you write more letters. Mandy became one prolific letter writer." She would include a copy of the ad with the offending words circled and send it to the advertiser with the words "You goofed" written across it.

Whether it was the giant Xerox Corporation, Sears, Dictaphone, or major insurance companies, banks, airlines, or department stores, nearly all the letters Mandy sent got prompt responses and promises to change. Those who wrote back gave some indication they would be more sensitive from then on about depicting women in positions subservient to men. And the letters from the larger companies often said or implied that women would be viewed as potential candidates for more substantial positions.

Whenever companies ran ads that featured photos of their sales staffs, executive officers, "Agents of the Year," or other leaders, Mandy always noted the number of faces of white males in relation to those of minorities and females. In almost all cases, the ads earned the same brief letter on her professional stationery: "It is obvious from your ad that your institution does not believe in promoting women. Do you have a logical explanation—or even a lawful one?"[159]

###

Sometimes Mandy undertook a letter-writing campaign to raise consciousness on a different level. If she did not plan to attend a law conference, for example, she did not simply throw away the announcements. When such events were being held in Illinois, Georgia, and other states that had not ratified the Equal Rights Amendment, she informed the sponsoring organization that she would be happy to attend if the event were held in a state whose legislature supported equality for women.

To even things up a bit, Mandy wrote the president of Avon Products to say thank you for its public support of the Equal Rights Amendment.

###

Only months before Attorney Stellman's services were required in the 1977 defense of Jennifer Patri, Mandy wrote to producer Norman Lear to offer her legal services to a character in the television series *Mary Hartman, Mary Hartman*.

This popular nighttime series was one of the first television programs to dramatize the issue of domestic abuse, but

Mandy felt it didn't go far enough. In the story, a woman who was battered by her husband stabbed him. Mandy felt that the script had the public defender offering inadequate legal advice to the woman. She wrote:

> It is my opinion the evidence will show: (1) that [the husband] committed suicide, and (2) that [the wife] has a full and complete legal defense to any and all alleged criminal charges.[160]

Mandy added that she looked forward to an early response "since I would have to clear my calendar in order to take on the legal defense."

Instead of "Yours truly," Mandy had the words "Sisterhood is powerful" typed above her signature.

Although her offer was politely declined, she received two replies. Each came from a woman in the production company's management. One mentioned a soon-to-be-aired TV movie, *Battered,* saying "light is coming in small rays."[161]

The other added the postscript: "I kno w sisterhood is powerful! I draw on it all the time!"[162]

###

Whenever Mandy observed insensitivity or exploitation where a serious issue was involved, her anger escalated.

"Shame on Miller Brewing," began her objection to an ad for beer featuring three Hispanic women in sexy poses. The ad appeared in the program book for the 1992 Milwaukee Hispanic Community Annual Awards Banquet—a family event that the Stellmans attended. Six people who sat at the same table with them added their names to Mandy's letter, which went on to say:

> We have to assume that there is a dearth of ideas by you and your advertising company...[if] you still have to use women in provocative poses to sell your product. Obviously all the recent public outcry about what these...ads

*do in putting women down hasn't had much effect on
your company....*

*Your ad was opposite an ad for the Sojourner Truth
House, the largest women's shelter for battered women
in Wisconsin. If you can't see the connection between
your ad and a shelter for battered women, then this letter will have little meaning to you....*[163]

A response came from the consumer affairs department.
"We are sorry that you disliked our ad. Although we do not
see the ad as inappropriate, your negative reaction is taken
very seriously and will be shared with our advertising agencies and upper management."[164]

###

An article in a local weekly paper, the *Shepherd Express,*
quoted a professor on the subject of domestic violence who
claimed that "a husband is as likely to be a victim as is a
wife."

Sam called the instructor, who taught at the same campus of the university, and said, "This is my field. You're in
my field and you're way off base."

When the instructor mentioned "radical feminists," Sam
straightened him out with some facts on the extent of battering of women by men.[165]

From then on, Sam started to read the *Shepherd Express*
regularly. He noticed how negatively the paper dealt with
certain stories making headlines at the time about cases of
alleged sexual harassment and rape brought against Clarence Thomas, Mike Tyson, and William Kennedy-Smith. He
noticed how the *Express* was handling a story in which Melissa Fotjik, a Racine firefighter, had accused a candidate
for Milwaukee mayor, Gregory Gracz, of sexually harassing
her at a firefighter's convention in 1990.[166]

Sam wrote to the editor objecting strongly to what he

saw as the anti-woman bias in the handling of such stories.

After his letter was published, several of the readers who began noticing a change in the paper's position telephoned Sam to congratulate him. He also received a note of thanks from Ellen Bravo, director of the Milwaukee Chapter of 9 to 5 and later co-director of the National Association of Working Women, who from time to time had been characterized by the *Express* as a mischief maker for her efforts on behalf of working women.[167]

In his letter, Sam said he felt the *Express* frequently implied that the women who brought such charges were lying. From reading the *Express*, one would have to conclude, he said, that all the men in the cases of sexual harassment and assault were "paragons of virtue" and all the women were "floozies." This colorful phrasing came directly from statements made in a local courtroom, which—Sam reminded the editors—led to severe criticism from the community.

Judge Ralph Gorenstein had made this sexist comment from the bench while hearing a case of prostitution that had also netted four businessmen. The judge had become angry as he'd read the charges against the men standing before him, and, as Sam wrote in his letter to the *Express*, had thrown down the sheet and said to the prosecutor: "I see that these men have been charged with soliciting a prostitute. It is so obvious to me that these men are good, upstanding family men. And the women are strictly floozies. Case dismissed!"[168]

What happened next is history. When members of Milwaukee NOW learned of the judge's statements, they got together and passed a resolution condemning him. Determined that no judge should get away with exercising such biased attitudes, they raised the next logical question: "Who is going to talk to Judge Gorenstein?"

Everyone looked at Mandy.

By the time she and Sam went to call on the judge a few days later, the press had picked up the story and the judge had begun feeling the heat from many sources. His phone rang incessantly, women and men kept appearing at his door, and neighborhood groups publicly criticized his comments.

Ready to make amends, he asked the Stellmans, "What can I do?"

Mandy suggested he visit a sexual assault treatment center to get a better idea of the issues, and he agreed. She also mentioned a special event being held by Milwaukee NOW at which he might express his regrets in person. He did that as well, going from table to table to apologize and talk to the women.

"He was willing to listen and learn," said Mandy. "That's all I ask."

On the national level, an instance of poor taste in a February 22, 1976, segment of *60 Minutes* led Mandy to direct a letter to Morley Safer. His reference to wife beating as "that sort of thing" showed considerable insensitivity about the seriousness of the issue, so Mandy, with great restraint, called the well-known journalist to task:

> I would like to believe that your choice of the words "wife beating...that sort of thing" was inadvertent. Surely 60 Minutes *does not place the vicious act of wife beating in the same category as a parking violation.*
>
> As a female attorney, I have had the sad experience of interviewing and representing hundreds of battered women.... I have learned that the problem is (1) worldwide, (2) passed on from father to son, and (3) not given a high priority by police, judges, politicians, and even CBS news journalists.

*Please—wife beating is not "that sort of thing." Other-
wise, your programs are excellent.*[169]

No answer. Some sixteen years later as the incidence of
violence against women continued to escalate, Mandy wrote
to the current moderator of *60 Minutes,* Mike Wallace, to see
about generating interest in reporting on the alarming increase. Beginning, "I might have better luck writing to you
than to Morley Safer," Mandy pointed out that because "wife
beating has led to a wave of homicides across the nation in
the past several years, I thought I would once more try to
elicit an answer from *60 Minutes* on this serious subject."

Facetiously, she added: "Or you might ask Morley if he
ever intends to respond. I appreciate your help, since a great
deal of my practice involves battered women, and currently
I see more of them than ever."[170]

Once more there was no answer.

Mandy had better results with the U.S. Postal Service. As
she waited in line at the city's main post office one day, she
could not help but notice a sign conspicuously mounted
behind the counter facing customers. In large letters it proclaimed: "Sexual harassment in this area will not be reported; however, it will be graded."

Having seen the serious effects of harassment on wom-
en's lives, Mandy did not find this sign at all humorous. She
knew that sexual harassment in its many forms—just like
sexual assault, from touching to rape—is often used to keep
women "in their place." As soon as she returned to her office she dashed off an angry letter to the city's postmaster,
with a copy to the U.S. Postmaster General:

*I can only assume that this was supposed to be a joke,
but I find it a very sick joke. Sexual harassment is a very
serious offense, and whether this posting was displayed*

*in jest or in seriousness, it is an affront to all persons—
women and men—-whether or not they are working for
the postal service.*[171]

Shortly after, she received both a phone call and a letter
thanking her for bringing the matter to the attention of
the postmaster. Immediately, a rule was instituted that no
personal signs of any kind could be put up, and sessions on
sexual harassment were begun for employees.

One letter had brought about change in a major governmental institution. This was in 1990, the year before Anita
Hill's testimony against Clarence Thomas led to similar training in workplaces throughout the country.

###

The legal profession once again became the object of
Mandy's ire when she protested an article in the September
1977 *ABA Journal*. It had been authored by one Burt Pines,
a Los Angeles city attorney, who seemed to regard wife beating as of little consequence. Pines had proudly cited two
kinds of cases his department would henceforth handle as a
minor misdemeanor: "a dog whose barking is creating a nuisance" and "a woman [who] reports injuries sustained during a domestic quarrel and wants to prosecute."

The drawings that accompanied Pines's article were just
as offensive. One depicted a dog with its mouth open; the
other, a woman with a closed eye and facial bruises.

Mandy was furious. "Assuming Pines knows enough law
to recognize that he is required to prosecute those who
beat others," she wrote to the ABA, "it has to shock women
and men equally to know that the Los Angeles city attorney
places so little value on women generally and battered wom-
en in particular."[172]

There was no response.

###

Sometimes the solitary act of writing a letter brings an apology and lasting benefits, sometimes nothing. Nevertheless, letter writing continues to be an effective individual action for creating change, and it's an easy first step. Although some issues require organized action to effect results, other issues generate so much public outrage that a groundswell of individual responses builds to swiftly engulf the offenders. That is what happened in 1983 to *Eve*, a slick magazine with a short lifespan.

The intent of *Eve's* Milwaukee-based publisher was to offer high fashion to the area's upper crust. The publisher had the idea that photographing little girls wearing expensive necklaces and earrings would sell jewelry and soon lead to well-paid ad placements by the city's major jewelers.

Most of the parents of the children used as models were flattered to have their daughters photographed wearing off-the-shoulder gowns, heavy eye makeup, and elaborately teased tresses. They were delighted that their little girls, some as young as three, were sensuously posed, their full pouty lips evoking a "come hither" look.[173] Only one set of parents backed out of the magazine before publication. They felt the photographs made their four-year-old daughter look like Marlene Dietrich.[174]

Meanwhile, the owners of several prominent jewelry stores thought the concept clever and agreed to purchase full-page ads in the debut issue at attractive introductory rates.

When 4,000 households received their complimentary copies of *Eve*, a public outcry ensued. For weeks after, the newspapers published letters to the editor and articles covering new angles.[175]

One article quoted the words of Iola Lockhart, at the time the director of the sexual assault treatment center at Milwaukee's Family Hospital: "Portraying children as adult sexual beings seems to lend approval to treating them as sexual beings rather than as children." She added that in the first seven years of the center's existence, it had treated 460 sexual assault victims between the ages of two and thirteen.[176]

An angry Elizabeth Matz, who had been speaking for some time on the issue of how media images exploit women, invited Mandy and several other women to get together and decide what action to take.

Individual letter writing by each woman in the group was a first step. The group also chose Mandy as spokesperson for the group, and she followed up the letters by telephoning the owners and managers of each jewelry store represented in the magazine.

Mandy found all of them courteous on the phone, some to the point of expressing concern, although a few at first "didn't get it"—like most of the parents of the seductive models. After Mandy explained how using little girls as sexy objects represented a form of pornography, the jewelers apologized profusely and decided against using little girls again in any of their advertising.[177]

The manager of the downtown branch of Bailey, Banks, and Biddle was particularly upset. "I had no idea! What can I do?" he asked.

Mandy invited him to a Sunday afternoon program led by Matz, whose slide presentation had been powerfully and unmistakably demonstrating for some time the pornographic aspects of numerous advertisements appearing in *Life, Time,* and other magazines.

"Pedophiles get affirmation from images they see in legitimate magazines," said Mandy, who knew that rapists often rationalized their offenses by blaming the victim, no matter how young or old.[178] Even more shocking, some judges—who "should know better," added Mandy—continued to let rapists go free because they concurred with the offender that the child was so "sexy" the rapist "could not help himself."

Milwaukee's reaction to *Eve* magazine in the early eighties occurred in the wake of a national controversy over the use of children in adult roles, which the 1978 movie *Pretty Baby* had set off a few years earlier. The movie featured Brooke Shields, a twelve-year-old cast in a provocative adult role.[179]

Over the years, the sexploitation of children has continued to increase, as images in all forms of media have become on the one hand more violent and brutal—on the other, more subtle and brutalizing. Anger and controversy erupted again in 1996 in the mysterious murder of Jon-Benet Ramsey, a "beauty queen" at the age of six.

Parallel to this increase is the unabated flood of sex crimes. The U.S. Justice Department reports that in the United States every minute of every day, more than one woman is raped. One of every four girls is sexually abused before the age of fourteen; one out of seven boys is sexually abused before the age of eighteen.[180]

Still the sexploitation of women and children of all ages grows, creating a lucrative tourist industry worldwide, most of it supported by willing businessmen, all of it sending a message about the sexual availability of women and children everywhere.

###

PART FOUR: TOWARD THE FUTURE

Political struggle is the most important thing any of us can do as citizens in a democracy....

The most important [thing] is for people who are still healthy and strong to get out and volunteer. Don't just donate your money, donate your heart, donate yourself.

Jonathan Kozol

13. Arrest Crime, Live Without Fear

It was a morning in late March that hinted at an early spring for southeast Wisconsin. Though Sam had retired, he remained as busy as ever, speaking and meeting with groups of all kinds.

Hardly any seats remained in the classroom that particular morning. In the front row of cramped student desks sat a large man, whom Sam recognized as a local political figure. When the man cleared his throat, Sam knew that the rest of the attendees—criminal justice personnel, professionals in related fields, community leaders, and interested citizens—were about to be treated to the minor official's simple solution to crime.

"The trouble with the system is that judges are too soft," declared the politician loudly. "Why should crooks be afraid? They know that even if they're caught, they'll just get a slap on the wrist and be let out to commit more crimes."

The man half-turned his massive shoulders so he could be seen by the others in the classroom—most of whom had signed up for Dr. Stellman's discussion because they knew

simple solutions did *not* exist. They had come to exchange
ideas about alternatives for dealing with the criminal offender. But the politician had his own ideas, and he was
building up steam.

"My constituents can't even walk down the street because
of these punks," he said, jabbing his finger in the air. "We
need tougher laws and longer sentences—or even capital
punishment. It'd scare the pants off these low-lifes if they
thought they were facing ten, twenty years in prison, or
even execution. Believe me, we'd see the crime rate go down
in a hurry."

"You're wrong," replied Sam calmly, taking in the faces
before him. "The threat of incarceration is meaningless to
the hard-core lawbreaker. We're not talking here about mandatory arrest for the guy who's beating up his wife, where
the arrest serves an immediate need for stopping the battering and keeping him away from her till he cools down."

The politician glared as Sam continued to quietly deflate
his faulty reasoning.

"The threat of jail might deter people from the middle
and upper classes—in fact, a few well-placed signs on college campuses would help cut down on date rape. A motivated kid, his whole career ahead of him, just might think
twice if he saw a sign in his frat house or in the taverns
that said, 'Rape is an illegal violent act that can get you
twenty years in prison.' And a woman might be more encouraged to warn her date that he'd be reported if he got
too aggressive. But for the vast majority of violent offenders, even the threat of capital punishment has no effect."

Standing before the politician, whose glistening forehead
suggested his discomfort, Sam explained that the states
with capital punishment often had the highest homicide
rates. He pointed out that when many states responded to
the rising crime rate with stiffer penalties and longer sen-

tences, prisons got more crowded but crime didn't let up. "So what did officials do?" he asked his listeners. "They got tougher. And crime rates kept rising. When I hear terms like 'soft on crime' or 'slap on the wrist,' I think of a talk-show mentality—someone who doesn't understand how judges hand out sentences. Blaming our law enforcement professionals for the high crime rate is like blaming the dentist for a toothache."

Perhaps it was the mention of a toothache that caused the politician to clamp his jaws and say nothing.

A latecomer entered the packed room and found a seat at the side. Dressed in the uniform of a police officer, she appeared to have just gotten off third shift. She looked familiar to Sam, but he couldn't place her. He'd worked with so many officers over the years.

He picked up his train of thought.

"You know the programs that try to scare people out of crime? They don't work. Ever hear of *Scared Straight?* Juveniles are taken to the state prison to hear prisoners talk about the horrors of incarceration. But it doesn't work."[181]

A brightly dressed woman in the third row nodded vigorously. "I wonder why no one ever asks why the repeat offenders weren't scared straight by their *first* time in prison!"

A man in a security guard's uniform spoke up. "I remember the documentary on TV called *Scared Straight.* I think it won an Academy Award or something. All kinds of celebrities were urging people to watch it. They thought a two-hour TV show would succeed where those of us working in the field had failed."

"Well, Ronald Reagan thought so, too," replied Sam. "He didn't understand why such a simple answer hadn't been thought of earlier."

Sam explained that *Scared Straight* had been based on
other similar attempts. "There was one in Colorado that reported a 'splendid success rate.' But the evaluation was in-
complete. It turned out that the success rate was based on
fewer than one percent of participants responding.[182] Today," Sam continued, "everyone agrees that attempts such
as *Scared Straight* haven't worked. It's like parents who talk
about the 'bogey man' to scare their children."

The politician's voice boomed out again. "Yeah, but what
about those boot camps they have for juvenile delinquents?
They really make those kids toe the line there!"

"As a way to turn people away from crime, boot camps are
a failure, too." Sam did not show his impatience. "Even
though inmates can get a reduced sentence for attending
the camp, the dropout rate is over sixty percent."

Sam was using his logical approach, which was almost
always effective. He never shouted. At times, he wished he
had a great voice, like Barbara Jordan's. But he believed
that everyone was born with certain faculties, and that people had to work with what they had. Whereas Mandy might
define herself as a steamroller, Sam's manner was low key:
speak softly and sell quality, like the Rolls Royce salesman
he'd once been compared to. It's the manner he used with
obnoxious people.[183]

An older woman raised her hand tentatively. "What do
you mean, 'boot camp'?"

"It's a program where young men, usually early offenders,
are put in camps where staff members act like the stereo-
type of a military boot camp sergeant. They scream at the
inmates and enforce a very strict discipline. Everything from
bedmaking to marching has to be done with precision...."

The politician interjected "...and violating the rules means
penalties, like push-ups."

"But almost two-thirds drop out," continued Sam. "They'd

rather serve their full sentence, because they feel that a degrading program like this questions their manhood. Most important, *nowhere* is there any plan to see that these men become adequately employed or educated when they return to the community." Sam's low-key rebuttal took on a sarcastic edge. "Just completing the program is supposed to make a juvenile more of a 'man,' and that supposedly assures him of being able to make it in society."

A pale woman sitting next to the overweight politician leaned forward. "Still, it seems to me that the concept is sound," she ventured, her voice barely audible. "Maybe the discipline isn't carried out correctly."

Sam had a way of using facts to shoot holes in theories without wounding the theorist. "These young men have been yelled at and punished all their lives for violating social norms and laws," he explained to the woman. "What they need most is someone nonthreatening to work with them to help them plan their future and learn how to stay out of trouble." Sam's pet theories began to surface. "As long as there's no program to turn these men around, they will be in and out of prison all their adult lives. I think the most effective way to keep them from becoming lifelong offenders is to have trained volunteers work one-on-one with boys in trouble and men coming out of prison."

Stepping to the blackboard, Sam drew a rough circle. "The problem affects everyone in the community. The police and the court system need the *community* to look at why there is so much crime, and then do something about the conditions that *cause* the crime."

The police officer who'd come in late raised her hand. "I agree. If they're put right back in the same situation, with the old neighborhood gang, all the old patterns may be repeated."

The officer's voice sounded familiar. Sam recognized her—

Rebecca, the former student who'd come to him about leaving the police force. It was the uniform that made her look different, he realized. She looked older than he'd remembered, and tired.

"It's going to take a lot of people and a lot of money," Sam told the group. "And the public has to understand that as a society we are responsible for each other's welfare."

"Hmmph" came from the front row. "More taxes!"

The pale woman in the next seat asked, "If jail or boot camp isn't appropriate for juveniles who commit crimes, what do we do with them?"

"The *first* time people come in contact with the law," Sam replied, "put them in a program designed to turn them around—one that stresses formal education and job preparation—with a part-time job as part of the program."

Pages rustled as several people began taking notes.

"I'd just like to add here," said Rebecca, "that it's important to choose candidates for such a program who will admit they have a problem and are committed to changing their behavior. Some violators I've encountered will participate in any program, knowing they'll get credit for good behavior and serve less time. But they don't change."

"That's why it's vital for a rehabilitation program to have one-to-one supervision by a trained volunteer," Sam added.

"You mean like the VIP program?" someone asked.

"Good example," said Sam, going on to explain how VIP—Volunteers in Probation—had been set up to pair adults and juveniles on probation with suitable volunteers from the community. The probationers had made a poor choice once in their lives. The volunteers would help them "go straight."

Introduced by Judge Max Raskin, a Milwaukee County circuit court judge in August 1969, the VIP program was one of the first to come out of Sam's Center for Social Services at UW-Milwaukee Extension. Sam designed the program, obtained the grant to fund it, conducted training, and oversaw operations. But because it was not the university's role to directly conduct community programs, the Salvation Army was designated headquarters for the local VIP program. In less than six years, as other communities picked up on Sam's idea, about 100,000 volunteers were involved nationally. Some 1,200 volunteers were involved in Milwaukee alone.[184]

Matching the probationers with suitable volunteers was a key to the program's effectiveness, and in that task, Mandy was a great help to Sam.

He chuckled as he told the class, "We matched a forger with an honest businessperson, a prostitute with a nun. I never would have thought of that combination myself, but the nun really straightened out the prostitute and got her a legitimate job."

Training was given to volunteers from every sector of society, men and women, white-collar and blue-collar. Mandy helped the volunteers understand the court system so they could be of greater assistance to their probationers.

Someone asked, "That kind of mentoring sounds ideal, but theory doesn't always work. What was the result?"

"The program had a high success rate," Sam replied. "A tremendous number of kids on probation stayed in school, and older people on probation got jobs."

Glancing at the politician, Sam explained how that success rate was amplified throughout the system. "Less tax money was spent because probationers were kept out of prison. And some of the burden of professional probation officers was relieved. When the VIP program began, the caseload of a Milwaukee County probation officer was over two hundred. The recommended caseload, nationally, is thirty-five or less. The probationers actually got more counseling from the volunteers we trained than they ordinarily got from their overburdened caseworkers."

"I'm wondering if there are any programs that attempt to raise someone's general education level?" asked a well-dressed man in the audience.

Sam leaned against the table at the front of the room. "Let me tell you about one. It had a positive payback, long-term, but it would be impossible to get support for it today.

"Back in 1973 or somewhere around then, we started Rehabilitation Aides. We took people either on probation or on parole and put them through a year of college. As much as I can remember, it started with my talking to some of the probation and parole people about whether education would do some good with these offenders. And they thought, well, it's worth a try. It was a creative idea, and when it's creative, I want to get it in. We wrote the grant to get federal money, and the federal people were enthusiastic."

The alderman snorted, stirring noisily in his seat. Sam continued.

"It wasn't complicated. The probation people screened the candidates to see if they might be college material. The Rehabilitation Aides were university faculty who taught standard college courses, and the program paid for a year of courses for each participant. The probationers also got some money for living expenses, because most were unemployed, and keeping up with classes took a lot of time. They got a check every month. Of course, at the beginning of the program, we had several who came only for the check. We threw them out. If they didn't come to class, they were out."

No one interrupted Sam's telling of the story.

"We did the teaching, and about half the probationers got through their first year. Probably a third of those went on to a second year on their own. Altogether, the program ran about three years or so with federal money. It was unique, and I wish we could have kept it going. Then the funding went out—which is typical."

Murmurs of understanding rippled through the room.

Sam chuckled. "Here's how someone once described federal programming. Let's say you want to keep minority kids from dropping out of college, and you want to see what kind of programming works best to do that. So you get a grant and start your research program, and the kids make it through the first year. You go back to the feds and say, 'It works. Now let's get enough money so we can help more kids with this successful program. They say, 'No, but if you'd said you failed, we'd give you money to find out why you failed.'"

Half the class laughed while others smiled and nodded knowingly. Sam chuckled again, but without humor. "Anyway, we started Rehabilitation Aides, we ran it, and it was effective. It was also very expensive, and today you'd never get money for that kind of thing. It's tough to get money for anything to do with criminals, like the programs I've encouraged where they run college courses right in the prison.[185]

"The public objects. They say, 'These guys are getting free tuition while my kids are paying.' Even the prison guards object. 'Why do I have to pay for my kids to go to college while prisoners I guard here can get free courses?'

"You aren't going to convince anyone that these courses will keep guys out of prison. Just like you can't convince people that paying for education is cheaper than paying for crime. If you say, 'for what you're paying now to keep them in prison you could send them to *Yale*,' people would still rather keep them in prison. And even when you tell them we have programs that cost about one-tenth of what it costs to keep a guy in prison, the public still wants him to go to prison. The public is not buying alternatives to building more prisons."

During the class break most attendees went off to find the soft drink machines, but many wanted to hear more. Gathered around Sam, they soon had him reminiscing about his travels throughout the state to set up fourteen more VIP operations like the one in Milwaukee. He told of Mandy's writing a letter to the *Milwaukee Journal* urging her fellow attorneys to ask that judges enroll probationers in the VIP program whenever appropriate.

Eventually, as with so many other good programs, federal funding for the Milwaukee VIP program dried up. Sam explained how the Salvation Army became involved and then transferred the program to another community agency, which was forced to limit VIP services because of a shortage of funds. Although the Milwaukee program ended, VIP programs in many counties statewide remained in existence, and more counties added similar programs.[186]

After the break, a young man raised his hand. "What do you think of prostitution, Dr. Stellman?"

Laughter rippled through the room.

The man reddened. "I mean, the way the system handles prostitution?"

"The only prostitutes who appear in court are the poorer ones," Sam replied. "Many cities have special vice squads whose job is to entrap prostitutes, but they seem to get only the poor ones, not the high-class call girls."

Rebecca, from her seat at the side of the room, spoke up, explaining how an undercover officer has to pass marked money to the seller before an arrest can be made.

Sam nodded. "Most police departments are reluctant to trust the officers with too much money. This means the officers simply don't have enough bucks to go after the prostitutes in the expensive apartments, so only the street-walkers ever appear in court."

A man about Sam's age spoke for the first time. "Don't you think we need to reorder our priorities so the police and the prosecuting attorney's office place their greatest emphasis on crimes against people—I mean, violent criminal acts?"

"Absolutely," Sam replied. "Too much emphasis is placed on whether taverns close on time, or on cases like prostitution, which involve entrapment by the vice squad. A change in priorities would go a long way toward restoring public confidence in the criminal justice system and its ability to control crime. What do you think, Rebecca?"

"I agree. Many of us on the force want to fight *hard* crime." She looked around the room. "So much is going on in the streets that it's overwhelming for us, and for judges, too, dealing with hundreds of misdemeanors when so many major crimes need immediate attention. Sure, minor crimes have to be addressed, but there are better ways than to tie up the courts. It might be best if the police weren't involved at all in crimes like gambling and prostitution. Assigning these to social services agencies would be one alternative."

The room was silent except for the muffled scratching of pens and the rustling of notebook pages. Because the group had come together to talk about alternatives to court, Sam began listing some of them.

"Intensive probation, with two conditions of probation: training in literacy, and employment skills. Home detention, sometimes combined with electronic monitoring. Fines. Restitution and community service. Individual and family counseling, including special counseling for alcohol and drug abuse, when needed. And early intervention programs for first-time offenders."[187]

He paused. Pages rustled.

###

For those whose flirtation with drugs turned into long-term abuse, Sam and one of his faculty members established a live-in drug treatment program in 1970.

He told about hiring Bill Priestly, considered an expert in drug abuse programming, and giving him the task of searching the country to find a program that successfully treated long-term abusers. The program had to not only involve treatment, but also enable staff members to keep an eye on their clients to make sure they stuck with the program and stayed off drugs. The assignment was a tough one, but Bill found just such a program in California called "The Family." Sam sent him there to learn how the program was run. Soon, he and Sam received a federal grant as seed money.

The home subsequently established in Milwaukee also received the name "The Family." It housed a limited number of heavy drug abusers. During the day they were gainfully employed, and evenings and weekends they took part in intensive drug counseling. Strict rules were established. Residents had to come home immediately after work. Drinking and drugs were prohibited, as was communication with known drug sellers or abusers. Those who violated the rules were dismissed from the program and the home. The program proved successful.

"The Family was the only agency recommended by the Milwaukee courts for referral of hard-core addicts," recalled Sam. It was ultimately turned over to the Wisconsin Correctional Service, which carried on the original program under a new name: Residential Treatment Center. It has been in

existence for more than twenty years—the longest-running
live-in treatment center for drug abusers in Wisconsin.

Sam next told the class about CCV, or Controlling Community Violence, an award-winning program that grew out of
a request by Judge Dennis Flynn of the Racine circuit court
in 1990. "Credit for developing CCV goes to Professor Kim
Baugrud, a creative, hard-working man who seems to have
almost built-in radar for ferreting out what a situation
needs." Sam always gave credit where credit was due.

"It's a program of education and therapy used by the circuit courts in Racine for people charged with criminal misdemeanors, such as criminal damage to property, battery,
or disorderly conduct."

"Disorderly conduct?" asked one counselor, grinning. "You
mean like the 'tavern fights' some of my clients get into?"

"Exactly," Sam replied seriously. "People who get involved
in these fights think they're harmless. Violent behavior,
unfortunately, has become a way of life for many people—
their reaction to any stressful situation. These men and
women need to learn the reasons for their violent behavior
and to understand the consequences of their actions. CCV
teaches some alternative approaches. The goal is to reduce
violence in the community."

"What actually happens to make these people less violent?" asked the pale woman sitting next to the politician.
He glared at her, and Sam surmised they were married.

"To begin with, they participate in group discussions."

"Discussion groups!" The politician smirked.

Pens became busy again as Sam described how people in
the group talked about the reasons people became violent,
the effects of violence, and what happened if they violated
the law again. Participants in CCV were asked to examine

their personal belief systems—why they resorted to violence for problem-solving.

"Those with drug or alcohol problems are referred to appropriate agencies," added Sam. Participants who paid the course fee, $125, and completed the one-day, eight-hour workshop, could get their fines or sentences reduced.

"More than one participant told me, 'It's a hell of a lot better than going to jail.' Best of all," Sam noted, "the program really seemed to work. Professor Baugrud followed more than five hundred offenders for eighteen months after their sentencing. Of those who didn't participate in CCV, thirty-four percent had one or more arrests. Of those who did participate, fewer than twelve percent had re-arrests.

"Tell me that's not a change in attitude! Not to mention a saving of the taxpayers' money."

A similar educational process occurred as part of Nevermore, a program to which batterers were referred by judges either as an alternative to sentencing or in conjunction with probation, fines, or other corrections.

"The men enrolled in Nevermore learned about being responsible for their behavior," Sam began. "They were confronted with the results of their violence on their female partners. Just as important, they learned about and practiced alternative behaviors that helped them communicate with their partners in nonviolent ways."

The politician's belligerence had reduced itself to loudly whispered comments to his wife. "Relationships. Programs. What about getting tough?"

Sam ignored the man and told of another successful alternative he initiated, Deprogramming Men Who Batter, which insisted that the violence must stop immediately and the abuser take full responsibility for his actions.[188]

A hand went up. "It sounds like using programs for certain kinds of offenders can be effective."

"It's not just programs," Sam replied. "You have to look at the causes and want to make real change. And you have to be outraged!"

Someone asked about the JAC program for shoplifters, and Sam explained how it worked.

"JAC stands for Justice Alternative Court. Judge William Panagis from the Milwaukee municipal court got the ball rolling on that one. The judge had been seeing all these first-time shoplifters in his court, people who'd ruined their lives because of one mistake. He went to a conference in Texas and met a fellow who'd started a program for shoplifters.

"So the judge and I got together with the police and the heads of security for all the big stores in Milwaukee and had one big meeting. I brought in the fellow who'd made the presentation at the Texas conference. After we brainstormed, I went back to the office, looked at the Texas program, did some major revisions to fit the Milwaukee scene, and we developed the JAC through the Criminal Justice Institute. That was 1981, and it's been running ever since.

"The judge gives the accused shoplifter the choice of paying a substantial fine or attending the JAC program," Sam continued. "Those who complete the program successfully often get their records cleared and don't have to pay the fine. The case is dismissed."

Sam picked up the chalk and scribbled some statistics on the board. He seldom wrote on a board because his handwriting was hard to read. He continued speaking:

"Our outreach specialist, Cherie Maris, did a beautiful job with the JAC program. She's so competent, it was a joy. She ran all over the state administering and setting up new programs. With her help, we expanded the JAC program to Stevens Point, Rhinelander, and Racine, with eighty to ninety classes a year in the four counties, as well as the programs in Manitowoc, Rhinelander, and Menomonee Falls. Anywhere from sixty to eighty people attended an all-day JAC class— we ran one a month—and the unique thing is that the people who came to it paid their own fees. That's why the judges liked it. Fees were fifty-five dollars to attend the program, including lunch, and that covered our costs."

Someone asked if the program helped chronic shoplifters.

"We don't knowingly let in repeat offenders. If they've been through the system too many times, they're beyond this stage and need more intervention. The program is for the person who is basically good and who just made a bad decision. I say, 'Look, you're not a criminal. You made a mistake. Let's learn from it.' These are first offenders. They're not dangerous people. The average age is about thirty-five, and includes every kind of person—even ministers and cops and security people!" Sam chuckled. "They're no different from other citizens. I haven't found one who is a 'klepto-maniac.' They know they're shoplifting. It's not an unconscious thing. Most of them respect the law and are afraid of the law. So we examine the law with them and also the consequences if they shoplift again. That's a key part.

"It's the most fascinating program for anybody to watch. One of the rules is that you must talk about what you did or you can't come to the program. We have them talk about the event itself, how they got picked up. At that point is when things begin to change. We see it. The moment they have to say it out loud, and they start to say things like 'I wasn't treated right,' they stop, and the whole group looks at them, because they're trying to put the blame on someone else. We make them accountable for what they did, and by the end of the day, you see a totally different group.

"It's remarkably successful," Sam added. "Since 1981, more than eight thousand individuals completed the course in Milwaukee alone. Ratings by participants in a JAC program have been over ninety-nine percent positive, and recidivism is under ten percent."

"Speaking of shoplifting..." began a social worker Sam recognized, "that reminds me of—we used to refer to him as 'Emil.' Maybe you ought to tell the folks about the MRO program, Sam."

Sam nodded at the bespectacled social worker. "You tell the story, George."

"Well, all right." George stood and adjusted his glasses. "This fellow, Emil, he's mildly retarded, you know? MRO stands for the mentally retarded offender. Anyway, one day Emil happened along just as one of his so-called 'friends' was about to get caught for shoplifting. Well, this 'friend' shoved the loot into poor Emil's hands and ran away, leaving him to take the blame. The police booked him, but luckily, the judge dismissed the charge after learning the truth."

George sat down, and Sam then described how the MRO program that he and Kim Baugrud pioneered came about. "A supervisor at the Southern Wisconsin Center for the Developmentally Disabled contacted Professor Baugrud. She was very upset because a Waukesha judge had sentenced a felon to serve his time at the Center. The man *was* determined to be developmentally disabled, but the Center was not a penal institution." The supervisor, Randy Hayward, felt the mistake was happening more and more. This suggested that something needed changing in the system.

"So we set up a meeting with eighty-five police officers, judges, sheriffs, agency personnel, citizens—we tried to include everybody. Based on that meeting, Professor Baugrud and I decided to incorporate information about people with developmental disabilities directly into the law enforcement training programs."

"Professor Stellman, that—forgive me for jumping in—" said an earnest young woman. "What you just said, incorporating something directly into law enforcement training— that sounds like an important difference between taking action for social change and just providing a service."

"Well, yes, you could say so. I'll give you a good example." Sam began, "One program that came out of our shop trained volunteers to mediate 'pittance' cases: two neighbors arguing, or a dog that goes on someone's lawn, or loud music, that sort of thing. The D.A. isn't going to prosecute, so the court throws these cases out, yet the police were called and there are costs involved."

Sam explained that although this volunteer mediation program[189] was successful, it was essentially a direct service to help the individual people involved who had a particular dispute. "There are hundreds and thousands of these situations. People don't always get along so well." He chuckled.

He went on to explain how a program that provides a service doesn't make a permanent change in the system; rather, the service has to be repeated for each of the hundreds or thousands of people who enter the system—provided the program's resources hold out. Resources, of course, go beyond funding when a program is headed by volunteers, because providing one-on-one service tends to burn out volunteers.

Sam then contrasted the mediation service for neighbor disputes with a training program that changes the way the system handles certain law enforcement problems right from the start. The MRO training, which was named "The Mentally Retarded Offender and the Criminal Justice System Professional," gave the police, sheriffs, and probation and parole officers the tools they needed to deal with offenders who had developmental disabilities. Making those tools part of police training was bringing about real change in the system: a problem was being dealt with at its source, and a solution was being implemented at the level where the same type of problem could be prevented from then on.

"The training was led by Professor Baugrud, and it helped the police understand the problems and become more sensitive in handling people with special needs."

The politician, quiet for some time, interrupted. "You're saying these programs excuse people who commit crimes?"

"Not at all. MRO programs advocate that any individual with a developmental disability who comes in contact with the law gets appropriate consideration from the time of initial contact until release."

George spoke up again, poking his glasses. "The training was videotaped, remember, Sam? And the police chief, Breier, arranged for the videos to be shown to all the rookies and officers in the city as part of their in-service training."

Sam nodded. "For the police departments around the state, we developed a training manual and audiocassettes, which the Knights of Columbus helped fund." A copy of the training program was also given to all police academies, vocational-technical institutes, and universities in Wisconsin. "We had a ceremony in 1984 where we literally handed the whole thing to Tony Earl, governor at the time.[190] The training program is being used at all the police academies in the state, at the State Patrol, the Department of Corrections, and the Department of Natural Resources. We also ran training once a year at the Criminal Justice Institute for other professionals who deal with the mentally retarded." Sam added, "More than seven thousand professionals have gone through the programs statewide."

###

"Sam, remember the young woman who always got caught?" George needed no prompting to tell the story. "She was a *terrible* shoplifter; she'd hit the same store five times in one week. Well, it took an expert in developmental disabilities to figure out why she did it. Because she loved to ride in the police cruiser!"

Sam laughed along with the class but quickly became serious again. "Cases like these show just how much a training program is needed to help police and security people understand the situation. You have to remember that nine to ten percent of the prison population is considered 'mentally retarded,' though only three percent of the overall population is. It's not because the individuals commit more crimes—it's because they get caught more easily in situations that people of average intelligence could avoid."

The pale woman raised her hand and asked how women are treated by the criminal justice system.

All at once, everyone had an opinion or a comment.

"They're not treated fairly at all," said the woman in the bright outfit. "Y'know the job training they get in prison that's supposed to give them a job skill? Supermarket checkout clerk! It just leads to lower-paying jobs than men get. How can that do much to 'arrest crime'?"

"How 'bout auto mechanic training?"

"Now you're talking."

Rebecca added a comment about so-called "status crimes"—not crimes at all but behaviors that ordinarily would be ignored if exhibited by males. "For example, a girl who runs away from home."

"Sounds to me like the old double standard again," said the brightly outfitted woman. "What else is new?"

Another participant commented, "The media blamed the

women's movement for the rising number of women in prison, as if women who become equal to men take on their
behaviors, too, like committing crimes. Yet I seem to recall
a study showing that almost all these women were the *girlfriends* of criminals and were in prison because they'd been
helping 'their man' in some criminal activity. They weren't
feminists at all!"

"That reminds me of an interesting thing that came from
another program, Second Chance," said Sam. "It's an early
intervention program we started for nonviolent first offenders. These are mostly boys, but a few girls are referred to
the program. When they are asked what brought them there,
the boys answer fighting, shoplifting, vandalism, or drinking.

"But nearly every girl was picked up for fighting. Fighting over what? In almost every case, fighting over boys."
Sam paused. "And the boy's role was to egg her on to fight,
not because he had any particular interest in the girl, but
because he enjoyed controlling her behavior. He could show
his buddies he could get 'his' girl to do anything for him."

"Seems to me," offered one of the women in the class,
"that a good dose of feminism would go a long way to reducing crime committed by women."

Rebecca replied, "It would go a long way to reducing crime
among men, too."

Only a handful of people snickered. Others nodded.

Sam then described an eight-session series he and Mandy
led in the spring of 1977. It examined the unique problems
of women in the criminal justice system, "which to my knowledge no one had done before." The series was sponsored by
the Extension's Institute of Governmental Affairs, and it
featured guest speakers Severa Austin and Shirley Abrahamson.[191]

###

Anyone sitting in this or any other workshop or discussion of Sam's could see that his greatest pride was reserved for the creative contributions Mandy made to his work.

"She thought of the name 'Housecoping' for one program," he said, explaining that it developed because too many housing violations in Milwaukee had been going uncorrected by homeowners. Fines were ineffective, as many of the homeowners didn't have the money anyway. A frustrated assistant city attorney, Tom Cooper, brought the problem to the attention of three municipal judges, Rudolph Randa, Beverly Temple, and Ted Wedemeyer.[192]

To find a workable solution, Sam set up a meeting among the judges and a few of the more discouraged building inspectors. Sam proposed a program in which volunteers would be appointed to work one-on-one with people charged with broken steps, missing railings, and other safety hazards. The volunteers would help determine which conditions needed priority attention, and they would help make the repairs with a small contribution from the city's development department. A pilot program to work with fifty clients began under the direction of Bill Winter, and a clinic was set up through the Center for Social Services that showed people how to maintain their houses.

It was Mandy who recognized that the problems often went beyond a lack of money or carpentry skills. She realized that many people guilty of housing code violations were completely overwhelmed by many different problems in their lives, such as juggling two jobs or lacking dependable child care. So she saw to it that volunteers were trained to counsel people about their personal situations as well as their housing problems. And she provided some of this training herself, emphasizing to the volunteers, "Whatever you see in your client is a symptom of problems he or she cannot cope with—it's not a failure of the human being."[193]

Sam began to describe some of the tough cases resolved through the Housecoping project. He told of the clients of Mandy's who raised dogs. The house had been cited for so many violations it was declared unfit for human habitation. The owners were cited for cruelty to animals because of the conditions under which their dogs were kept, such as restricting them with extremely short leashes in a small, crowded yard.

Sam encouraged another social worker to add her comments. He knew that Elaine had counseled some of Housecoping's clients.

"Okay," began a tall, slender woman. "Well, anyone referred to municipal court for housing code violations had the option of fixing up their place, paying a fine, or being referred to Housecoping. If the individual eliminated the, y'know, violation with help from the Housecoping staff and volunteers, okay, charges were dropped. The individual got counseling from volunteers, like me, to help them in whatever personal situation was getting in their way. And they got help from architects, plumbers, carpenters, and so on— all on a volunteer basis. In some cases, community groups with larger workforces lent a hand."

Turning to look at the politician, Elaine explained how, at times, city aldermen called the Housecoping staff for help in getting a whole neighborhood involved in a clean-up campaign, and how the Housecoping staff also conducted clinics about health hazards and dangers associated with failing to maintain a sanitary home.

Sam added, "We saw great success with Housecoping. In the five years we had the program, thousands of people got the help they needed. Hundreds of homes were saved from demolition. The relatively small cost of Housecoping saved the city a great deal of taxpayers' money." He glanced at the politician. "Unfortunately, the funding ran out."

Elaine offered a concluding note. "When you save a house, you often save a neighborhood from going downhill, y'know? And if we can keep our neighborhoods up, Milwaukee will be a better place to live."

Sam smiled ruefully. "I'll admit though, among all our successes, we've had the occasional failure. There was one woman." He chuckled. "Everyone called her the Cat Lady. She kept dozens and dozens of cats in her house, and it became completely unfit to live in. It was a nice house in a nice area. The smell was so awful the neighbors complained, and when the building inspectors got a look at the place, they were horrified. They recommended she be evicted. But she brought suit to stop the eviction.

"Mandy agreed to meet with her—though she wasn't a client—provided she came to the office without her cats. They met, and the woman promised to fix things up, but nothing ever happened.

"The city ended up evicting her, condemning the property, and pulling down the house because it was beyond repair. Most of the cats were emaciated and obviously sick, and they went to the Humane Society. It took about a week to air out Mandy's office."

###

Although the day's topic focused on options for dealing with criminal offenders, Sam was never one to stick to a script, especially when members of an audience represented agencies with dismal track records in helping those they were designed to help.

"All agencies that are supposed to help people should ask themselves, 'If we went out of business tomorrow, would we be missed?'"

Heads nodded as the professionals in the room recognized the truth in Sam's question.

"Billions of dollars are spent both nationally and locally. The money comes from public and private sources. But much of that money doesn't go where it should go and doesn't do what it should do. Agencies aren't always held accountable and asked to prove their value. Meanwhile, other agencies that have substantial needs and make good use of their money are underfunded."

This is an issue Sam returned to again and again. "You know, I'm a goal-oriented person. So I always make it clear to anyone I work with what the goals are. Three things have to be there: establishing a clear goal, determining what means we will use to get there, and then actually accomplishing that goal. Often, only the first two take off—setting the goal and doing it. Then people forget about accomplishing anything. It's a case of confusing the means and the ends. The means run the show—because people aren't outraged enough. Over and over I've seen that."

Sam continued, "If agencies are to continue receiving money, they must be asked, 'Are you helping people get out of poverty—or whatever your purpose is—or are you simply making them feel comfortable about being poor?' I keep hearing agencies say, 'If we help only one person, we got our money's worth.' No! Not when the agency has a budget of half a million dollars a year! That's not much of a success rate. At that rate, helping one person isn't worth a damn. It's an outrage!"

###

A dozen or so people clustered around Sam at the end of the session.

"Two-thirds of your hundreds of programs still going after so many years! It's something to be proud of," said one.

Added another, "And with over twenty-thousand served over the lifetimes of the JAC and Second Chance programs, and I think the Alcohol Education Awareness program, too."

"That last one, I wasn't involved in it..."

"But you definitely inspired it, Sam."

"Thank you for the ideas you've given me," interrupted a man on his way toward the door. "I'm going to start some educational programs like you did."

"Programs are not what I'm all about," Sam called after the man, shaking his head and wondering if he'd failed to make his point in class. "Programs are a means to an end," he said to the few remaining people. "It disturbs me that some programs turn into an end in themselves. The 'ends' have to be very meaningful and very tangible in affecting people's *lives*. And the means of getting there have to be *very clear*, not vaguely identified."

The room gradually emptied except for the police officer.

"Rebecca, I cringe whenever someone labels an educational program 'successful.' Mandy and I could be doing 'successful' programs forever, but if the results are simply internalized by people going through a program, without some radical change as the outcome, to us such programs are meaningless."[194]

"I want to make real changes in people's lives, too, Sam. That's why I've been rethinking where I put my energies."

"I recall your having some doubts the last time we talked."

"Yes, well, I've continued to have doubts, Sam. I've been trying to figure out where and how I could do the most good." She smiled. "You know, for a long time I thought I'd follow in Mandy's footsteps and become a lawyer, and then maybe a judge. But now I've changed my mind...."

The gray-haired professor and the police officer gathered their things and left the empty classroom.

"It's taken me ten years in uniform to realize that I want to try turning people around *before* they come into the criminal justice system—to get them at a younger age." Rebecca grinned. "I've decided to become a teacher, Sam. I've already enrolled in classes. This is my last year on the force."

"Congratulations! That's just the reverse of what Mandy did. She started out as a teacher and moved into the law."

"And is probably a better lawyer for having been a teacher. I'm hoping I'll be a better teacher because of my police work."

"In a way you *are* following in her footsteps. And mine. You keep looking for better ways to improve the lives of greater numbers of people. Too bad more folks can't see the difference between the means and the end." Sam often worried that his life's work might be summed up as a series of programs.

"At first it was the cynicism on the force that got to me, Sam. That, and so much else made me wonder if *anyone* can make a difference, with crime getting so bad and all."

"Your being on the force had to make a difference."

"Well, I know I raised the consciousness of some of the macho officers I work with. And maybe I made them a little more sensitive in their dealings with women. Actually, I hope more women will go into police work."

As the pair left the building they stopped on the steps a moment, the sun directly overhead. A warm spring breeze came from Lake Michigan.

"There's no one path, Rebecca. Anyone can make a difference, no matter what their job, if they feel a sense of outrage at injustice *and act on it.* As Mandy says, no one has to 'cope with crap.'"

"I think of you and Mandy when something really gets to me and I'm tempted to just forget it. But then I think, 'What would the Stellmans do?' And you know what? The outrage you talk about gets stirred up in me, and I feel full of energy!"

###

14. The Check Is in the Mail

The deejay leaned over the mike. "This is WTOS, Milwaukee's best underground radio station. We're opening up the lines for requests now. What do you want to hear?"

The phone lines lit up.

"Hello? Yeah, man, I—uh, my fingers are disappearing, and I don't know what to do...." The caller sounded scared, and younger than usual.

Barbara Hoerl rubbed her forehead. It was 1969, and this part-time disk jockey, secretary, newsperson, and college student was getting calls like this one with overwhelming frequency.

"I talked another one down today," she told a friend afterward. "Lois, he was so strung out he couldn't even tell me what he'd taken! Little green pills with lines—how am I supposed to know what those are?"

"I guess they call the station because there's nowhere else to turn," said Lois, who was married to Bob Reitman, the regular deejay for the station.

"Listening to this caller reminded me of that Wisconsin kid I saw at Woodstock last week. His withdrawal was so bad he was on his knees begging for downers—anything to calm himself down. Man, his parents probably put him in a psych ward when he got home. There *has* to be someplace we can send these people, Lois. Somewhere they can call anonymously and just say, 'Help me.'"[195]

Barbara Hoerl (now Barbara Labrie) and Lois Reitman (now Lois Hoiem) decided they'd have to start a helpline themselves. For a long time, each had wanted to do something for young people on a bad drug trip or in some other personal crisis. Each was a catalyst for the other, and together they formed an effective team.[196]

First, they decided they needed help from a professional. But Barbara had a hard time asking for help. "I was twenty-two and scared stiff. I felt very young and naïve. I wasn't sure what I was doing."

A friend's roommate, a student majoring in social work at UW-Milwaukee, had a suggestion. "Sam Stellman's a good person. Why don't you talk to him?"

Barbara found Sam easy to share her thoughts with. "I'd like to see a confidential hot line where we can help people in crisis right away. And Lois wants to start a free health clinic where people can walk in off the street and get help immediately. Otherwise, Dr. Stellman, I'm afraid many of them will die. And I'd like the police to lay off and stop harassing those who need help, give them a chance to get well. I want some way we can tell those who insist on using drugs they will be hurt by them, and more than that, I'd like the message to get out, somehow, about what drugs are out there on the street that they ought to stay away from."

"That's a big package you're asking for," said Sam, who saw that Barbara had a lot of good ideas. "But as you know, there's no money to support your ideas at this time." So Sam suggested that Barbara and Lois start small, perhaps with just the telephone helpline. If they found volunteers and a place for the phone, Sam would then see if the university's Center for Social Services could provide free training and help with the set-up. "If you get enough people willing to staff the phones, and you start having meetings to organize this, call me and I'll be there."

Sam had realized the seriousness of the problem for himself after riding with a police officer along Brady Street, the center of Milwaukee's hippie culture. "It really opened my eyes to the runaways and the drug culture."

What happened after that is a success story of the kind Sam most enjoys, because by providing the right kind of support at the right time, he made it possible for others to carry on and achieve their goals. The result was Milwaukee's Underground Switchboard.

Together with other faculty members, Sam consulted in the design of the training for the helpline, and he gave Barbara a list of other professionals to call on.

Bob Reitman broadcast the call for volunteers over what was probably the most listened to rock station in Milwaukee in the sixties. And the two young women got a group of volunteers together from among their friends.[197]

"We were all in our late teens or early twenties—young, inexperienced hippies," recalled Barbara.

When the volunteers showed up for the first session, Sam found them eager to learn. But not every one of them seemed in the best condition for learning. "I thought some of them had been experimenting with drugs. I was firm," recalled Sam. "I told them if they really wanted to help people, they'd have to come to the training sessions squeaky clean. Sure enough, the next time they all came back ready to go."

During the fall of 1969, Sam was involved in the training, concentrating on getting the volunteers to respond to crisis calls in ways that would keep them from being liable. Mandy's legal expertise made an impact.

"If we simply gave advice on what to do," Barbara said,

"and something happened to that person, we could be in trouble. We had to say, 'The experts say you should do such and such, but please contact a doctor, too.'"

In addition to Sam, the instructors included Bernard Weiss of the UW-Milwaukee School of Social Work, an expert on counseling who had extensive knowledge of the street scene. "He was the best damn trainer," recalled Sam, who also saw to it that the university helped pay for some of the volunteers to attend a conference in California on how to operate a helpline.[198]

Medical information was provided by Dr. Alan Reed, who had just returned to Milwaukee to complete his residency in psychiatry after working in a free clinic in Haight-Ashbury. Clinical psychologist Larry Kipperman helped with the phones and provided counseling. The volunteers were also given a list of the current, though limited, resources available in the community—churches, counselors, emergency rooms, and so on.[199]

The phone was installed in a volunteer's apartment, and a philanthropic businessman donated money for the first few months of phone bills. "The operation was pretty much a folding table and a couple of chairs and a telephone," recalled Deb Billings (now Deb Billings-Nelson), one of the first volunteers.

On December 19, 1969, the Underground Switchboard set up shop—and was flooded with calls right from the beginning. It was a time of national angst over Vietnam, civil rights, and student protests. Callers were experiencing great stress, and the Switchboard did a lot of suicide counseling. The phone's extra-long cord reached to the bathroom so a volunteer could concentrate in privacy when dealing with an especially frightened caller.

At first, only a handful of volunteers could be there consistently, so to keep the lines open twenty-four hours a day, some of them managed to put in as many as sixty hours a week—each.

Callers were told they could contact the Switchboard for anything—not just problems. "We kept track of all the rock festivals," Deb added. "And if a certain type of LSD was on the street that people were having bad trips with, we put out alerts. The community trusted us because we were their peers, not part of the 'establishment.'"[200]

The Switchboard outgrew its budget, the small apartment, and the two-line telephone. More volunteers came forward, most of whom never learned of Sam's early role. And that was fine with him, for it signaled independence.

As volunteers held a benefit rock concert to raise funds for a free medical clinic, Sam's role became one of watching with pride and writing personal checks. Early in 1970 the Switchboard was able to move to space offered by St. Mary's Hospital, where multiple phone lines began receiving more than three hundred calls a day. The free clinic became a reality, and an Alternative to Drug Abuse program began, with Alan Reed, Andy Kane, and other doctors obtaining federal funding from the Safe Streets Act for a walk-in counseling center.[201]

"The people who ran the Switchboard were the most dedicated people you ever want to see," commented Sam. "You need movers and shakers to start things, but for something to be a long-term success, the community has to care and has to be involved."

"Sam didn't put himself in the forefront," Barbara pointed out. "He stayed in the background—that's the role he wanted." Today, the Switchboard is still in existence. Renamed the Milwaukee Help Line, its ninety-plus volunteers currently answer 25,000 calls a year on a wide variety of personal problems in addition to drugs—from depression and troubled relationships to homelessness and suicide.[202]

"Sam sure started something that lasted with very little further connection from him," Dr. Kipperman added. "If more people would do that, the world would be a better place. I like to say, 'You can do a lot of good if you don't care who gets the credit.'"[203]

During the sixties when young people in large numbers began experimenting with illegal substances, many Jewish kids also got strung out on drugs. They'd eventually come out of it, Sam recalled twenty-five years later, but for a long time the Jewish community tried to figure out why so many were going in that direction. The phenomenon puzzled Sam because, in general, "you don't see Jewish kids in trouble with the law. Or if you do, you know they won't be repeat offenders, because the family will immediately develop a program or call a psychiatrist." He laughed.

"And the lawyer will go talk to the judge and say, 'He's a Jewish kid and we have a program.' The judge wouldn't dismiss the case but would let the community try it for a while."

Sam was alternately thinking aloud and scribbling notes— which are virtually indecipherable to anyone but him. Sitting in the sunny family room at the rear of the Stellman house in Glendale, he was talking with an editor about developing a newsletter, something he'd been wanting to start ever since he retired.

Not surprisingly, Sam's ideas exceeded the time he had available to act on them. His packed calendar was evidence of his efforts to fulfill another post-retirement dream, helping kids. As a member of the board of the Milwaukee Jewish Community Center, he helped establish a youth center in the northern Milwaukee area and acted as chair of its Youth Activity Committee. He served as chair of the education committee of the Milwaukee Council on Alcoholism and as a board member for Milwaukee Legal Services, which is the anti-poverty "legal" agency renamed Legal Action of Wisconsin. He was a member of the Milwaukee Urban League, a consultant to the Urban League Drug Abuse program, and a member of the board of directors of the Milwaukee Women's Center. When not attending committee meetings, Sam was writing letters, phoning for information, and calling upon people to get their support.

"Parents, the schools, and the community have to work together to build strong families," he explained, having grown up with the YMHA and the Workmen's Circle as examples, and having spent the first twenty years of his career working within the tradition of the Jewish Community Centers. Sam had absorbed the values of social outreach organizations devoted to eliminating poverty, supporting unions, and fighting for justice as the means for improving people's lives.

He was always quick to object to the use of the expression, the "deserving" poor. "The concept is more in keeping with an attitude about low income people that's anti-welfare—and, in most cases, non-Jewish. The Jewish credo and Jewish heritage recognize only that the poor are poor, and they do not place adjectives like 'deserving,' 'cheating,' 'lazy,' etc., before the noun 'poor.' It is contrary to the *tzedakah* philosophy of 'what is just' to use such terms."[204]

It was for the purpose of empowering parents that Sam designed classes for parents of teenagers and offered them for about five years throughout Wisconsin. For the class called "How to cope with your teenager," he involved Patricia Costello, a social worker in private practice, to talk about a child's socialization, and Mandy, to give her views on some of the legal issues as well as on raising children. All three of them presented a similar program for the department of probation in Racine to help parents understand why their children had been cited and what resources were available. The Stellmans' goal was achieved when the probation department took over the program and continued to run it. Yet so much remained to be done, especially with juvenile offenders. How much of the background of the Second Chance program should he write about in his newsletter, he wondered aloud to the editor—who was trying to keep up with the shifts in focus that Sam's fertile mind produced.

Sam thought back to the early eighties when Second Chance began.[205] It grew out of a judge's frustration with the ineffectual fines the law permitted him to assess on the juveniles who appeared before him for nonviolent offenses, such as shoplifting, vandalism, underage drinking, curfew violations, and loitering. The fines were too low to make an impact on those who could afford them, and the kids who couldn't afford even the small amounts paid nothing, since there was no penalty for not paying. Judge Jeffrey Wagner, a municipal court judge,[206] was so frustrated he called Sam, his friend of many years.

What Sam did was adapt the JAC or Justice Alternative Court program, which worked so well with adult shoplifters,[207] to create Second Chance, an early intervention program for nonviolent juvenile offenders coming into the system for the first time. The program began in April 1982, and after Sam retired Cherie Maris administered Second Chance for four years. It continues today, an incredibly effective program with a recidivism rate of less than ten percent.[208]

Kids are referred by judges, law enforcement officials, city attorneys, and professionals in health and social service agencies. During its first ten years, Second Chance made a positive impact on more than 9,000 young people in seven

Wisconsin counties—suburban as well as urban.

The youths attend a one-day educational session designed specifically to stop the behavior and change the underlying beliefs that got them into trouble initially. Sam explained: "We charge them a small fee. Not much, but enough to make them feel more serious and responsible for their actions and the consequences to them, their families, and the community."

Mary Esser, a trained counselor, conducted the sessions from the beginning. In a typical Saturday session, one of the young people always asked her, "What's the big deal?"

"The big deal is that you now have a juvenile record that won't go away. If you get in trouble again," Mary Esser would tell them, "your record follows you to court, and it can be used against you even as an adult if you are sentenced for another offense."

However, if these first-time offenders successfully complete the program and stay out of trouble for as long as the judge determines, their records, for all intents and purposes, are wiped clean. Technically, they have not been convicted of a crime, and they don't have to mention it on their job applications. The program gives them a second chance—literally—a chance to start over as if they had never made that one mistake.

The counselors also help the young people look at the reasons for their behavior, the importance of being more responsible, and how their conduct affects them, their families, their community, and their future.

Based on the success of Second Chance, shortly after his retirement Sam proposed adapting the program to the school setting. "I'm a firm believer in early intervention," Sam often said. "If you can catch 'em early, or the first time, you can turn 'em around. We have a saying in criminal justice: 'the further a juvenile penetrates the system, the harder it is to dislodge the juvenile from the system.' And then they commit more violent acts."

The idea had the support of three respected Milwaukee municipal court judges: William J. Panagis, Stanley A. Miller, and James A. Gramling Jr.[209] The grant for funding was written by Bill Winter, who by that time had succeeded Sam as chair of the Criminal Justice Institute (CJI).

Winter also helped design the experimental program, which began in 1989 and operated in three high schools and one middle school in inner-city Milwaukee. It was aimed at the kind of in-school transgression that a student could be arrested for if it occurred outside the school: battery, vandalism, or theft.

Instead of an arrest, the student was given a ticket marked "Second Chance," and the penalty was suspended. If the student successfully completed the Second Chance program, the action was dismissed.

The program's greatest weakness was that its maintenance depended on key personnel from multiple institutions— school principals, court administrators, and law enforcement people. Unfortunately, during the grant period the positions of school vice principal and assistant D.A. experienced high turnover, and every few weeks Cherie had to meet with new people to explain the program. After a year that saw some favorable results, the in-school program was allowed to die because of lack of time and attention from harried administrators.

You win some, you lose some. But Sam knew that times change, new people come along to make their energies felt, and a good idea from the past can be adapted to changing

situations. Most of the Stellmans' ideas have been ahead of
their time, some more so than others.

"Time...there's so much yet to be accomplished." Sam was
continuing to identify themes with the editor. He thought
back some years to another outreach program aimed at reducing juvenile crime, Home Detention. His department had
developed it together with the Wisconsin Correctional Service and the Junior League.

Its goal was to reduce the number of incarcerated juveniles by qualifying some as able to stay in their homes under strict supervision whenever they weren't in school.
Because of the home supervision aspect, the program had
to involve parents, many of whom, Sam recalled, turned
out to be alcoholics.

"So in addition to the program for the kids, we ran classes
on parental responsibility. I think it was effective, and so
did some of the judges, who made it part of the court order
that the parents go to our classes." But when the judge in
Racine who supported the program left juvenile court for
another court, "the next juvenile judge wasn't interested in
the program," said Sam, and it died out. "This happened
fairly often."

But a judge in Prairie du Chien, a rural community near
the Iowa border, asked the university's extension people
there for help. "In a place like Prairie du Chien," said Sam,
"it's not uncommon to have a very high alcoholism rate—
which we found when we got there. A lot of the kids were
in trouble, and we had to deal with both the kids and the
alcoholic parents. So we designed a program based on the
realization that we were getting a lot of parents who had
their own problems.

"In the sessions with the parents, we talked about the
nature of the law, bringing up kids, and the dangers of a
kid getting in trouble with the law. When we talked with

the kids, they often reflected on how their parents handled them." Sam felt the program was effective, and the judge was pleased with it.

One of Sam's strategies was to get a judge involved in a program whenever he could. As for the financial support for the Prairie du Chien program, "The people there got a grant to pay us—which is a little different."

"I have trouble understanding someone going to a bar as a *way of life*," confided Sam. "I'm not talking about now and then. But a father who regularly goes to the tavern right from work or who goes home and then to the tavern...?" Sam pondered the notion for a moment. "I have trouble with that, particularly if you're an adult male with a family at home. Jewish families rarely do that."

The values Sam held were not necessarily grounded in religion, but in ethnic and family traditions, which he and Mandy learned, lived by, and passed on to their children.

"If you're a parent, you're a parent and a role model all your life," Sam insisted. "As parents and grandparents, we need to ask, 'Do you know where your *grown-up* children are and what they are doing?' The role model your adult son or daughter sets will remain with your *grandchildren* all their lives." Sam jotted down some notes, then looked up.

"Concern for our children and grandchildren is part of the fabric of Jewish philosophy," he said. "I'd call it a concern with the concept of equal justice for all. That's a simplistic way of putting it, because justice does not come easily."

Sam chuckled. "By the way, that's one of Mandy's favorite expressions. When I drive her to work, she says, 'I'm going to the courthouse to look for justice. I'm not going to find it, but I'm going to keep looking!'"

What motivated the Stellmans was the search for a justice

that they knew *ought* to be there. What ought to be there but *isn't* is what Sam called "the check-is-in-the-mail philosophy." This phrase encapsulated the promises society makes but doesn't keep.

"Society doesn't keep its promise about children being the future of this country. Absolutely not. Not when there are millions of abused children. Not when no one wants to pay for education. The conservatives come up with a simplistic answer like 'school choice.' That's not going to make a difference in the public school system. We're always fighting to get them to come up with an 'honest' check, to make them really provide the money and support to benefit all children."

This is only one example of a promise that won't be kept.

"I'm annoyed when we criticize the educational system and teachers," continued Sam. "The fault is in the business community that won't inject itself in local issues. We have to start with that group."

One businessman who did inject himself in local issues headed a task force studying the Milwaukee schools. Like many others, this man was fond of saying schools should be run like businesses. "Yet this same businessman," said Sam, "announced some weeks later that he was moving a chunk of his operations to the southern part of the country. With it, he was taking a great number of jobs from this area."

Sam wondered if people saw the contradiction. "What job prospects was this man offering the students whose education his task force was charged with determining? I want to expose this kind of thinking, and that's why I want to publish a newsletter and call it, 'The Check Is in the Mail.'"

###

Six words, "The Check Is in the Mail," sprawled across the front of a large manila envelope that Sam handed to the editor. It bulged with materials he had been collecting for some time for his dreamed-of newsletter: clippings from newspapers and magazines and announcements of community programs on self-esteem. The Stellmans had little use for the self-esteem movement that became popular in the mid-eighties.

"Look at this." Sam handed the editor a "Sally Forth" cartoon from the local paper. It showed Sally reading a book and realizing what she didn't like about the whole self-esteem trend: "I think a lot of times it's just a way of passing the buck," she says to her cartoon-husband, Ted. Observing that people are blaming their problems on things that happened to them many years earlier, she asks, "Why can't we just act like adults, take responsibility for our shortcomings, and work on doing better?"

Ted replies, "You mean like actually admit something is our own fault? Sounds pretty un-American to me, Sal."[210]

The Stellmans had little difficulty distinguishing between an individual's responsibilities in facing the consequences of a bad choice, and the consequences visited upon whole categories of people because of unjust social policies. They saw the shift in emphasis to the individual's self-esteem as a way of relieving business and other institutions of the responsibility for addressing the social and economic problems they created.

Partly because the Stellmans had never experienced low self-esteem themselves, the self-help movement seemed like another unwritten check. Even in their darkest moments—for example, when Mandy was rejected by a nursing school because "we already have one Jew"—pain was seen as coming from external events, not from internal flaws.

By conceptualizing problems as external, the Stellmans could see how social problems grow out of unjust, uncaring social systems. With that clear vision, they had no patience with any program or agency that placed the building of self-esteem at the core of its efforts to address social problems.

Never having been tormented by the self-doubt that afflicts vast numbers of Americans, they never expended any of their energies on unproductive self-flagellation.

"You have to be tough enough to know you don't take these issues personally," Sam explained.

They saw the *system* as inadequate, not the individual. Nor did they become depressed by injustice; they became outraged.

Because they had no need to either search for their identity or assert supremacy over others, they did not resort to game-playing when dealing with people. This honesty enabled them to be as straightforward as possible in communicating their ideas and motives, freeing them to go after results. They could channel their energies toward positive strategies for reaching their goals.

They scoffed at the notion that programs and agencies could justify their existence without showing results.

Sam recalled one agency administrator telling him: "We can't tell you now if we are doing any good—the results won't be seen for years." Another time he heard, "We are always ready to help people in need. Just remember our hours are nine A.M. to four P.M. Monday through Friday."

At a meeting of alcohol and drug abuse professionals, he heard a director declare: "We take the war on drugs very seriously. By the way, our agency will be closed June, July, and August."

Sam originally exposed such check-is-in-the-mail attitudes in a speech he made in 1984 before the Wisconsin Mental Health Association Training Institute and Forum. "The applause was not deafening," he commented afterward. "In fact, most of the participants looked puzzled."[211]

###

The Stellmans were equally contemptuous of programs that were totally out of sync with the needs and interests of young people.

"Why do we identify the primary interests of modern teens as the telephone, television, cars, music, 'hanging around,' and relationships with the opposite sex," Sam mused, "yet the programs we plan for them revolve around athletics and table games? And for that matter, when are we going to eliminate the myth that athletic programs are a major factor in keeping youths from becoming delinquent?"

Ruefully, he added, "Some of the best athletes in Wisconsin live at our reform schools."

He recalled making that remark while attending a civic fundraiser. His comment didn't go over too well with a high school wrestling coach standing nearby.

"Sports programs are a great way to keep kids off the street," the coach protested. "They get to burn off some excess energy."

"But can you point to one single sports program that's done that?" Sam countered. "I've heard the same claim made for basketball, boxing, wrestling, and a program involving go-carts. There's even a Milwaukee teacher who promoted the game of checkers as an alternative to drug use. Sorry, but the argument just doesn't hold water. These programs are supposed to build self-esteem, but the kids can gain much more status in the neighborhood by joining a gang."

Sam grinned as he recalled the scene. "That coach didn't care for me too much. I'd punctured his pet theory in front of everyone, and he couldn't think of a word to say back."

It was another example of simplistic solutions to complex problems. "Every time you get a new piece in the paper saying we've now discovered a problem in the inner city, suddenly they start a basketball league. The Spanish Center, for example, runs boxing programs. Every time you talk to the people who run 'em, they say boxing keeps kids off the street, it's wholesome, it builds character, it improves their self-esteem. And all that kind of garbage. They won't talk about the possibility boxing will damage their brains. Nine-year-olds? They say they're protected because they wear helmets, but if they take one punch here," Sam said, pointing to his chin, "it shakes the brain up."

When asked whether these types of programs can be successful simply because they put kids in contact with caring people, Sam replies, "These are not role models. No. Generally kids go into a boxing program because in their culture it's an acceptable program. It's built into the African-American and Hispanic communities. You don't see it in the white community. It used to be on the campuses and then some fellow got killed boxing over at Madison. So they took it out of all the campuses in the country. You see it only in the minority communities. The irony is these so-called experts think if we can get the kids in the program we'll be able to talk to them and guide them."

But the goal is soon forgotten, Sam believed. "Boxing, which started out as a means, becomes the goal. Not straightening the kids out, not making a better life for them, not helping them back home with the problems there."

He was just as critical of the argument that sports keep many youths in school because that's the only place they get recognition for success. Even if true, what does that say about the school's central purpose? He added, "If athletics is the only reason children come to school, the school has failed in its educational mission."

The promise to build character also struck Sam as hollow. "Even when I was a student in Minnesota doing field work at a settlement house, I saw that when the kids weren't shooting baskets, they were rifling the lockers downstairs."

He reiterated, "No, there is no simple answer. You're talking about poverty. No basketball program will get you out of poverty unless you become a pro, and there are very few of those. What the kids need are family relationships, a safe place to live, and encouragement to go to school. Athletics isn't the answer to anything."

Most people who know of Sam's work in criminal justice don't know that he spoke with some authority in these matters; they don't know that until his mid-forties he was a well-respected professional developer and director of community athletic programs.

He fingered a yellowing proposal he received in 1973 from a national group promoting wrestling combat centers. "They call it an 'unqualified solution' to urban youth violence, a 'major breakthrough.' They use statistics like, 'within eighteen months, the number of gang-related deaths will be reduced by at least fifty percent, and very possibly seventy-five percent.' Where do they get this from?"

Another related belief of Sam's that bucked popular opinion was his opposition to peer counseling among teens about problems that could be life-threatening.

"One of the biggest fights I had was over at Nicolet High School at a social gathering. I said to one of the teachers, I understand you're sending senior high kids down to tell the junior high kids about drugs. That's one of the stupidest things I can think of. She got so mad at me."

Then he'd asked her, "What kind of maturity does a fifteen- or sixteen-year-old have to cope as counselors to other kids facing problems with drugs and alcohol? Or with thoughts of suicide? How could a kid be able to answer a tough question another kid might have about family—or whatever—that could have long-lasting effects on someone's life?"

Other ideas that Sam criticized included the practice of having ex-addicts, former drug dealers, and recovered alcoholics speaking to schoolchildren. He felt that only positive, not negative, role models should speak in the schools.

"One of the common problems for children in the inner city is that their role models are usually the local drug dealer. So why is it that we bring these same drug dealers into the school under the guise of 'ex-addict' or 'recovered alcoholic' to advise kids?"

The Stellmans found that one agency often worked wonders with children and families that other social agencies had given up on as hopeless. The Youth Development Commission was willing to work with children who were difficult cases—youths who do not get along in regular school settings, juvenile offenders, abandoned and abused kids, and high school drop-outs—or, as Sam would say, high school "kick-outs."

Many times, Mandy called on its founder and executive director, Jeannetta Robinson, to see about creating an individual program for a juvenile client she had. Involvement by Robinson's agency was often effective in convincing a juvenile court judge to consider probation instead of sending the youth to an institution. As a result of this kind of intervention, some of Mandy's young clients, boys as well as girls, even went on to college in spite of their troubled, anti-social backgrounds.

Identifying the major safety issues in the schools became the focus of a 1990 survey of school personnel. The Criminal Justice Institute, together with CESA, the Cooperative Educational Service Agency, surveyed twenty-one school districts in the Wisconsin counties of Milwaukee, Washington, and Ozaukee. Sam was the survey's chief investigator.

It came as no great surprise that drugs and alcohol were named the number one school safety concern by 150 out of 167 school personnel. The surprising result was the extent to which that issue outstripped thirteen other issues. Sexual assault in the schools turned out to be rather low on the list.

Of the middle and high school administrators and counselors responding to the survey, 84 percent felt that most courts do not communicate adequately with the schools about cases threatening school safety. An equal number agreed that the general public does not understand the nature and extent of school safety issues.

The following year, 180 school staff, law enforcement officials, and other professionals came together to discuss potential solutions. They recommended teaching acceptable school behavior in the first and second grades, identifying disruptive students and developing effective programs for them, training middle and high school personnel in controlling fighting among students, and establishing policies in each school district about when to call police to the school.

The action that came from the 1990 survey was admirable, but Sam wondered how many of the programs conducted in the name of prevention and intervention had any real effect. "Do school personnel know, or are they guessing?" he mused, turning back to the notes rapidly accumulating in his check-is-in-the-mail folder.

Sam suspected that students knew of the dangers of drinking and using drugs. "But how do we reach them so they change their attitudes and behaviors?"

He wrote: "What we really need is a way of imparting

ethics to students. Every student's academic program should include ethics classes emphasizing the legal and moral aspects of breaking the law. Maybe then we wouldn't have such a problem with date rape on our college campuses.

"It should make people angry," he wrote. "So much happens in and around the school that interferes with children learning and teachers teaching. The goal of schools is to educate our children to reach their potential. Whatever interferes with that goal should be dealt with severely!"

Sam thought of the low marks earned by parents in the survey of school personnel, and he recalled the family issues complicating the home detention program for Prairie du Chien. "Our society is fond of bashing the schools and the criminal justice system, but based on the problems the schools, the police, and the courts have to face, I think the most popular sport ought to be 'community bashing.'"

If there is a high rate of violence in the community, Sam knew there would be a high rate of violence in the schools. He knew that schools reflected a community's high rates of drug and alcohol abuse, violence, sexual abuse, hostility, and lack of respect for authority.

In exposing the check-is-in-the-mail philosophy, Sam intended to coach the sport of community bashing through the pages of his future newsletter.

"Violent crime by teen boys has escalated out of sight," Sam scribbled for a possible article. "And there's very little social or legal control that might stop them—other than locking up boys and men for every transgression."

Sam was dismayed that so little was being done to address root causes, other than the so-called attempts to wage a war on drugs. He saw that war as one more hypocritical example of saying "the check is in the mail."

Sam put down his notebook and pen, booted up his PC, and quickly turned out his first newsletter article: "The War on Drugs is an Industry."

What was once the war on drugs has become an industry that employs people as in every other large industry. Hundreds of thousands of people all over the world depend upon drug sale and use to earn their livelihoods. Where the materials to make addictive drugs are grown, governments look the other way because drugs, in many cases, are their most important export.

Sam's article chastised the United States as the largest contributor to the drug market because so many people were earning their livelihoods from the "war on drugs"—and therefore had a stake in the status quo—such as hundreds of thousands of law enforcement personnel at all levels of government, the "snitches" who go underground to identify drug dealers for law enforcement, and thousands of "chemical dependency counselors" employed by the schools to educate children about the evils of drugs.

As Sam hunted and pecked at the computer keyboard, he continued to list the beneficiaries of the war on drugs.

Tons of literature are printed by pharmaceutical houses and others for distribution to children and their parents. Certified counselors supply treatment to addicts and others who have become drug dependent. Hospitals set aside beds just for drug-dependent people.

Sam wrote of the hundreds of people employed in turning out one film or television show that uses stories involving drug dealers and the police who seek them out.

He acknowledged the special courts that handle nothing but drug cases, with judges who specialize in such cases.

So many people—legitimate and illegitimate—benefited from drug distribution, use, education, enforcement, and treatment, that thousands of jobs would be lost if drug use and abuse were eliminated. He concluded, "The reality is that the drug industry has made so many people dependent upon its existence, it is a self-perpetuating operation with no chance of going out of business."

Moreover, none of the programs had made much difference, "from Nancy Reagan's 'just say no,' to the parade of 'recovered' addicts before the children, to a federal drug czar addressing children about the evils of drugs." These programs should all be eliminated, Sam insisted. He felt that treating addicts should be a primary goal of any drug-treatment program. "At the risk of sounding naïve," he said, "the slogan for a 'war' on drugs should be, 'Stop the seller and treat the user.'"

###

Moving from the computer back to his easy chair, Sam resumed his discussion. "School has become a lot more important in children's lives in ways that were never intended," he told his editor. "It has superseded the family as the problem-solving institution."

He observed that school was the place children formed the peer groups in which they often made life decisions—from what they wore to who their friends were—whether their parents liked their choices or not. These days, "it's where teens decide about drinking, smoking, using drugs, having sex, going truant, and joining gangs."

School law, which used to be primarily civil in nature, has become more attuned to criminal offenses, Sam observed. "Today we have a totally different image of school as a safe place for children. When they go to school, most junior high and high school students worry daily about two things: getting punched, and having something stolen." He added, "How can kids be educated when they're worried about being hit or losing their property?"

Traditionally, the courts hesitate to enter the realm of school law, and rightly so, he believed. Yet in some areas the school and the courts do overlap. In the mid-eighties Sam helped co-found a group that attempted to address these areas: the Milwaukee Police Department-Milwaukee Public Schools Task Force on School Safety.

At various times this task force included police captains, social workers, school administrators, community leaders, officers from the Milwaukee Police Department School Squads and Gang Squads, and Sam, who acted as an unpaid consultant.

Members met once a month to see how the different agencies could work together in curbing violence in the schools, and they discussed issues such as new truancy programs or the use of metal detectors at school entrances. They also followed legislation and recommended passage of bills that enhanced school safety.

It was at one of these task force meetings that Sam met Dr. Melanie Moore, an administrator with the Milwaukee Public Schools, and her husband, John Steen, an officer with the Milwaukee Police Department. Years later, this couple shared their views of these early meetings.

Right from the start, they were impressed by Sam's commitment and his no-nonsense approach. "At the meetings we had, Sam was very unassuming," Dr. Moore recalled. "He'd talk to people and clarify things, but he wasn't gung-ho. He always brought a rational side to the discussion, plus an understanding of the law in relation to the school system and to the police. Three different points of view had to be brought together."

John Steen added, "Sam didn't try to run the committee, but he was a very important part of the group. He should have been a more important part. I always enjoyed dealing with Sam because he was easy to work with. He didn't use big words and try to talk over you, like a lot of people would. He was frustrated about many of the issues. We would go to meetings and listen to a lot of lip service, and yet nothing got done. Then we'd go to another meeting and nothing got done there, either. Sam tried to get back to the basics. But not everyone wanted to listen. After, we'd wonder, 'What got accomplished here?'"

"Sam was interested in the bottom line," Dr. Moore recalled. "He wanted to know, 'Is this going to make a difference?' So many programs that people throw out there—federally funded, state funded—may not really work long-term. Either it doesn't happen because the money gets cut off too soon and you never know if it was really going to work or not, or it might look good—you can make a lot of things look good on paper—but maybe in the long run it isn't really achieving what it's supposed to. Sam wanted results. And he wanted them *now*."

Sam, for his part, remembered the meetings as sometimes fruitful, sometimes frustrating. "We never did solve the problem of confidentiality. It's a tough problem. When a kid gets in trouble, often the people in the school system are not told he's been through the juvenile court system. They wouldn't know a kid might be on probation for rape, so they couldn't help protect others."

That was because state and federal confidentiality laws said juvenile records could not be shared.[212]

With characteristic frankness, Sam admitted to changing his views on the issue of confidentiality as he learned more about it. "Ten years ago I would have been on the other side, supporting total confidentiality of records." But Sam was a practical man. "The more hands that get into the picture, obviously the more potential for abusing children's rights. But principals and teachers have to know when they have a dangerous kid in school." So Sam worked to find a solution that would not violate the law. But the committee could never agree on any recommendations. The task force discussed confidentiality many, many times. It was one of their biggest stumbling blocks, and Sam kept bringing them back to it.

John Steen recalled that the committee seemed to talk about everything but the real issues. "Sam would say, 'Okay, that's good, but let's get something done that actually deals with the problem.'"

The task force did produce one concrete outcome, however: a one-page set of guidelines[213] for the Milwaukee Police Department School Squads.

Wanting to know more about these School Squads, Sam took the opportunity to meet with Steen after a task force meeting. As they talked, Sam asked how the School Squads functioned, and whether all the troublesome students came from dysfunctional families or if the kids from "good" families were causing trouble, too. And he was curious about how John saw his role.

Because John was dealing with problems on a day-to-day basis, Sam realized that the police officer could make an impact on the situation. Sam was intrigued by the man's positive attitude, his ability to control a potentially violent situation calmly, and his willingness to look for the root causes behind each problem. Sam learned to value his insight and his ability to mediate between the kids and the administrators.

John found it interesting that Sam took the time to explore these issues with him. From their talks together, Sam produced a report for the Criminal Justice Institute.[214]

In it he discussed the history and growth of violence in the schools, and the need that led to establishing the School

Squads. That need was painfully evident: in 1992 alone, Milwaukee police were called to city schools, public and private, more than 10,000 times. The School Squads, whose function was to respond to those calls, became a necessary and integral part of managing violence and other problems in the schools. They were called to the schools for "disruptive behavior," defined as anything that interfered with school operations. To put it another way, "The police are called when nothing else works," John told Sam.

Yet the whole point of the School Squad was to take the time to deal with a situation rather than just come in and write tickets or make arrests. Because such views exactly paralleled Sam's own, in his report he concluded, "The School Squad is an important part of the operation of the Milwaukee Police Department, and its importance is more and more being recognized by school personnel. Police have a positive contribution to make to the school."[215]

For those students who cannot behave properly in school, Sam believed in alternatives, such as dormitory-type schools in which selected students who needed considerable help could live and be educated away from home—but only if the program paired such students with an adult on a one-to-one basis.

Sam stood and went to his desk and pulled a photocopy from a stack of papers. One sentence was underlined: "The delinquent rarely knows it, but the school is his or her ticket out of the problems that encourage delinquency."

###

15. Stick Your Neck Out

"If you are deeply concerned with the future of our young girls today...then you have to be supportive of us feminists." So spoke Sam in accepting the Feminist of the Year Award from the Milwaukee Women's Center in 1992.

"My definition of a feminist is someone willing to stick their neck out so that women, who for so long have been looked upon as second-rate citizens—particularly if they are homemakers full-time—can gain some sense of respectability and equality."

Sam was the first person to receive this award from the Milwaukee Women's Center, and he was prouder of it than of any other honor he received in his lifetime.

###

The summer of 1992 was known in Milwaukee as Abortion Summer. National leaders of a group calling itself Missionaries for the Pre-Born, together with other similar groups, launched a campaign targeted against the city's family planning clinics, just as they had against the clinics of Wichita, Kansas, the summer before.

Anti-abortion demonstrators from Wisconsin and other areas of the country descended on five Milwaukee family planning clinics, blocking traffic and harassing everyone attempting to enter—including the frightened and confused pregnant women who were exercising their legal rights.

Day after day, week after week, demonstrators clashed with pro-choice advocates, who had vowed to defend the clinics and escort women safely through the lines. Repeatedly defying a court order against blocking access, 105 anti-abortion protestors, including thirty-two children, were arrested on June 16 by the Milwaukee police.

Week after week, Sam and Mandy, long-time advocates for the reproductive rights of women, joined the staunch defenders of the clinics. July 11 was no different, even though it was the Stellmans' forty-ninth wedding anniversary. What better way to mark the occasion, they felt, than "on the line" at the women's health care clinic on Brown Deer Road?

Whenever the Stellmans marched, they took pleasure in antagonizing the anti-abortion army with their senior status and the signs, which Mandy had crafted, proclaiming: "Grandparents for Choice."

These same words were mounted on a small sign hanging in Mandy's office, along with others that read "Pro-Family, Pro-Choice" and "Against Abortion? Don't Have One."

"The next time I march," declared Sam, chuckling, "my sign will say 'Veterans for Choice.' That should really upset 'em!"

By August, the number of anti-abortion protesters had swelled to nearly 4,000 at the Brown Deer Road clinic alone. On August 8, the police arrested 546 demonstrators, most of them anti-abortionists.[216]

As the Stellmans continued to encounter the displays of intolerance and venom directed at the clinic defenders, they grew angrier and more determined. Sam found the most obnoxious act of the anti-abortionists to be their facsimile of the entrance to a concentration camp, Nazi symbol and all.

"These zealots," he said, "are primarily the same sort of church people who ignored the Holocaust and the murder of six million Jews. This is the same church that has supported every war since the Crusades. And they call themselves 'pro-life'? Who are they to tell my granddaughter what she can do with her body?"

The Stellmans' beliefs, Sam explained, "are part of the Jewish concern for the quality of families, which is based on small families. We believe firmly in birth control and individual choice."

Mandy added, "Too much money is being spent in the wrong direction. So-called pro-life activists should be spending it putting money and food into the homes where girls are getting pregnant. Then we wouldn't have unborn 'babies' to rescue."

The cost to Milwaukee taxpayers for salaries and overtime for the police that summer exceeded half a million dollars—and kept growing.

Mandy's greatest hope was that with a generation of women who were taught to be more self-sufficient than women of the past, more marriages would become equal partnerships, like her own. "I see young boys being brought up by women who are asserting their own rights. I'm hopeful we will raise a generation with respect for the other sex. One day young girls will have a lot more respect for themselves and not let boys get them pregnant."

Mandy and Sam sat at their dining room table being interviewed for a women's history project. On the table and several chairs were piled thick loose-leaf binders of every description, each packed with news clippings and copies of program announcements, letters, and reprints chronicling the many causes that had merited the Stellmans' efforts. Their interviewer, an enthusiastic history major, discovered she barely needed to ask questions to keep the discussion moving—the Stellmans were at no loss for words.

"One of the benefits of the women's movement," Mandy was saying, "is that it enables women to respond to a changing economic climate in which their earnings are not viewed by the courts as belonging to their fathers or husbands—as they were in the days when women fought for the right to vote. As a result, with the growing need for women to work, whether or not they are married, more women are gaining equality in marriage. Independence has raised their self-esteem.

"Historically, women, minorities, and children have *always* had to live their lives according to certain roles: little boys mustn't cry, little girls mustn't get dirty; minorities know their place and so do women; a woman shouldn't be pushy or masculine, and she should take care of her hubby.

"It was as if they were actors and actresses—given a role and having to follow it. Few people had the guts not to play their assigned roles, and those few have been looked upon as uppity women and uppity blacks who don't know 'their place.'

"White men were always told, 'You can achieve anything you want to if you work hard.' Women could put their heart and soul into it, blacks could put their heart and soul into it, and they'd only go so far."

Sam agreed. "If you are deeply concerned with the future of young girls today—and that future *will* be in the workplace, whether anyone likes it or not, often as working mothers—then you have to be supportive of us feminists."

He pointed out to the researcher that "Another problem comes into play when the government forces poor mothers of small children to take a job or job training." He pulled from one of the binders an article he'd written decrying the Learnfare proposal of Wisconsin Governor Thompson. "These mothers must then be away from their children, who are often looked after inadequately. Better that the children have a mother present in the formative years than make the mother leave the home for a poorly paid job that neither supports the family nor gives her a chance to help her children grow."[217]

As for counseling, Sam was disdainful. "Counseling can't raise the poor out of poverty," he said. "Poverty is a shortage of money, not a state of mind. For years, welfare workers have been 'counseling' people on public assistance about their status and what they have to do to be able to live better on what they receive. The reality is that no amount of counseling will make any difference to people in poverty. Only if there were some way to get them out of poverty so they would have enough to sustain themselves adequately could the welfare worker help them. And if that were the case, they wouldn't need a welfare worker to counsel them."

Sam went on. "Parenting classes for poor women wouldn't be necessary if the women had enough money to support their families. Because poor women must depend on others to provide them with the necessities of life, they're under the control of public employees who make it a requirement to attend parenting classes. It's assumed that because they are poor, they need to learn how to bring their children up 'properly.' It's easy to be a good mother if you have enough money for maintaining a 'good' life. Being a good mother means you have the means to adequately feed, clothe, house, and educate your child."

Added Sam, "This is a generous nation when it comes to

raising money or gathering food for the poor. But there's some confusion here, because food banks are designed to alleviate immediate hunger, not poverty. They don't help in the long run. What's needed are programs to get people *out of poverty*. But it's so much easier to just give food."

"So many problems are caused by male behavior and attitudes toward women," Sam told the women's history major. "Boys are brought up to expect to dominate and control female attempts to gain equality, yet equality is basic for a good life for everyone."

These attitudes, he observed, have led to a tolerance of violence against women and children. "I say we will never get rid of assaulters of women until they know we mean business. Sexism is the cause, one hundred percent.

"It's the lack of social control, as well as lack of legal control of violent activities by males, that results in the wanton attitude some men have that 'nothing much can happen to me anyway if I get caught.'"

Mandy expanded on the law's pernicious leniency toward men: "The law bends over backwards to give a man the right to see the kids at the expense of the emotional and physical well-being of his wife. No one wins in these situations. If he's a wife beater, he's hitting the mother of his children. And the children are seeing him getting away with it."

Being brought up in a domestic war zone is the single greatest reason little boys become adult batterers and little girls become the women battered by them.[218]

Sam believed it's a male society that lets the abuse continue. "If we can get all the D.A.s to prosecute, then it becomes part of their system," he pointed out. But this means women must also come forward and keep the pressure on until the system picks it up.

"Mandy had a case once in which the woman kept starting divorce actions and then changing her mind."

Mandy took up the story. "She kept telling me, 'I'll make it work.' I tried to tell my client she has rights, she doesn't have to tolerate the man's brutality. I didn't hear from her for a long time. For weeks and weeks I phoned and sent letters. When I finally got hold of her, she explained that she avoided me because she was embarrassed about changing her mind again. 'I knew you'd be angry,' she said. 'I was afraid to tell you that I took him back.'

"I told her, 'I'm not angry. I'm concerned about you and don't want to pick up the paper tomorrow and find out your husband killed you.'"

Mandy could never forget what had happened to the frightened woman to whom she'd given sanctuary many years before. Teresa had hidden in a back room of the lawyer's office all day but gone home the same night. A few days later Mandy read in the newspaper the gruesome details of how Teresa's brutal husband had murdered her.[219]

Mandy was not angry at her clients, she was angry at the system—at the economics that keep women and their children in dangerous environments. She was outraged by the religious systems that make a woman believe it's her duty to stand by her man no matter what. "And if she left?" Mandy asked. "The shelters are crowded."

Mandy always made it clear to the women who came to see her that a man who batters his wife is likely to batter his children. If he doesn't batter them physically he brutalizes them emotionally because they see their mother getting beaten up.

If that isn't battery, what is? They cower in the corner when he's mad. They hide in closets. Many women I've represented tell me he's battered them for five years, six years, the whole marriage.

*Now they're coming for a divorce. I ask them what makes
it different now?*

"He hit my kids," they say. "That I won't tolerate."

*So I ask the women, "Why do you think he should hit
you?"*

"Well, that's different," they say.

###

"How will change come about?" asked the researcher.

Sam replied, "We need our leaders to react with outrage
to crimes like child and sexual abuse. Educators have to
talk to students about women's rights and little girls' rights
and little boys' rights. The power people must come forward."

Although the Stellmans believed men and women must
work together to solve problems such as spouse abuse, rape,
and other feminist issues, they pointed to men as being in
a position to make the greatest difference.

"In the 1980s when Tony Earl was governor of Wisconsin
and Henry Maier was mayor of Milwaukee," recalled Sam,
"they told people wherever they went they would not tolerate the abuse of women and children. They brought that
message no matter where they spoke, on what subject, or
to whom. Every community needs a male advocate to stand
up and say he won't accept the abuse of women and children."

###

Sam was furious at clergymen, lawyers, doctors, and other professionals who saw the abuse of women and children
and did nothing, despite their having the opportunity to
do something.

"I'm a secular Jew," said Sam, though he and Mandy al-
lied their religious beliefs with those of the conservative

sect. "I'm uneasy about how Jewish values sometimes leave women out of the picture. For a long time women were not allowed on the platform during praying time, and Mandy and I resented that."

When a newspaper article quoted the rabbi of their temple as opposed to allowing women to become rabbis, the Stellmans resigned from their temple and joined another.

"The role of feminism within Judaism is a mixed bag," continued Sam. "The service groups women are involved in, such as the National Council of Jewish Women, are active in community change. But the synagogues and temples are not. I'm critical of the rabbis. They should be fighting more."

Mandy said, "I keep pushing the men in our community to take seriously what is happening to females—adults and children—and to act on it. It surprises me—no, it angers me, when political leaders and corporate executives make critical remarks about 'those feminists.' They don't seem to want to understand that it is 'those feminists' who've opened the doors for their own daughters and granddaughters to become doctors, lawyers, accountants, stockbrokers, college professors with tenure, plumbers, carpenters, and electricians."

Mandy added that most of these fields were closed to women until "we, the looked-down-upon feminists, forced the doors open. We picketed, we sued in the courts, we sat in, and we did so many things, all legal under our Constitution, to see that women could move up the ladder in jobs which paid decent wages."

"America has to be ashamed of how it treats its children," Sam admonished. "Particularly its female children. We are not treating them as if we consider them the future of our nation. It's reflected in the lack of investment America makes in education, in children's health, in the families that need help bringing up their children, and in the lack of support for families when parents divorce or one of them dies.

"We should be appalled at the amount of domestic violence in this nation," he insisted. "We should be repelled by the amount of child abuse and neglect, and by the vast amount of sexual abuse of children, especially female children. No, we can't say America treats its children as its greatest asset and the hope for its future. It's a myth. Millions of American children live in poverty, their families have no health insurance, and they are given a third-rate education. Many of them are battered and abused, physically and sexually assaulted."

Sam always managed to convey vehemence without ever raising his voice.

"This nation needs a complete change of attitude about its children, and more important, a new commitment to see that its children are healthy, well-educated, free from violence and abuse, and valued as first-class citizens."

Sam described learning of a district attorney in a Southwestern Wisconsin county who would not prosecute a man accused of abusing his six- and four-year-old daughters.

So Sam told the mother to "fill the courtroom" with friends and other supporters whenever sexual abuse and child abuse cases came to court "to get the message across that this will not be tolerated."

Without hesitation, Mandy said, "I think the biggest obstruction to making this a safe society is local business people, industrialists, and politicians. They should publicly commit themselves to making the city safe for women, for the elderly, and for children. But I find that the people in power, who are ninety-nine percent men, show absolutely no outrage when a crime takes place against a woman. They are outraged when a bank is robbed or a building is burned.

But if a woman is raped in a downtown parking lot, there will not be a great deal of public comment."

To illustrate, she told of the rape of a seventy-three-year-old Milwaukee woman. "Women weep when we hear that. But where is the president of the chamber of commerce or other important men in the community who will come out and say, 'Enough already!'"[220]

When people in a position to take a stand fail to raise a finger in protest, those figures became the focus of the Stellmans' greatest outrage.

"Despite progress for women, the necessary reaction from male leadership is still not forthcoming," Mandy said, explaining that until violence against half the human race was regarded by society as a priority human rights issue, real progress was not possible—for women or men.

"You have to be outraged twenty-four hours a day when you see the horrendous way our society handles women, minorities, the poor, and the powerless," added Mandy. "A woman is beaten by a man every fifteen seconds in this 'civilized' nation. Every minute of every day more than one woman is raped by a man in this 'civilized' nation. You *have* to do something about the inequities. To constantly complain and not fight for what is right puts you out of the picture."

"The point is," said Sam, "a few people can bring about some big changes, including laws that affect big corporations. Look at the changes in attitudes about smoking. It doesn't take a whole onslaught of people to change things."

Sam believed it was harder to change people's attitudes than their conduct. That's why he and Mandy worked hard to get legislation passed, because through legislation, people's conduct would have to change, and a change in attitude would follow.

The older Sam grew, the more convinced he became that the law was the answer to social problems.

"Despite the hackneyed comments you hear all the time that 'you can't legislate morality,'" Mandy observed, "we think, yes, you *can*. If you underpay someone, the labor laws force you to comply and raise the pay. That changes conduct. Then maybe a generation or two later, the conduct becomes the morality as attitudes change. One problem is that it's very important to get the right president who picks the judges."

"You can't have a Clarence Thomas interpreting the laws," Sam insisted.

The north light filtered into the Stellman's dining room through blue sheer curtains. The variety of loose-leaf binders piled on every surface created a crazy quilt of colors and patterns.

"How would you define your philosophy?" asked the interviewer.

"Realism," Sam replied. He turned one of the loose-leaf binders around to face her. It lay open to display a full-page article about the Stellmans headlined, "Couple fight crime, believe in justice." Sam pointed to a line in the article that described him succinctly: "Samuel D. Stellman, a criminologist who has spent twenty years in the academic world, still appears as realistic as a street cop."[221]

Sam explained his credo for a realist's approach to criminal justice: First you put a stop to it—whatever it is, and whatever it takes. After that you look at prevention, rehabilitation, and other things.[222]

Throughout their lives, the Stellmans felt that outrage was an essential emotion in bringing about change. Indeed, outrage was the powerhouse pumping energy into all their efforts. "Why else would two people in their seventies go out and spend four to five hours standing in a line at an abortion clinic?" Sam asked. Then he supplied the answer. "You've got to be outraged. It's not an objective, intellectual exercise." He went on to emphasize that outrage is not the same as anger. "You have to be outraged by the behavior against women and children, against blacks and minorities, and against poor people, in a society where it's mostly males who have brought this about or are leading it.

"Moreover, this outrage has to be channeled into fighting for what you believe in. It has to be used creatively." Sam reiterated, "There's a sense of outrage we have in everything we do. When we pick up an issue, it's because we are incensed. Whether it's the abortion issue, discrimination against women, sexual harassment, sexual assault—we can't be cool about it. No way. You have to be outraged. If we weren't outraged, we couldn't do what we've done all these years."

"How do you manage to act on your outrage with so many injustices needing correction?" asked the researcher.

"Our method is not to take on everything," Sam answered. "You take on pieces you feel most comfortable with. Not necessarily the ones where you can make the most impact, but where you feel most comfortable, and where you have something to say and know something about it."

He identified the national organization 9 to 5 as "a beautiful example of when a focus on one kind of change works well. It's the best darn agency in terms of a clear goal and sometimes abrasive methods. Another is Planned Parenthood. They take criticism from all sides, but the goal remains steady and clear, and they go at it."

When Michael McGee was the director of Project Respect in Milwaukee's inner city, he contacted Sam to learn how to get his project off the ground. "I suggested a program I had just read about called Neighborhood Watch. He jumped on to it, starting the first Neighborhood Watch program in Milwaukee."

McGee later became a Milwaukee alderperson and a controversial figure in the area, hated and feared by many for his unorthodox tactics. Sam nevertheless admired the man for setting a specific goal and going after it.

As to Sam's underlying strategy for activism, he always declared himself a follower of Saul Alinsky, the community activist who fought against Chicago's destruction of its urban neighborhoods and became well known during the civil rights movement.

"Alinsky said you have to first create pain to get people to want to make change. Either you blow up a building—and create real physical pain—or you make people *think* you will—and create mental pain."

Sam added his own metaphor: "Don't get ulcers, give them to others."

Mandy offered a sober observation. "You'll never get rid of social problems. You'll ameliorate them, bring them down to a little more palatable level." To be effective in doing so, "you have to stay current and keep your methods updated. It never ends."

Reflecting on when she was young, she said, "I had this ambition to cure the world of its evils. Now I know you can't cure all the evils at one time. Though I've still got the guts to do it, I don't want to put so much time and energy into it any more. I want to spend more time with my husband, visiting my children and grandchildren. So I just can't take everything on."

The Stellmans hoped that what the two of them have done will be an inspiration to others. Said Mandy, "It's time for others to come forward."

The loose-leaf binders that have been piled in the dining room for this interview bulge with clippings and announcements representing a small part of the Stellmans' half-century of activism. The materials are waiting to be made accessible to others.

After two heart attacks in five years, Sam had been feeling a more urgent need to pull together the many different threads of this activism. At the same time, he was continuing to plan new strategies to deal with ongoing issues.

So much remained to be done.

When asked what they would like others to know about their experiences fighting for social change, Mandy replied, "I'd like to share the techniques we used. I'd like someone else to know it can be done. That one or two people *can* fight city hall. That you can *win*. That you can make a major change. And that you can inspire other people to do it, too."

Sam replied, "Young people should be able to read this and say, 'Yeah, I can do certain things with my life, and it doesn't have to be a sacrifice. It can be *fun*.'"

###

Epilogue

Sam was paying one of his frequent visits to his old office on the UW-Milwaukee campus. While Mandy stopped at the campus bookstore, Sam went ahead to see his former co-workers at the CJI—the Criminal Justice Institute.

"Retirement for Sam was only an official thing," observed Bill Winter. "He was in the office all the time. We talked about programs, and he always had a lot of ideas about things he thought the Institute should be pursuing."

About 2:50 in the afternoon on Tuesday, December 14, 1993, five weeks after his seventy-fifth birthday celebration, Sam was waiting for an elevator in Enderis Hall of the university with Kim Baugrud, his long-time friend and colleague from the CJI, when he was stricken with a massive heart attack. The paramedics were called immediately, but they were unable to revive him. By the time Mandy returned from the bookstore, Sam was dead.

###

"He was there to deliver a Christmas gift to our secretary," said Cherie Maris, who worked with Sam at the CJI for many years. "That was Sam. The way he passed on—I reflect on that a lot—he died with a gift for someone in his hand. That defined his entire life. He was one of the most thoughtful people...thoughtful behavior, compliments, finding people's potential and trying to bring them out more. He gave and he gave, and he gave, and he gave. He and Mandy didn't even celebrate Christmas."

###

Sam's colleagues and the community responded with an outpouring of tributes and honors. Among them...

The Milwaukee Common Council passed a resolution expressing "sincere condolences to the family of Sam Stellman, a beloved and model citizen." The Common Council enumerated a few of his many contributions to the community, taking official note that Sam had been a champion for women's rights and had received the Milwaukee Women's Center Feminist of the Year Award.[223]

The National Women's Conference Center immediately established, through the generosity of an anonymous donor, a fund to honor the man "whose work and writings have created a legacy of wisdom on issues for women, including rape, domestic violence, divorce, victim's rights, probation, teen crime, family law," and more.[224]

Among the leaders of the National Women's Conference Center at the time were such national and local luminaries as Bella Abzug, Kathryn Clarenbach, Catherine East, Sarah Harder, Carmen Delgado Votaw, Allie Hixson, and its president and good friend of the Stellmans, Gene Boyer.

Chief Justice of the Wisconsin Supreme Court, Shirley S. Abrahamson, wrote these words: "Dr. Stellman deserves to be honored for his long and distinguished service to the university. He truly understood its urban mission and was a vigorous and effective champion of that mission throughout his career.

"Dr. Stellman's skill in gathering community forces for the betterment of society was nothing short of splendid."

###

The staff and volunteers at the Milwaukee Women's Center were devastated by the loss of one of its most beloved leaders. Sam's memory was honored with an annual Justice for Women Award.

Carey Tradewell, the center's executive director, told of Sam's always being available to her as a mentor. "Sam taught me the right path to take and the right fights to fight, and when to back away from an issue. He was very politically astute, a community educator who understood we needed to educate the criminal justice system. He knew all the judges in town and he knew the criminal justice system inside out.

"One of his favorite lines whenever the center faced a tough fight for funding and support was: 'So did you get a bloody nose? Well then, be prepared, because you'll get another one next week.'

"Sam believed in fighting against racism and sexism for a population that didn't have a voice, no matter how long it took. He really believed that despite the injustices perpetrated against women and girls, we could bring about justice, though it would take years, maybe not in our lifetimes.

"He'd say, 'You're working in a field with issues that are going to lend themselves to your feeling discouraged.' So he came to every meeting and event, and he always had a word of encouragement for each of us. He had a wonderful sense of humor. He also shared his frustration and anger, and he'd feel hurt at things happening that were unjust. He definitely showed his feelings."

William J. Panagis, a Milwaukee County municipal judge, said: "Those who knew of Sam's contribution to his profession, [to] his family, and to his fellow man found a man of warmth and determination, intelligence and loyalty, and unselfish accomplishments in those things that are right."

E. Michael McCann, Milwaukee County District Attorney, wrote: "He was a man of extraordinary dedication, very high competency, integrity beyond compare, rock solid common sense, and uncommon goodwill.... I not only deeply respected Sam but also had a keen affection for him.... Sam labored long and hard at the relatively thankless effort of improving the criminal justice system. He provided innovative ideas, implemented excellent programs, and generously made time to discuss problems and provide forthright critiques of operations.

"He was a man whose presence was a delight. He was never inconsiderate and was always unfailing in his graciousness. Sam Stellman was an extraordinary human being, a credit to the human race, and a credit to UWM."

Victor Manian, a Milwaukee County circuit court judge, wrote: "Professor Stellman was the embodiment of the outreach mission of the university. He didn't just suggest programs; he had a unique ability to recognize a need...then put a solution into action. He went into the community to draw together diverse actors of the criminal justice system and put them to work creating solutions.

"The areas he addressed involved the most difficult segments of society. The problems he encountered seemed almost unsolvable. In his quiet, persistent, and persuasive manner, he could win over the participants with the simple logic of his proposals. Professor Stellman never claimed credit for the programs he initiated. Like a true leader, he always stepped aside and let the participants take credit for the success." The judge added, parenthetically, "He was too busy preparing the next project."

November 4, 1994, a marker was placed in the Ernest
Spaights Plaza on the campus of the University of Wisconsin-Milwaukee following a ceremony recognizing Professor
Emeritus Samuel D. Stellman's "rare gift for bringing together diverse groups in the community to work on common problems."[225]

###

Endnotes

PART ONE: OUTRAGE

1. Pam Hanson, "Women Organize to Combat Rape," *Bugle American* 6/27–7/11/73, pp. 8–9, quoted by J. M. Dombeck, "The Women's Coalition of Milwaukee," Master's Thesis, 1987, p. 24.
2. When the Women's Crisis Line later incorporated, LMS and Atty. Karen Case handled them. By-laws for the Women's Coalition and Women's Crisis Line were created by several women, including LMS and Libby Peckarsky. The Crisis Line, initiated as a project of the Milw. Women's Coalition, later affiliated with the Counseling Center of Milwaukee, was administered by Good Samaritan Medical Center, and is now part of Milw. Women's Ctr.
3. William Bablitch became a Wis. Supreme Court justice in 1983; Mary Lou Munts served in the state legislature 1972–84, then with Public Service Commission 1985–91; now retired.
4. Anita Clark, "West High Rapist Given Year of Supervision," *Wis. State Journal* 5/26/77.
5. *Facts on File* 9/17/77, V 37, #1923.
6. This author included.
7. Moria Mackert Krueger became Madison's first elected female judge. Her campaign received a boost when it was reported on 8/27/77 that the rape defendant released by Simonson was arrested on burglary charges. *Facts on File* 9/17/77, V 37, #1923.
8. The first nat'l conference on battered women was held in Milwaukee 1976, sponsored by Milw. TF on Battered Women.
9. Commissioner Michael E. Kehoe.
10. Alaska workshops, 1979.
11. For information on long-term effectiveness of treating male batterers, *see* R.A. Storeur and R. Stille, *Ending Men's Violence Against Their Partners,* Sage Press, p. 272; Michael Groetsch, *He Promised He'd Stop: Helping Women Find Safe Passage from Abusive Rela-*

tionships, ed. Chris Roerden, CPI Publishing, 1997.
12. Doubleday 1983.
13. Englund, *Man Slaughter,* p. 186.
14. Ibid.
15. Appellant's Brief #78-187CR, Ct. of Appeals Wis. District IV.
16. Annie Laurie Gaylor, in *The Feminist Connection* n.d.
17. "Wives Who Batter Back," *Newsweek* 1/30/78.
18. LMS letter to K. Graham 1/26/78.
19. *Newsweek* 3/29/93, p. 27.
20. Englund, pp. 282–83.
21. Ibid, pp. 283–84.
22. AMA statistic from Clothesline Project at Univ of Toledo Catharine S. Eberly Ctr. for Women. Battering is leading cause of death for women 15–44 and major cause of injury, more common than auto accidents, muggings, and cancer combined; from Response to Violence website, Family Violence Clinic at SUNY Buffalo School of Law.
23. Approx. 37% of women seeking injury-related treatment in emergency rooms were injured by a current or former spouse or partner; from Nat'l Crime Victimization Survey by Dept of Justice 1994. Battering is most frequent reason women seek medical attention at emergency rooms, and battering accounts for estimated 25% of female suicide attempts; from FBI figures cited by Family Violence Clinic at SUNY Buffalo School of Law. Domestic violence kills 58,000 people every 5 years, the same number lost in the Vietnam War; from Antonio Novello, former US Surgeon Gen'l.
24. LMS, "In My Opinion," *Milw. Journal* 9/26/76.
25. LMS, "Battered Women Encouraged to Expose Brutish Men," *Milw. Sentinel* 9/8/77.
26. *Milw. Sentinel* n.d.
27. *Milw. Sentinel* 9/19/77.
28. *Milw. Sentinel* 9/24/77.

Abbreviations used in these notes and in the index are listed on p. 338. Information not annotated or attributed to another source was furnished by L. Mandy Stellman and Sam Stellman from their personal archives and from extensive interviews conducted by Pat Meller, Julie Kleppin, Chris Roerden, and Kathie Manglos.

PART TWO: SOURCE

29. *Toronto Evening Telegram* 3/11/41.
30. Univ of Toronto *PHE Alumni Update* 9/93, p. 2.
31. 2/27/46.
32. Aaron Beckwith letter to Emanuel Berlatsky, Dir., Bureau of Personnel & Training, Nat'l Jewish Welfare Board 5/24/49.
33. *Columbus Jewish Chronicle* 9/6/63.
34. 9/61.
35. At Zelionople, PA, sponsored by Nat'l Council of Jewish Women and YMHA of Pittsburgh. Camp directors were Moe and Libby Kotovsky.
36. *Columbus Dispatch* 7/21/61.
37. Letter in Stellman archives.
38. Clipping in Stellman archives.
39. Dave Hess, in *The WRFD Commentator* (Ohio) 5/13/65.
40. Original handwritten letter April 24, no year; stationery is imprinted "Ronald Reagan, Pacific Palisades."
41. Martha Brian, 5/16/65.
42. William Cramer, in *Ohio State Lantern* 2/17/66.
43. Mary Lou Ringle, in *Ohio State Lantern* 7/27/67.

PART THREE: ACTION

44. "L. Mandy Stellman: Grandmother Clause," *Marquette Mag.* Spring '93.
45. *Marquette Mag.* Spring '93; Draga Meyer, *NE Post News* 3/24/76; Dorothy Austin, *Milw. Sentinel* 11/3/70.
46. Office was located on State St.; later, both attorneys moved to 238 W. Wis. Av., Ste. 800.
47. See Ch. 3.
48. The original was painted at the White House in 1864, engraved by A.M. Riche. L-R: Stanton, Sec'y of War; Chase, Treasury; Lincoln, Pres.; Welles, Navy; Caleb Smith, Interior; Seward, State; Montgomery Blair, Postmaster Gen'l; and (behind the superimposed photo of Mandy Stellman) Edward Bates, Atty Gen'l. The original hangs in the White House Treaty Room.
49. LMS letter to Roger Simon, *Chicago Sun-Times* 2/1/84, responding to article about attorneys.
50. "L. Mandy Stellman: Grandmother Clause," *Marquette Mag.* Spring '93.
51. Emma, dau. of Steven & Jeanne, grad. Bryn Mawr (physics major) & Stanford Univ; married; teaches high school science in Cambridge MA. Andrew, 1 year older, grad. Carnegie Mellon (math & computer science) is a programmer in NYC. Michael, only child of Les and Judy, is working on degree in culinary art & hotel management in Providence, RI.
52. *Milw. Sentinel* 6/20/91.
53. Patrick J. Lucey, Democrat, Wis. governor 1971–77.
54. *Inside Outreach* 7/86, internal newsletter of UW-Ext. Milw.
55. A degree in criminal justice is offered by UW School of Social Welfare, not connected with UW-Ext. Ctr for Social Services nor UW-Ext. CJI.
56. Dave Begel, "Leave it to Begel," *Milw. Journal* 7/2/82.
57. The woman was Lois Torkelson, per J. M. Dombeck, "The Women's Coalition of Milwaukee," Master's Thesis, 1987, p. 12.
58. Held at The Abbey, Fontana, Wis.
59. Milw. Board of School Directors and Milw. NOW entered into an agreement 5/19/78, case V-77-53.
60. Kenneth Stoffels, "School Board Signs Pact for Sex Bias Ban," *Milw. Sentinel* 6/7/78, p. 5. The first, 6 months before, was Mnpls–St. Paul.
61. "Wrong Role for NOW," in *Milw. Sentinel* 6/16/78.
62. LMS, "NOW School Case Challenged Injustice," *Milw. Sentinel* 7/5/78.
63. Gene Boyer also served 15 years as pres. of Nat'l Women's Conference Center 1981–96; nat'l pres. of Jewish Women's Coalition, Inc., in '96.
64. Priscilla J. Kucik, "'Outraged' attorney 'makes things happen,'" *The Feminist Connection* 4/81, p. 4.
65. In Stellman archives. Earl joined 11/26/80; his dues, $13, were processed by the author, NOW state pres. at the time.
66. Paula Brookmire, "Family Unit Gets New Definition," *Milw. Journal* 1/17/73.
67. Applies to all banks, retailers, etc., that regularly extend credit; no one can be refused credit on account of sex or marital status; a woman's income or savings are to be counted in determining eligibility for credit.

68. Alex Thien, "Shopper insists Social Security unlisted number," *Milw. Sentinel* 7/8/92.
69. LMS letter 1973.
70. Some progress occurred when Wis. Supreme Court said if it can be *proved* a spouse is shirking for sole purpose of not paying court-ordered support (by not working or by taking a job at much lower salary)the court can order the spouse to pay larger amount.
71. Ralph D. Olive, "Life went sour; times got tough," *Milw. Journal* 10/27[or 28]/82.
72. See also Jeanne Rudolf Weber, "Divorce Aftermath for Women," *Wis. State Journal* 4/21/74, §1, p. 11.
73. Ibid. Also, Jo Banko, "Warning, hope given on being 'Suddenly Single,'" *Capital Times* 6/6/74, p. 14.
74. Timothy Harper, "Divorce Class for Men Only," *Wis. State Journal* 10/13/74.
75. Banko, "Warning."
76. Barbara Dembski, "Divorce Is a Part of Real Living," *Milw. Journal* 5/6/73, §6.
77. Dorothy Austin, "Divorcees Helped to Build Future," *Milw. Sentinel* 12/23/74, §1, p. 6.
78. Wis. Gov. Commission on Status of Women, *Real Women, Real Lives*, 1978, p. 63.
79. Chief operating officer was Herb Kohl, Democrat, elected to US Senate 1988.
80. Dorothy Austin, "Job Bias Flouts Law, 4 Agree," *Milw. Sentinel* 7/9/74.
81. Alida Johns, "Minority, Women's Fire Jobs Ordered," *Milw. Sentinel*, 10/18/74.
82. "Fire Breier, he's a liar" was chanted at early Take Back the Night marches to protest police indifference to assaults of women. The Stellmans and this author were among the nearly 3,000 Milw. demonstrators for many years, beginning in 1979.
83. Alida Johns, "Judge Rips City Delay in Bias Suit," *Milw. Sentinel* 3/26/75, quoting Milw. Fire Chief William Stamm.
84. "13 Women Suggested for UWM Post," *Milwaukee Sentinel* 11/1/75.
85. "Woman Pushed for UWM Job," *Milw. Journal* 11/9/75; lists 14 candidates: UW-Ext. Prof. Kathryn Clarenbach,

chair, Gov. Commission on Status of Women; UWM Prof. Carol Baumann, Dir., Institute of World Affairs; Aileen Cavanaugh, Amherst College, former nat'l pres. of Soc. of Women Engineers; UWM Prof. Beverly Cook; Leila Fraser, ass't. to UWM vice chancellor; Fannie Hicklin, ass't. dean of faculty, UW-Whitewater; UW-Ext. Ass't Prof. Sarah Ettenheim; UWM instructor Marian McBride; Karen Merritt, academic planner for UW System; Laureen Fitzgerald, dean of graduate school, UW-Oshkosh; Milw. Alderperson Cynthia Kukor; Wis. Sen. Kathryn Morrison; UWM Dir. Developm't. Evelyn Petshek; and Atty. Mandy Stellman.
86. Case #7605438 filed 3/24/76 with Equal Rights Div., Wis. DILHR.
87. Dorothy Austin, "UWM Accused of Sex Bias," 4/9/76, §1, p. 6.
88. Robert M. Huppertz, Reg'l Dir. DILHR, letter to LMS 9/13/78.
89. *Milw. Journal* 5/7/93, editorial page.
90. *Dick and Jane as Victims: Sex Stereotyping in Children's Readers,* Women on Words & Images TF, Princeton NJ.
91. *Shell News,* house organ of Shell Oil; no response from company to identify date of its tearsheet.
92. Chris Roerden, letter to editor, *Syracuse New Times* 6/74.
93. Banko (*see* n. 73).
94. "More Warfare on Sexless Laws," *Milw. Journal* 10/20/73.
95. 1974, took office 1975.
96. Amy Rinard, "Voters keep Constitution as is," *Milw. Journal Sentinel* 4/5/95, p. 14. Votes in favor: 266,095; against: 305,845.
97. Richard P. Jones, in *Milw. Journal* 4/8/95.
98. Harold A. Schwartz, letter to LMS 3/19/75.
99. Neill Hollenshead, Research Group, letter to LMS 7/6/73; reply 7/18/73.
100. R. C. Lawrence, Jr., Pitney Bowes, letter to LMS 10/10/75; handwritten note from LMS.
101. Stan Andersen, Provident Mutual Life Ins., letter to LMS 10/3/73; LMS handwritten note.
102. Atty. James D. Zakrajsheck, EMBA, letter to LMS 8/25/75; LMS to JDZ 8/26/75; JDZ to LMS 8/28/75.

103. Transcript 9/12/83, Milw. County Circuit Ct. Branch 12, Judge Michael Skwierawski presiding; Alex Thien, *Milw. Sentinel* 10/7/83, §3, p. 1.
104. 1976 or 1977.
105. 1973, 1974, 1975 in Stellman archives.
106. Stanley Balbach, Webber Balbach Thies & Follmer, form letter to LMS 10/26/73.
107. Balbach, handwritten note to LMS 11/13/73.
108. LMS letter to *Bar Leader* 11/1/78, re Dr. James G. Carr article in May-June '78 issue.
109. LMS letter to Frank W. Norris, Bank of Commerce 9/30/72; Norris letter to LMS 10/6/72.
110. LMS letter to pres. of Dictaphone, 7/31/75.
111. E. Lawrence Tabat, pres. Dictaphone, letter to LMS 8/8/75; D. D. Doar, district mgr Dictaphone, letter to LMS 8/21/75.
112. LMS letter to Jerry A. Klein, v-p Dictaphone, June 17, 1976.
113. LMS letter to WISN-TV 4/8/75; Ronald R. Anderson, Dir. Public Affairs, WISN-TV letter to LMS 4/23/75.
114. LMS letter to pres. Wis. Bar Ass'n 5/29/74; Patrick T. Sheedy, pres-elect Wis. Bar Ass'n letter to LMS 6/3/74; Richard Best, Chicago Title & Trust Co. letter to LMS 6/13/74.
115. St. Francis Savings & Loan letter to LMS 7/29/75.
116. Milton L. Neister, Circuit Ct. 24th Judicial Circuit, letter to LMS 8/7/74.
117. Anthony Scudellari, pres. Callaghan & Co. letter to LMS 7/17/84.
118. William Proxmire, US Senate, letter to LMS 9/20/84.
119. LMS letter to Barbara Walters, ABC News, 10/14/76.
120. Barbara Walters letter to LMS 12/6/76.
121. LMS letter to Barbara Walters, copy to Abigail Van Buren 12/29/76.
122. Undated note.
123. *Milw. Sentinel* 4/4/74.
124. AVB letter to LMS 5/1/74.
125. "'No-cost divorce isn't," *Milw. Sentinel* 5/31/76.
126. LMS letter to AVB 6/1/76.
127. AVB letter to LMS 6/14/76.

128. *Milw. Sentinel* 9/22/76.
129. AVB undated note to LMS received 9/30/76.
130. "Beard Raises Fuss," *Milw. Sentinel* 10/2/76; LMS letter to AVB 11/24/76.
131. See Ch. 11, pp. 231–32.
132. LMS letter to AVB 12/29/76.
133. AVB reply written on 12/29/76 letter from LMS, n.d.
134. "No case for rape but slate not clean," in *Milw. Sentinel* 4/28/77.
135. LMS letter to AVB 5/4/77.
136. AVB reply to LMS, n.d.
137. AVB letter to LMS 11/17/77.
138. SDS letter to AVB 5/1/79.
139. *Milw. Sentinel* 7/18/79.
140. *Chicago Tribune* 9/19/79, §3, p. 5.
141. Ibid.
142. LMS letter to AVB 8/28/79.
143. AVB letter to LMS 9/4/79.
144. LMS letter to AVB 11/20/79.
145. Dorothy Austin, "Judges toasted, and nobody roasted," *Milw. Sentinel* 11/12/79, §1, p. 8.
146. AVB to LMS (written on 11/20/79 letter from LMS).
147. "Commandments Point Way to Happy Marriage," *Milw. Sentinel* 2/14/92.
148. "Protest a bit late," *Milw. Sentinel* 2/19/76.
149. LMS letter to AVB 2/19/76.
150. *Milw. Sentinel* 5/14/76.
151. LMS letter to AVB 5/14/76.
152. 1/29/92.
153. Michelle Anderson, customer service, *Time*, letter to LMS 2/27/92.
154. LMS letter to Stephen Wolfe, pres. Republic Airlines 9/10/84; Marlene J. Krogstad, dir. consumer affairs Republic Airlines to LMS 9/18/84.
155. LMS letter to Marlene J. Krogstad 9/20/84.
156. MJK letter to LMS 9/24/84.
157. Linda Hall Daschle, Civil Aeronautics Board letter to Sen. Wm. Proxmire 10/10/84.
158. LMS letter to Wis. Gov. Lee Dreyfus 8/16/79; Gov. Dreyfus letter to LMS 9/6/79.
159. LMS letter to Heritage Bank Milw. 2/20/75; LMS letter to New York Life, Milw. & NYC 2/17/75.
160. LMS letter to Norman Lear 2/8/77.
161. Brooke Buhrman, ass't to v-p TAT Communications, letter to LMS 4/4/77.
162. Virginia L. Carter, v-p Creative Af-

fairs TAT Communications letter to LMS 3/15/77.

163. LMS to Leonard Goldstein, CEO Miller Brewing 10/26/92.

164. Erma J. Politoski, Consumer Affairs, Miller Brewing, letter to LMS & SDS 11/6/92. [A letter to Politoski 8/27/96 for update not answered].

165. More than 90% of victims of domestic violence are women; from Milw. Fighting Back Initiative "Take Back the Night" brochure 1996. *See also* Resources, p. 339.

166. Story was made public during the 1992 mayoral campaign.

167. To contact, *see* Resources, p. 339.

168. *Oshkosh (Wis) Daily Northwestern* 4/29/78, p. 10.

169. LMS letter to Morley Safer 2/23/76.

170. LMS letter to Mike Wallace 8/5/92.

171. LMS letter to Milw. Postmaster Gen'l 3/29/90, copy to US Postmaster Gen'l.

172. LMS letter to *ABA Journal*, n.d.

173. Jean Towell, "Magazine's ads raise eyebrows," *Milw. Journal* 2/20/83, pp. 1, 20.

174. "Parents wouldn't let girl appear in 'offensive' ads," *Milw. Journal* 2/24/83.

175. *Milw. Journal* 2/20, 21, 24, 27, & 3/5/83.

176. Carolina Garcia, "Groups decry magazine's use of child models," *Milw. Journal* 2/21/83.

177. LMS letters to Schmitter-Burg Jewelers, Bailey Banks & Biddle Jewelers, Rohr Jewelers, 3/10/83.

178. Carolina Garcia (*see* n. 176).

179. Jean Towell (*see* n. 173).

180. Clothesline Project at Univ of Toledo Catharine S. Eberly Center for Women; Response to Violence, Family Violence Clinic at SUNY Buffalo School of Law.

PART FOUR: TOWARD THE FUTURE

181. "Scared Straight: A Second Look," Nat'l Center on Institutions & Alternatives, Washington DC, n.d.

182. SDS, "In My Opinion," *Milw. Journal* 6/25/79.

183. Priscilla J. Kucik, "'Outraged' attorney 'makes things happen,'" *The Feminist Connection* 4/81, p. 4;

184. Dorothy Austin, "Housecoping: Help Wanted," *Milw. Sentinel* 7/1/75. Prof. Wm. Winter points out that Housecoping was part of CJI at the time CJI was under CSS, and SDS was part-time acting dir. of CJI as well as dir. of CSS. At first it was hard to distinguish Housecoping from VIP, but later they became separate programs.

185. Program operated at Green Bay and Waupan state prisons.

186. Stu Driessen, Dir. Volunteers in Offender Services, Outagamie County, intrvw by KJW 1996.

187. *See* Second Chance, an early intervention program for juveniles, in Ch. 14 pp. 293–94.

188. See Ch. 2, pp. 24–32.

189. The Milw. Mediation Center was a CJI program directed by Carlisle Dickson, federally funded; taken on by Wis. Corrections Service.

190. State Standards Bureau of Wis. Dept of Justice created a 400-hour training program, "Uniform Standard Student Performance Objective," which included CJI's audiocassette course material on MRO, 7/91. KB intrvw by KJW 6/17/96.

191. Severa Austin headed Wis. Planned Parenthood until 1/97. Shirley Abrahamson was first woman appointed to Wis. Supreme Court, 1976; elected to a full term 1979; reelected 1989; first woman Chief Justice 1996; reelected again 1999.

192. Tom Cooper became a circuit ct. judge; Rudolph Randa became a federal judge; Beverly Temple is a Milw. ass't city atty; Ted Wedemeyer Jr. serves on Wis. ct. of appeals.

193. Dorothy Austin, "Housecoping: Help Wanted," *Milw. Sentinel* 7/1/75.

194. SDS letter to CR 7/29/92.

195. Barbara Labrie intrvw by KJW 8/27/96; articles in *Shepherd Express* 7/7 & 7/14/94, and *Milw. Journal* 2/8/70.

196. Lois Hoiem intrvw 8/26/96 and Barbara Labrie, supra, by KJW.

197. Deb Billings-Nelson intrvw 7/1/96 and Lois Hoiem, supra, by KJW.

Dave Hess, in *The WRFD Commentator* (Ohio) 5/13/65.

198. Barbara Labrie intrvw by LRC 8/31/94 and by KJW 8/27/96; SDS intrvw by JK 10/89.
199. Deb Billings-Nelson intrvw 7/10/96 by KJW; Barbara Labrie and Larry Kipperman 8/27/96 by KJW; *Milw. Journal* 2/8/70; *Milw. Journal* 6/24/94.
200. UWM *Post* 2/20/70.
201. Barbara Labrie intrvw 8/27/96 and Lois Hoiem 8/26/96 by KJW; *Milw. Journal* 6/24/94.
202. *Milw. Journal* 6/24/94.
203. Larry Kipperman intrvw by KJW 8/2796.
204. SDS letter to editor, *Wis. Jewish Chronicle* 3/3/77.
205. *See also* Ch. 13, p. 279.
206. Jeffrey Wagner later became a circuit ct. judge.
207. *See* Ch. 13, pp. 273–75.
208. Cherie Maris intrvws 1997 and 1999 by KJW.
209. Stanley A. Miller became a Milw. Co. circuit ct. judge; James A. Gramling Jr. is a municipal ct. judge; Wm. J. Panagis is deceased.
210. Greg Howard, "Sally Forth," *Milw. Journal* 5/2/92, © 1992.
211. Stevens Point, Wis. 11/1/84.
212. FERPA, the Family Educational Rights & Privacy Act, enacted 1974 by Congress to correct abuses in the handling of student records by educators; provide for student and parental access to student records; and protect records from improper release outside school system, including law enforcement officials without proper authorization.
213. "Procedures Regarding Police Involvement/Support in Schools."
214. "The Milw. Police School Squad: Reinforcing Safety in the School," 2/25/93.
215. John Steen and Melanie Moore intrvws by KJW 7/31/96.
216. *Milw. Journal* 8/9/92, p. A12.
217. Changes to Wis. welfare system have been touted for saving public funds. It also created a large, cheap labor pool for certain employers— by pushing tens of thousands of poor women into minimum wage dead-end jobs. To survive, thousands of women hold two or more part-time jobs. "And those are the able-bodied. Women with disabilities and their children are dying," said Patricia Gowens, dir. of Welfare Warriors. Lengthy commutes and long hours cause many women to be gone 13 hours a day or more, leaving children as young as 18 months—the cut-off age for eligibility for welfare. Without quality, affordable child care, substandard, unlicensed facilities have come into existence to exploit desperate women.
218. Groetsch, p. 103 (*see* n. 11).
219. *See* Ch. 4, pp. 54–55.
220. Priscilla J. Kucik, "'Outraged' attorney makes things happen," *The Feminist Connection* 4/81, p. 4.
221. Anita Black, "Couple fight crime, believe in justice," *Milw. Sentinel* 6/9/82, §1, p. 6.
222. Ibid.
223. Resolution, Milw. Common Council, 1/25/94.
224. Gene Boyer letter to LMS 1/24/94.
225. *Invictus,* bulletin of the UWM Black Student Union 10/31/94.

ABBREVIATIONS USED IN ENDNOTES, INDEX, RESOURCES

ass'n ...... association	dept ...... department	nat'l ...... national
ass't ...... assistant	div. .... division	n.d. .... no date
atty. ...... attorney	ext .... extension	PM .... Pat Meller
AVB .... Abigail Van Buren	intrvw ... interview	SDS .... Samuel D. Stellman
CJI .... Criminal Justice Institute	JK .... Julie Kleppin	SUNY ..... State Univ of New York
	KB .... Kim Baugrud	
Co. .... company or county	KJW ...... Kim J. Wilson	TF .... task force
CR .... Chris Roerden	LMS .... L.Mandy Stellman	univ ...... university
CSS .... Center for Social Services	LRC .... Leah Carson	UWM ..... Univ. of Wisconsin-Milwaukee
	mag. ...... magazine	
ct. .... court	mgr .... manager	Wis. .... Wisconsin
ctr .... center	Milw. ..... Milwaukee	WW .... William Winter

Resources

BATTERING & RAPE

RAINN (Rape Abuse & Incest Nat'l Network), 635-B Penna. Ave. SE, Washington, DC 20003: 800-656-Hope (4673); www.rainn.org

Nat'l Domestic Violence Hotline: (nationwide database of shelters) 800-799-SAFE (7233); TTY: 800-787-3224; http://www.ndvh.org/

Nat'l Resource Center on Domestic Violence: 800-537-2238

Jewish Women's Coalition, 608-273-9760 summer; 954-389-1879 winter; jwlegroups@aol.com

CAVNET (Communities Against Violence Network) (also lists videos, books): www.cavnet2.org

Battered Women's Justice Project: 800-903-0111

Health Resource Center on Domestic Violence: 800-313-1310

Jewish Women Internat'l, 1828 L St. NW, Ste. 250, Washington, DC 20036: www.jewishwomen.org/domestic.htm

Response to Violence, SUNY at Buffalo School of Law: www.violence-response.net/facts.html.

CHILD CUSTODY

Resource Center on Child Custody & Protection: 800-527-3223

JOB DISCRIMINATION

9to5, Nat'l Ass'nWorking Women: 800-522-0925; www.9to5.org

SPECIAL INFORMATION

Career Youth Development, Inc., 2601 N. Martin Luther King Dr., Milw. WI 54212: 414-264-6888

Justice Information Center, Nat'l Criminal Justice Reference Service: www.ncjrs.org/

Criminal Justice Institute, Univ of Wisconsin-Ext., Drawer # 491 Milw. WI 53293: 414-227-3370 www.uwm.edu/UniversityOutrea ch/catalog/Criminal_Justice/gninfo

WOMEN'S RIGHTS

NOW (Nat'l Org. for Women), 733 15th St. NW 2nd floor, Washington, DC 20005: 202-628-8669; 202-331-9002 TTY; www.now.org

NOW Legal Defense & Educ. Fund, 395 Hudson St., NY, NY 10014: 212-925-6635; fax 212-226-1066

WOMEN IN POVERTY

Welfare Warriors, Pat Gowens, Dir., 2711 W. Michigan Ave., Milw. WI 53208: 414-342-6662 (MOMA); fax 414-342-6667 (MOMS) www.execpc.com/~wmvoice/

SELECTED READINGS

Cantrell, Leslie. *Into the Light: A Guide for Battered Women*

Freeman, Jo. *A Room at a Time: How Women Entered Party Politics*

Faludi, Susan. *Backlash: The Undeclared War Against American Women*

Groetsch, Michael; Chris Roerden, ed. *He Promised He'd Stop: Helping Women Find Safe Passage from Abusive Relationships*

Lee, Ilene, & Kathy Sylvester, illus. Carol Deach. *When Mommy Got Hurt: A Story for Young Children About Domestic Violence*

Storeur, R.A., & R. Stille. *Ending Men's Violence Against Their Partners*

Warshaw, Robin. *I Never Called it Rape: The Ms. Report on Recognizing, Fighting, & Surviving Date and Acquaintance Rape*

Index

D

D.A.'s office 5, 8, 52
DAR 102
Deaconess Hospital 211
Dept of Industry, Labor & Human
  Relations (DILHR) 203
Deprogramming Men Who Batter
  22-32, 272
Deutsch, Sue 156
developmental disabilities, *see*
  MRO
Dewson Street school 87
DIAL 157
Dickinson, Florence 156
Dictaphone Co. 229, 245
DILHR 203
Dinitz, Simon 119
Directory Identity Action League
  157
diSalle, Michael V. 98
district attorney 55, 331
  D.A.'s office 53-54
divorce counseling training
  189, 190
divorce reform 180-81, 184-85
doctors 23, 48-50, 108-11, 145-
  46
Dreyfus, Lee 243
Dundas Street 74, 76

E

Eagle Forum 186
Earl, Tony 168, 277, 320
East, Catherine 329
Edhlund, Sandra 14, 16
EEOC 203, 210, 213
Eisenberg, Alan 33-34, 38, 48,
  143
EMBA 196-97
Emma Kaufman Farm Camp 98
Employers Mutual Benefit Ass'n,
  see EMBA
enforcement 46, 48, 52, 54
Englund, Steven 35, 40-41, 50
Equal Credit Opportunity Act 171
Equal Employment Opportunity
  Commission, *see* EEOC
Equal Rights Amendment 159,
  161, 181, 246
Ernest Spaights Plaza 332
Esser, Mary 294
Extension, see University of Wis.

F

fair housing 101-102
Family Hospital 253
Family Life Center 190
family structures 170
Family, The 270
Fancher, Dr. 109
Fawcett, Novice 118
FBI 204
Federated Department Stores 118
Felger, David 56
Feminist of the Year Award 313,
  329
Fire and Police Commission, Milw.
  203-204
*First Reading of the Emancipation
  Proclamation* 144
"firsts" 7, 82, 125, 138, 158, 166,
  183-84, 187, 194, 313
Flynn, Dennis 271
Foley, Mary Pat 207
Fotjik, Melissa 248
Franklin County, Ohio 118, 121
  Franklin County Home 123
Franklin Law School 129
free speech 104, 111-12, 210
Future Teachers of America 102

G

Genesee Street 91
Girls Sports Clubs 97
Golden Age Club 98
Good Samaritan Medical Ctr. 333
Gorenstein, Ralph 249
Gracz, Gregory 248
Graham, Katherine 39
Gramling Jr., James A. 295
grandmothering 147-48
Green Lake 93
Greenfield, Wis. 207-208
Groppi, Father 101
guardian ad litem 148

H

Haberman, Donald 225
Haig, Alexander 227
Harbord Collegiate 80-81
Harder, Sarah 329
Hayes, Woody 96
Hayward, Randy 275
Heinemann's Restaurant 155-56
Helms, Jesse 111